D1035576

*Psychoanalytic Studies
of the Sighted
and the Blind*

Psychoanalytic Studies of the Sighted and the Blind

DOROTHY BURLINGHAM

INTERNATIONAL UNIVERSITIES PRESS

New York

Manufactured in the United States of America

216575

PREFACE

To the prospective readers, the articles collected in this book may seem to be in the nature of a haphazard assembly of presentations giving evidence of an analyst and child analyst changing subjects of interest during a lifetime of work. In fact, this impression is misleading. Even though the concern is with apparently differing subjects, my main interest was always concentrated on a major point: the relationship between mother and child.

I explored this subject first in the general realm of child analysis, treating children of latency age where I was fascinated by certain remnants in them of much earlier functioning, namely, deep and rather obscure areas of contact between mother and child, which I attempted to describe under the title "empathy."

I moved from there to the opposite, i.e., to a rather unusual disturbance of the close mother-infant tie through the constant presence of a third in that partnership which is usually confined to two people: to twins. Since it has been my good fortune to explore several pairs of twins either in analytic treatment or supervision, or observation, I was able to show that subtle but fateful repercussion in the individual's love life, in cases where the first object relationship is made not to the mother, but to a peer. The paper on "A Study of Identical Twins: Their Analytic

Material Compared with Existing Observational Data of Their Early Childhood" (with Arthur J. Barron) gives evidence on this point which I pursued further in my book on twins.

Finally, and this is the bulk of the book's content in the second part, I tried to trace the difficulties of the child building up the tie to the mother in cases where one important interpersonal link is missing: vision. The blind child sees neither the mother's face nor her smile, nor her affectionate or warning glance, nor does the mother find an answering response in the child's face. What this does to the mother-child relationship and what has to be done to compensate for the sensory lack is again a fascinating study which has sustained my interest all through the difficult and exacting work with, and study of, blind children.

London, March, 1972

Dorothy Burlingham

CONTENTS

Part II
Development of the Blind

Part I
Child Analysis and the Sighted

Chapter 1

CHILD ANALYSIS AND THE MOTHER

There are certain difficulties which arise in the analysis of a child that are not encountered in the analysis of an independent, nonpsychotic adult. There is, for instance, the child's relative inability to express himself in words, and his frequent use of other means of communication. Furthermore, the child's emotional relationship to the analyst is complicated by many factors, among them his natural attachment to and dependence upon his parents. In turn, his dependence upon his parents forces the analyst to keep the child's parents in a favorable attitude toward the analysis. It is this last problem which will be the chief topic of this paper. To maintain the sympathy and the cooperation of the parents throughout the entire analysis of a child is a difficult and trying problem; and yet if one does not succeed in this, the analysis moves inevitably to an abrupt and premature interruption. In this paper I shall talk chiefly of mothers, because it is almost exclusively with them that the analyst must deal.

First published as "Kinder Analyse und Mutter." *Zeitschrift für psychoanalytische Pädagogik*, 6:269-289, 1935. The English translation was published as "Child Analysis and the Mother." *Psychoanalytic Quarterly*, 4:69-92, 1935. Excerpts of this paper also appeared as Chapter 17 in *Psychoanalysis and the Occult*, ed. George Devereux. New York: International Universities Press, 1953, pp. 188-191.

There are two kinds of mothers, those who are completely ignorant of analysis and those who know something about it and who perhaps have themselves been analyzed. Those who are informed about analysis are at first easier to deal with, for they understand the analytic process. Nevertheless it is inevitable that difficulties should arise, for the analyst's suggestions often conflict with the mother's unconscious needs. Mothers who are in analysis at the same time as their children will often unwittingly allow their attitudes toward their own analyses to influence their behavior toward the analyses of their children. Those who know little or nothing of analysis cannot help making difficulties, no matter how hard they try not to. Mothers in general, therefore, have to be dealt with as part of the treatment. They must be appealed to and their interest must be gained. The analyst must find out just how much of her child's analysis the mother can stand. Upon her ability in this direction may depend the success of the whole treatment.

A mother can make countless small difficulties for the analyst. Thus she may not see to it that the child comes punctually to the hour, and may often let him miss a session without any adequate reason. She may make derogatory remarks about analysis in general or about the child's analysis in the presence of the child, and may treat it all as a jest. Or, on the other hand, she may expect miracles and anticipate that the child's difficulties will vanish as soon as analysis begins. Or during analysis the analyst may with great difficulty bring the child to a better understanding of his mother; and the mother may then at the first opportunity act in such a way that everything that the analyst has explained to the child must seem like nonsense. For instance, the analyst may have to prove to the child that his mother really loves him, and the mother may just at that moment treat him in an unusually harsh manner. Or if the child has become freer in his attachment to his mother so that he can turn to other people as well, the mother may react with intense jealousy. The analyst may ask the mother to behave in a certain manner toward the

child, and the mother may not be able to carry out this suggestion; or else may so overdo it that it cannot have the desired
effect.

The analyst must therefore consider the mother as part of
the little patient's environment. Even before one has seen the
child, one knows that the parents have had a large share in
forming the neurosis. Whether the parents are narrow-minded
and "conservative" or broad-minded and open to outside influences makes a difference, not merely because of their overt
behavior toward the child, but even more because of their own
inner tensions. Therefore it is necessary to keep in mind the parents' attitude toward religion. A mother may cling to her religion
not as a faith alone, but as a vitally necessary solution of her
own problems; she may therefore wish to foster it in the child
by every means in her power. In the same way, a mother's attitude toward sex and the strictness of her own upbringing are
reflected in the way she trains her child. It is hard for her to
give up ideas about sex that had been instilled in her when she
was a child and that she has maintained ever since. The mother
has surely had her own difficulties and peculiarities; and out of
them, without help, has had to form her own character and
work out her own adjustments as best she may. She will cling
to these solutions defiantly and desperately; and they in turn
are bound to play a large part in the formation of the child's
character.

The power of unconscious forces is especially marked in its
interplay between parent and child. It is so subtle and uncanny
that it seems at times to approach the supernatural. The analyst
knows this, and knows that this quality is more marked in some
people than in others, and that if it is found in a child, it must be
taken into account as an unknown quantity that will bring many
uncertainties into the analysis. Therefore, when the analyst first
comes in contact with a mother, there are many things to be
watched and to be kept in mind. One must wonder in what way
the mother cares for her child, whether the child is not an outlet

for very complex feelings, and how these feelings will play into the changes that the analysis will bring about in that child. One wonders whether the mother will cooperate, and if she will be amenable to the analyst's influence, and will yield to guidance so that in the end she will help to foster the growth which the analysis made possible. Or, on the other hand, is this perhaps a mother who cannot be influenced, and who at the first difficulty will turn against the analyst?

On the other hand, let us consider the mother who brings her child to an analyst for treatment. Usually this step is taken only after every other measure has been tried. She comes to the analyst because she cannot cope with her child alone and is much relieved to find someone who will help her. Nevertheless once the analysis is under way she may become astonished and frightened when her desire to have the symptoms removed is not all that is achieved by the analysis. She sees all sorts of things being taken into account that she would much prefer to have left out. She sees the child suddenly behaving in a quite altered manner, and even treating her differently. She feels herself being dragged into the analysis. Her relationship toward her child, her actions and behavior toward him, what she says to him, and how she says it, her moods and her tempers, everything is studied from the analytic angle. That is bad enough, but when she realizes that her whole private life is also being brought in, she naturally feels abused. She can understand why all that concerns the child is necessary material for the analyst, but when it comes to her private life—that seems to her to be going one step too far. She will not stand for it and struggles against it. Naturally, she feels injured, criticized, misunderstood. Furthermore, she feels jealous even of the attention which is now being given to her child. It was she who suffered from her child's behavior, and now it is her child who gets all the sympathy and help. She, who was most affected by his difficulties, now not only is not being considered, but an even more difficult situation is being made for her. Moreover, she feels her child loving someone else more than herself, turning to someone else with all his troubles as he previously did to her. It does not make it easier for her to realize that this person really does understand her child better than she does. She feels humiliated. And then, added to all of this, the child begins to look at her, his mother, with newly opened eyes, even criticizing her, her actions, her very thoughts; and she knows that her child finds sympathy in all of this with his newfound friend, the analyst. Is it astonishing that the mother resents the analyst's efforts? Is it strange that analysts often lose cases just because parents cannot stand the analysis and suddenly break off the treatment?

Analysts have tried to meet this situation in several ways. Some ignore the parents and confine themselves purely to the child, interpreting his unconscious expressions and the transference relationship. They leave out all of the child's daily life and his reactions to his surroundings, except that which comes into the hour as necessary material. They prefer not to know the parents or to have them report on the child. Some prefer, when it is possible, to remove the child from his parents and to place him in more impersonal surroundings during the analysis, and to return him to his parents to adjust as best he can when he has completed his analysis. Still others try to take into consideration the child and his surroundings, his parents and his reactions to them as a part of the analytic treatment. They try not only to show the child his reactions to his parents, but also to take the parents with them through the analysis, showing them step by step what they are trying to accomplish with the child and giving them an insight into the child's troubles so that they can change certain outer and inner conditions which tend to increase the child's neurosis. Their hope is that as the personality of the child is freed through the analysis, the parents will then be enabled to guide the child away from the neurosis instead of repeating the old mistakes.

There are difficulties in each of these three methods. One cannot carry through an analytic treatment without the parents' consent, because they can break off the analysis at any moment, they can disturb it, and when the analysis is completed they can make it impossible for the child to make use of the freedom he has just acquired. When an adult has successfully completed an analysis, he knows what to do with his released potentialities; but a child, just because he is a child, still has to be guided and helped and given opportunities to use these released powers. In the development of a child, this is a part of his normal education.

When one examines the three methods and takes into account the drawbacks and advantages of each, one must bear in mind the further development of the child. Where the analyst ignores the parents, according to the first method suggested, how will the child behave during his analysis and how will he adjust to his environment at the close of the treatment? There is no question but that to ignore the parents makes the situation much easier for the analyst. At best he has enough difficulties to cope with. Why should he add one more to the others? If he is able through his treatment to uncover the child's unconscious and to interpret it to him and to understand the mechanism of his actions and thoughts, will the child not lose his symptoms? Why should he take the trouble to understand the mother who will only make difficulties for him and, should he not succeed with her, probably cause him to lose his patient? He risks more if he tries to win the mother than if he completely ignores her. Let us see, however, how the child is after he has been treated in this manner. When one talks to him he can recite to you at length all the conscious and unconscious reasons for all his actions and where they come from; but if one watches him in his surroundings, he seems like a ship at sea. He has no connection with reality. He cannot use his newly acquired understanding of himself to adjust to reality, even if he has lost his symptoms. His world is changed for him only so far as his symptoms interfered with his ability to meet it; but his environment, the atmosphere which was conducive to the formation of his neurosis has not changed. He still has the same situations to fight against even though he can meet them less neurotically. He cannot try out new lines of thought and action; he is still tied to the old difficulties—perhaps not in the same way, but they are still absorbing his energy.

If according to the second method one takes a child away from his parents and puts him into another home for the duration of the analysis, he will at first have much fewer difficulties; but after a certain length of time the child will transfer to the new setting the difficulties that he had at home. Again one has, as before, the choice of one of the two methods, either to try to gain the cooperation of the foster parents or to ignore them. Nevertheless, there may be certain advantages in transplanting the child into a new home. The child's own parents may be so neurotic that an analysis at home would be impossible. Or from the very beginning one may realize that the parents could not stand the child's analysis and would make it impossible. The child in his new home might not have such neurotic adults to deal with, nor would they necessarily react to him with the neurotic intensity of his own parents. For the analyst it is surely easier to understand the child's neurosis in this less complicated home. The child can, as he becomes freer through his analysis, adjust more easily to his new parents. He can see the part that he has played and often the part his parents played in forming his neurosis. Here in his foster home he can become better adjusted to his environment. But when the child at the close of his analysis returns to his own home, he finds it very difficult to adjust there. He has felt so contented in this less neurotic atmosphere that he cannot adjust himself to the old situation. One often hears of a child begging to be sent away to school because he feels his home problems too difficult to meet. He cannot stand being put back into the home of his neurosis. Children who have lost their symptoms in their adopted homes often produce them again immediately after returning to their own homes.

The third method, that is, to try to gain the cooperation of the parents in the treatment, is by far the most difficult. It is, for the duration of the analysis, an added complication. One knows from the very beginning that one is carrying not only the child's difficulties but the parents' as well. The mother is bound to bring in her jealousy, her criticism, and her hurt feelings. One cannot forget her for a moment, for one has really come between her and her child. Even though this is only for a short time, she feels that she must protect her rights.

One has means, however, with which to meet this difficult situation. Obviously, one must give the mother something to make up for her loss. The analyst must show her that he is interested not only in the child but also in the mother. She must be encouraged to join in the treatment of her child. She must feel that any information she brings about her child is important. She must be urged to observe everything the child does at home, not only in his general activities but in his relation to her. She must feel that she too is taking part in a piece of research work, so that her interest is awakened. Then she will bring in material about herself, making comparisons between herself and her child, and finally taking as great an interest in the analysis as the analyst himself. In the study of her child her own natural interest in herself is approached, for her child is often an image of herself and her interest in her child is indirectly an interest in her own personality. There is another important trait that the analyst can count on for help in their relationship; namely, the mother's feeling of guilt toward the child. A mother almost always feels that she could have done more for her child. She quickly calls to mind all of the occasions on which she has made mistakes with him and turns to the analyst for help in undoing the harm which she has done. By means of these two approaches one can usually reach a mother, keep her from harming the analysis, and even gain her assistance during the treatment.

At the same time that the analyst is winning the mother's cooperation in this way, he must initiate her into each phase of the child's analysis in order that she may not be unprepared or too shocked by each step of the analysis through which the child has to go. If she is told of each improvement, she can help the child make use of his new freedom. As the end of the analysis draws near, the analyst should feel that there is someone who is adequately prepared to resume the parental role in the emotional life of the child, which the analyst had partly usurped. This, of course, should be a gradual process continuing throughout the terminal phases of the treatment.

Perhaps this consideration of the three methods of dealing with the mother during a child's analysis will enable us to decide on the best method of introducing the mother to the subject. We see both the analyst's difficulties and the mother's. The analyst wants to start his treatment and to have it proceed without interruption. The mother wants the analyst to start the treatment, but naturally she resolves in the back of her mind that if she finds that she does not like what is going on, or if it does not seem to help the child, or (as we can add ourselves) if she cannot stand the strain, she will simply take the child away. She does not realize that to start a treatment and break it off might be harmful. How then should the analyst proceed? Should he decide which method he should use only after having seen the mother a few times? This would seem to be the sensible thing to do; but the difficulty is that if he starts with one method, he must usually continue it. Should the analyst introduce the mother to her child's analysis as one introduces an adult into his own analysis, telling all the difficulties that lie in the way? Should he enumerate the child's difficulties, his possible reactions to the treatment, his probable bad behavior at home? Should he mention the necessity of enlightening the child concerning religion, babies, sex, masturbation, and intercourse? Should he prepare her for the turning of her child's affection to the analyst, and for her own probable reaction of jealousy and hate? Should he tell her of the necessity of bringing all that concerns her private life into the analysis, everything she says, does and feels, and of her inevitable self-protective impulse? How many mothers would put their children into analysis if the analyst told them all of these facts? Or should one first give the mother a few weeks in which to get used to the analysis and to the analyst and then tell her of the difficulties that await her? Would this increase the chance that she would keep her child in analysis? Should one tell the mother only a few of the difficulties at first, and prepare her step by step as the difficulties appear, hoping to be able to carry her along as her interest in the analysis and her confidence in the analyst grows? Or are there some cases which, no matter how suitable the child is for analysis, must be refused at once, because it is evident from the start that the mother's resistance to analysis is too strong to stand the treatment? Or should one tell the mother in such a case that it is impossible to analyze the child in his home, and that if she wants an analysis for him, she must put him in another home for the duration of the treatment?

Such problems are familiar to all, and specific examples have not seemed necessary. However, illustrative examples of a few special points are perhaps not out of place.

The first two clinical episodes are examples of how a well-intentioned mother can render the analyst's advice absurd, by naïveté or exaggeration. The third episode shows a mother driven by a sense of guilt into what might have been a serious false accusation against her own child. The next group of examples illustrates the kind of embarrassment that adults must be prepared to endure at the hands of little patients while they are working out some of their primitive impulses. Then the difficult problems of sexual curiosity, speech, and activity is illustrated in a series of short episodes; and, finally, a tragic case history is given, the analysis of which was interrupted because of the mother's inability to accommodate herself to the child's growth.

The first is an interview between a mother and her child's analyst, after the latter had had the child in analysis for a few weeks. The analyst was able to tell the mother something of her child's neurosis and could show her where she had aggravated her child's difficulties through her behavior. She had been too hard on him and had expected too much of him. As a baby, the child had had a very strict nurse. This nurse had been able to manage him so well that the baby was always good; he was always quiet and never cried. For instance, it had been her custom at bedtime to hold his head pressed into the pillow until he fell asleep. When the nurse left, the mother tried to follow the nurse's methods, because she had seemed so successful with him. Here the analyst was able to tell the mother how unhappy the child really had been at this time. He had felt that she much preferred his older brother to himself, believing indeed that she did not love him at all. The mother was very unhappy over this report. As she looked back over these years, she could see for herself that the analyst was right in what he said. Therefore she took the analyst's statement to heart and made up her mind to follow his advice. She began to pay the child a great deal of attention, fondled him, kissed him, and gave him his way in everything. The result was anarchy. From being too docile, the boy became unmanageable, self-willed, and stubborn, and had violent tempers. He would refuse to dress, would throw himself in tantrums on the floor, would eat only certain favorite foods, and would get into endless battles with his mother. The mother felt she had behaved as the analyst had wanted her to and was naturally dissatisfied with the result. She lost confidence in the analyst and did not believe that he would be able to remove her child's symptoms through the analysis.

In a similiar conversation another mother was told that the obsessional neurosis of her child had been intensified because the mother did not show the child much affection. The mother asked in reply: "If I go home now and love my child very much, don't you think the child will be cured?"

A mother can place the analyst in a serious dilemma. The mother of a twelve-year-old girl telephoned her child's analyst in great excitement that the child had again done something dreadful. A telegram had come to the house, and her daughter had opened it, read it, and destroyed it in order to keep the telegram from her mother. The child denied having done this. The analyst was cautious; she wanted to be certain that what the mother had said was correct. The mother insisted that it was quite in keeping with the unsocial behavior of her child. The analyst knew how very serious it would be for the analysis if she should suspect her little patient falsely. She therefore suggested calling up the telegraph office. The mother did so and was told that the signature was written in a child's handwriting. Still the analyst hesitated and sent the mother to the telegraph office to look at the signature. There, the mother to her amazement recognized the signature as her own. She must have received the telegram, signed for it herself, and then forgotten it. It was clear that the mother needed to prove to the analyst that the child was in the wrong and that she was in the right.

On the other hand, there are times in an analysis when the mother's fears for her child seem to be justified. It is well known how often adults act out their analytic reactions in the outside world instead of bringing them into the analysis. For children this is the usual behavior. That is one reason why it is important for the analyst to keep in touch with the child's activities at home, and why the contact with the mother can be so useful to the analyst. With children the transference is not so clear and the results of interpretations often are seen only in the resultant activities at home. If the mother has been analyzed, she can easily follow the various phases of the analysis. To the unanalyzed mother this reactive conduct can mean only that her child is going to perdition. Even to the analyzed mother these activities are not always interesting or amusing. The following incident may serve as an illustration. A few children had been invited for supper. One of the children, who was in analysis, had the brilliant idea of gargling with her soup. The other children were fascinated with the idea and all followed suit. When the mother came on the scene, she found all the children in various phases of gargling. Some of the children had their heads bent back and from their throats came wonderful noises. Others were spitting the soup back into their plates, and still others were choking from laughter. It was a hilarious party, but no mother could quite enjoy the scene completely. The mother reported the episode to the analyst, to whom it was a welcome and interesting piece of information because it fitted into the phase through which the patient was struggling.

Another child, who had never been particularly difficult, suddenly became entirely unmanageable. To every demand she answered, "I won't." She carried her stubbornness to such a point that it was necessary to leave her sulking for hours on the floor, or to use force to make her do what was essential. She was a big child and when she was being picked up, she made herself so rigid that it took two to lift her. She gloried in her power. It was necessary to carry her upstairs, to lift her into her bath, or into her bed. She became unbelievably dirty, her hair unkempt, her dress full of spots even if she had been cleaned only a few minutes earlier. At the table she was revolting. All around her plate was a circle of spilled food, and her face and dress were one large smear. During this period, she and some friends decided to give a play. They asked the grown-ups to leave them alone. They wanted to make a beautiful surprise. After what seemed a very long time the grownups decided to enter the room where the children were. The children had forgotten all about the play. Our little patient had suggested "making up," and they had painted each other's arms, legs, and faces, every bit of bare skin, without any rhyme or reason. It was a revel in paint. The floor was a muddy mess of paint and water. The costumes that the children had collected were lying in the mess. Of course, all children can do such things at times, but such an extreme orgy is rare. It happened just then because the little girl was in a phase of her analysis in which this behavior played a significant and even therapeutic role. At the same time that the child was behaving in this outrageously dirty fashion at home she was drawing the most charming, delicate tiny flowers in her analysis for her analyst. It is evident, then, that the mother, or substitute mother, may have to bear the brunt of the analysis.

One thing that mothers fear is that when during an analysis their children begin to talk openly of sex at home, they will begin to perform as well as talk. This fear is not entirely unjustified. An example of this is the case of a five-year-old child who in his analysis had been discussing the question of intercourse at great length. The information that he received was evidently not sufficient, for it did not satisfy his curiosity. Whereupon he suggested to his little girlfriend that they should play marriage. She thought it might be amusing and they made their first attempt at intercourse. The analyst takes such an experience calmly, although without liking it. To the analyst it is a phase of the child's analysis; but to the mother it naturally means much more.

The following is the account of a child who was actually lost to analysis because of the mother's resistance.

Gerti, a five-year-old girl, has been in analysis over a year. Her jealousy of her brother and of her sister, her penis envy, her castration fear, had all been analyzed, but above all her attachment to her mother, which in the transference showed itself in her acting the part of a little baby for months. I am presenting here certain selected parts of her analysis to show the interplay between mother and child and how it affected the analysis.

Picture this proletarian mother, ignorant of analysis, but with an urgent desire to do all she can for her three children. She has difficulties with her little girl. Gerti is in a kindergarten, where she is considered odd because she sucks her thumb, daydreams, and does not join the other children at play. The mother worries about her, goes to school lectures on children, and tries to follow "the modern ideas" (as she calls them) in bringing up her child. Gerti's kindergarten teacher suggests to the mother that Gerti might be helped by an analysis, and even goes to an analyst with the mother for consultation. The analyst too considers that an analysis would benefit her, and the mother agrees immediately. When she comes it is explained to her that the analysis will be long, that she will become very impatient, and will often have difficult times with her child because of the treatment, and that the symptoms which her little girl has may even become more intense for a while. The mother is not to be put off; she is now quite determined to have the treatment for her child, and she wants its passionately.

The analysis begins. Gerti is an actress. She acts father, mother or child. In a short while it appears from this play-acting (which of course may or may not be based on facts) that her father is a wicked man, that there is peace at home only when he is out of the house, that he is always demanding money, that his wife refuses to give it to him because she has none to give him, that he then gets angry and beats her, and that the children stand around with their hands to their ears, crying. The first reaction to this period reaches the analyst through the mother. She cannot understand what has happened to Gerti; she is so changed, so cross with her, she plays with all kinds of dirt and talks of dirty things. The superficial meaning of this is very clear: Gerti is critical of her home. She tells dirty things about it, feels guilty about doing so, and gives herself away to her mother by doing dirty things there. The mother was told only that it was natural that Gerti should react in some such way at home, and she is encouraged by an expression of gratitude for her cooperation in telling about Gerti's actions.

For weeks now Gerti is silent. She does not answer when I speak to her, sticks her fingers in her ears so that she cannot hear me talk, runs to her mother in the next room, until finally she suggests a new game. I am the mother, she is a robber, and the three cushions on my sofa are my three children. She bursts into the room in the role of the robber, frightening me, seizes my three children, stamps on them, murders them, and runs away. I, as the mother, have to be overcome by grief and cry. Then she comes back into the room as a little fairy being, saying she is the Christ child bringing back my children. She hides the children so that when the robber comes again he will not be able to find them. Now she comes to lead me and the children up to heaven. There I will be able to wash without being disturbed (her mother does washing), and my children will be protected. Next she tells me that the Heavenly Father wishes to be introduced to me, she brings Him to me, and He tells me I will not have any more troubles. At this moment she runs to the window. The Heavenly Father has after all almost let the robber in.

For days Gerti acts out this fantasy. If I try to get her to talk, she just sits and looks unhappy. Finally, I tell her I am sure she has something to tell me and that her mother would surely like it if she told me. At that remark she prepares to leave, picking up her things and going out of the room.

I send for the mother, who tells me that Gerti seems unhappy, and that at home she plays one game continually, namely, that her mother is sick. I explain to her that I think Gerti is hiding something from me and that I cannot help her when she keeps things from me. Perhaps she can guess what it is, because I have the impression that the mother is not quite open with me. She then tells me she has a lover, that the children know him and love him and that she never takes him home because if she did her husband would surely kill her. However, on Sundays he often accompanies them to the country. Now it is easy to understand why Gerti was so silent. The mother had an all-too-well-founded fear of her secret being found out. She told me how she managed the children so that they would keep her secret: she had threatened them with her own death if they told anyone, and told them that their father would set the house on fire if he found out that she had a lover. Gerti has seen her father beat her mother and wound her, so that these are not idle threats. Nor is it difficult to see how Gerti's fantasy was built up. The robber is the father who does wicked things. He is also the seducer who runs away with the children. The robber may also be the lover who prefers them to the mother. Her mother shows her great love of the children through her grief when they are torn from her. Gerti's love for her mother is too great to stand her mother's grief; so she brings back the children. Heaven must be life with the lover. The children have surely heard him say how he would protect their mother and give her a life without troubles. But Gerti cannot quite allow her mother to enjoy herself while she is left out of it. The loved father must therefore return to punish and to seduce.

Little by little the mother tells me a good deal about her difficulties at home with her husband, how her life is full of troubles, that she has had nothing but misfortune, that her only pleasures are when she can be with her lover, what a wonderful person he is and in what a lovely way he cares for her and for her children. She tells me that her only wish is to bring up the children so that they will not have the difficulties she has had. They are her whole life. She takes a great interest in everything they do. She asks me about analysis, is interested in all I tell her of Gerti, is anxious to cooperate, and asks me how she should behave with the children. Surely I am getting on very well with the mother. And Gerti? What is she doing now? She is making great strides in her analysis. All of her drawings are full of penis symbols, people with long noses, animals like elephants, horses, and dogs with long tails. I explain to her what she is thinking about. Then she rapidly draws a man leaving out the penis and asks me, "What is that?" pointing to where the penis ought to be. I draw the penis in the picture, she seizes my pencil and scribbles over the picture saying it is "dirty." She hands me back the pencil and tells me to draw an angel. At home she does everything her brother does, sticks out her tongue, and uses bad language. Next she takes up playing doctor. She has a doll and this doll is sick. Through this play I learn that she was in a hospital with scarlet fever when she was three. It was evidently a trauma in her life. She will not let her mother take her drawers off and insists on washing and dressing herself alone, screaming if her mother tries to do these things for her. She asks me whether my child wears drawers in bed, whether I do, whether I wear a nightgown and how long it is. Then she asks for a piece of paper and draws an oval with a line through it and a diamond-shaped figure with a line through the middle of it. She says, "I have two holes," and scribbles over the figures. "Make a drawing of my brother. I have seen my father; he has hair there." A short time later her mother tells me she is much improved.

I do not need to go into the analysis of this material; it is transparent: her interest in the penis, her penis envy, her identification with her brother, and later the shock in the hospital and her awareness of the differences of the sexes. My purpose is only to point out that at this time the mother had a good relationship to me. When she talked freely of herself and was interested in the analysis, Gerti's analysis went well; furthermore, when Gerti had a quiet time, undisturbed by actual happenings at home, she could bring out much analytic material. Can that all be merely a coincidence?

Then came an important event. The mother was left by her lover. The children were present at the farewell scene. The mother, beside herself with grief, told the children that her lover was going to America in a few days. Gerti begins to have fears, especially at night. The moon shines on her bed and wakes her up; she is frightened and cannot go to sleep. She will go crazy; she will walk on the roof; her mother told her so. She must not look at the moon, she says. She thinks of her mother's lover. He has gone to America, he will die, he will never come back; there will be a war and he will be shot. If there is a war here, she will not live, she will kill herself with a long knife driven into her head. Everyone will do it before a war comes, but only where there is war. She tells me she sometimes has the dreadful dream that her mother has died. She says: "Sometimes when one dreams something, it really comes true. For instance, I dream my father dies and he really dies." She talks of God. "He is everywhere, He can see everything that we do. You will go to heaven but I won't." At this point Gerti wants to leave me to go to her mother. I told her her mother has her so much of the time that she should at least give me this one hour. At this Gerti gets very angry. She says that is not true. She is in school in the morning and her mother is always away every evening now.

A period now begins when Gerti does nothing but washing and it is hard to get a word out of her except a request for more things to wash. I soon realize that this means that her mother is washing and she is left to herself a great deal. Her mother corroborates this. Gerti tells me she is afraid she will be stolen. A child has been stolen from his parents at night. I reassure her by telling her that she has bars at her windows; but she answers that robbers can hack their way through bars. What can children do when their parents leave them alone at night? Our new game is the abduction of the Lindbergh baby.

Gerti knows that her mother is unhappy because her lover has left her. She feels it to be her fault because of her jealousy. She has dreadful dreams, death wishes against her mother because her mother does not think of her, but instead thinks so much of her lover, and death wishes against him because he has made her mother so unhappy, or rather because she does not want him to come back and wants her mother for herself. Besides her jealousy, there is another secret she has kept hidden from her mother, viz., her masturbation. For this she feels that she deserves the most awful punishment. Now follows her struggle against masturbation: if she masturbates,

her mother will leave her to go to her lover. For her wicked
thoughts and deeds, the moon will punish her. God sees everything. She will kill herself because everything is her fault. She
blames her mother for leaving her to herself; she needs her
presence to keep her from masturbating. She is constantly afraid
that her mother might really leave her for her lover. We can
see here two struggles going on in Gerti at the same time, the
actual situation caused by her mother's emotions over the loss
of her lover and the struggle against masturbation. The two
are so intertwined that it is hard to separate them.

Now let us observe the mother. First she is unhappy because
her lover has left her; and she goes through a period of real
mourning. She tells me that the children seem to understand
because they are so quiet. Nevertheless, at the same time she
also says that she cannot stand the children, because they disturb
her so much. She throws herself into her work in order not to
have time to think. That is why she does so much washing.
Then her interest in the children gradually revives and she is
interested only in them and in what she can do for them, and
now for the first time she begins to tell more about her husband.
She cannot understand what is suddenly changing him. He is
being so nice to her, trying to do all sorts of things for her, trying to relieve her of the cooking. He has even brought her
some money, and of all unheard-of things, he has for the first
time in his life joined the ranks of the unemployed and shoveled
snow all night long. She thinks that perhaps the girl he lived
with has left him, and she wonders whether he wants something
from her. She has not had intercourse with him for three years
and has no intention of starting again now. I tell her that I
think it must be very hard for her now that her lover has left
her: surely she has troubles that she does not usually have. She
denies this passionately; but the next minute tells me how nervous she is nowadays and how impatient. She tells her husband
to go walking, and she cannot stand him in the house; his efforts

to be nice to her infuriate her. Of course, she takes it out on the children and is cross and irritable with them.

With this situation of the parents in mind we go back to Gerti. Her mother tells me that Gerti had a dream. "A doctor came and bored into my hole with an instrument." Gerti told the dream on waking, in front of the other children. They said, "Aren't you ashamed? One does not talk about such things." Gerti was hurt and said: "All right then, I'll never speak again." Later the mother told her that such thoughts were dreadful. If one did such things, one would become dreadfully sick. When the mother told me this, I asked her to tell me once more how she had really treated the children about masturbation. She told me with pride that they never masturbated. She saw to it that they did not. Even when they were babies she never let them go without diapers; the minute she took one off she put another on, and when they were older they always wore drawers in bed. In this connection one recalls how Gerti did not let her mother dress and undress her or take off her drawers. The mother told me further that she had the greatest horror of masturbation and had never resorted to anything like it, although some of her friends had told her that when they suffered from sexual privation they turned to it. I tried to tell her that masturbation was no longer considered so dreadful and that now one realized that all children masturbate. She told me that she knew that, that she had been to a lecture and had even heard that doctors considered it was harmless. A doctor in the hospital where Gerti was had told her not to be too severe about the thumb sucking, for if she was, something worse would be the result. However, in spite of all this knowledge, when the children touched each other, she told them that it was the same as putting dirty things in one's mouth, and that if one did, one would get dreadful sicknesses. It is interesting that Gerti will never use a spoon that anyone else has ever used, except her mother's. This creates difficulties at home, as they have only four spoons. The mother told me her husband had had gonorrhea, and that she had a horror of the disease. Although he had been cured, she never felt safe from infection. When I suggested that he could go to a doctor again, she admitted that she was sure he was well but that she was glad of an excuse to refuse to have intercourse with him.

In the meantime Gerti in her analysis was talking of babies; saying that they come from the stomach, girls from the mother, boys from the father. When boys are born, they are immediately given to the mother to nurse. She gives the babies milk from one breast, blood from the other. (This was of interest because the mother had told me previously that before her own marriage nothing had been explained to her and she had imagined just what Gerti's analysis had brought out. Perhaps her mother had told Gerti this, but it seemed scarcely possible.) During the same period the mother told me that Gerti was lying; and Gerti herself told me that she had so many sins, lying, stealing; and, I added, putting her hands to her genitals. She talked more freely now of the children and how they played with each other, and above all and with the greatest pleasure of the boys' "tails." The next day the mother came to me in great excitement. Gerti had talked of her hour at home; the children were horrified and she is afraid that when Gerti begins to talk of such things, she will begin to do them. She is sure that I do not understand her milieu and the temptations for the children. Through the windows of the house across the way they can see all sorts of things going on. Her husband, when he does not have enough money, urges her to go on the street, to be a prostitute. I try to quiet her by telling her that the best protection for the children lies not in ignorance but in knowing about such things.

Throughout the whole next hour, Gerti asks how much longer she can stay with me. Can she come tomorrow, the next day, this spring, next year? I did not realize it would be her last hour; but the next day a letter arrived from her mother saying that she would not send Gerti anymore since one could not have an analysis without being enlightened about masturbation and sex, and she did not wish that for her children.

Between this part of Gerti's analysis and what was happening in the mother's life there must have been a connection. The mother is having difficulties, missing her sex life. Her husband suddenly behaves differently toward her and makes advances as if he instinctively felt her need. What does Gerti do at this time? She dreams of intercourse. She talks of babies and is interested above all in the penis. She feels that someone is lying to her, not telling her the truth as it really is—surely her mother. She is excited and shows signs of greater freedom at home. She is also on the point of being very open in her analysis. How does the mother react? With horror. Gerti should be given the freedom to do that which the mother does not allow herself to do, to masturbate? Gerti should always remind her mother of her own desires? She has always turned away with disgust from such desires and such thoughts. We know how she kept the children from masturbating. She has previously protected herself from temptation. Now she has to struggle against the desires caused through the loss of her lover and those which her husband has stirred in her. But above all she must protect herself from Gerti. She cannot stand Gerti's having thoughts so like her own. If her daughter begins to have such thoughts, even to speak openly of sex, how will she avoid the next step, actually doing things? She must protect her as she has protected herself. She must not for a moment forget the temptations of their lives, the difficulties due to their milieu, and to her husband's urging her to go on the street. Above all, she must not forget the consequences of giving in to such temptations, the dreadful illnesses. She must shut the door to these thoughts completely. She knows of only one sure way, through ignorance and through repression.

I have given only a small part of Gerti's analysis, and have omitted periods where only straight analytic material was to be seen. It was my intention to describe only that part of the analysis in which the two trends could be seen side by side, i.e., the simple analytic situation on the one hand, and on the other hand the more complicated situation, which was the result of the mother's actual life with its conscious and unconscious emotional reactions continually intruding into Gerti's problem.

We must bear in mind that not all cases are like this one. There is not always such a close contact between mother and child. There are many such cases, however, and in all of them one is struck by the interplay of emotions between the two. One does not know the extent of this influence on a child's life; but the following examples illustrate a phenomenon which demands investigation.

1. A mother had just had the idea of giving her child a bicycle for Christmas. The child was in the room with her and called out, "I know what you are going to give me for Christmas —a bicycle."

2. The child guesses that her mother is pregnant before she is sure of it herself, or that she is in love with someone before she is aware of it herself. (Instances of this kind are not rare in analyses.)

3. Here, however, is an example where the child is in no way emotionally connected with the mother's thought and yet follows her thoughts in his actions. A gold piece had played an important part in a scene in the mother's childhood. This scene had just been brought out in her analysis. After her hour she went home. She had been there only a few minutes when her little boy brought her a gold piece to hold for him. She asked him where he had got it, and he answered on his birthday which had been several months ago. There seemed to be no reason why he should have remembered it just then. A few weeks later, just as the mother was writing down some notes about this scene of the gold piece, the little boy came in to her and asked for his gold piece. He wanted to show it to his ana-

lyst. Again there was no connection with this material at this time in his own analysis.

4. The most striking example that I know of a child being influenced by his mother's thoughts is the following. The mother was in analysis and in her hour she had a fantasy of throwing a jug of boiling water over someone when in a rage. She had witnessed a similar scene in her childhood. An hour later she was sitting at the table with her children. The younger child quarreled with his older sister. He suddenly left the table and returned a few seconds later carrying a glass of steaming water. He advanced on his sister crying: "You will see what I will do to you," and he threatened her with the water. The action was entirely unusual and unexpected from him. Where would such an occurrence fit in the child's analysis? Had it really anything to do with the child? If not, what is this strange form of communication?

I would like to close with one more remark. We all know how necessary it is for teachers and educators to be analyzed, so that they will not bring their own conflicts into their work with children. We can understand how important this is when we realize that even the analyst finds it difficult to remain aware of all the forces of the transference situation which is here a double one. The transference relationship with the mother plays the same role as that of the child. It is hard for the analyst to keep his own emotions free. He is tempted to side either with the mother or, as is more frequently the case, with the child. To keep sufficiently detached, to be just to both, is a real problem. In a child's analysis one has often to take decisive steps in one direction or another: one cannot always remain an inactive observer. One can often observe how analysts try to protect adult patients from criticism. Certainly, the female child analyst is apt to have that protective impulse to an even greater degree; for criticism will at the same time stimulate both her professional pride and her natural maternal instinct to protect her child.

Here, however, there is a real danger; for the protective instinct,
which would often be directed against the real mother, might
become more highly charged emotionally than the protection
of a helpless patient would demand. This would arise especially
through the analyst's desire to posses the child herself, or to the
wish to prove to herself that were she the child's mother, how
much better a mother she could be.[1]

---

[1] Other aspects of the role of the mother in the treatment of the child
are discussed in Chapter 8.

Chapter 2

A CHILD AT PLAY

Gerda was a little girl of seven who entered analysis because of persistent thumb sucking and other behavioral difficulties. Although it was hard to make her talk, she showed an excellent ability to express her thoughts in actions which were easy to understand, as the following example shows.

I chose for playing with her tiddlywinks, a game where each player has a number of small round men of a specific color. With these he has to jump the opponent's men, and "kill" them, and take them off the board. When we began the game, Gerda sat opposite me on a low chair, very quiet and very well behaved. When asked to choose her color, she said, "You take the black ones; no, take the red ones!" During the game, whenever one of my men was in danger, she herself saved him from being killed by sending hers far beyond it or in the opposite direction. Since this always assured my winning, I said in a casual tone: "It is quite funny to play with you. Whenever I play with other children, it is always they who want to win." She did not answer to this, but from then onward she never failed to jump on my men and succeeded in winning the next six games.

Next day she refused the black and red men and took the

First published as "Ein Kind beim Spiel." *Zeitschrift für psychoanalytische Pädagogik*, 6:245-248, 1932. The English translation, by Anna Freud, is here published for the first time.

green and yellow ones instead. While playing she became very excited, rose from her chair, and followed each move of the men with close attention. Her finger was in her mouth, and sucking became all the more violent the more she became engrossed. Whenever I missed one of her men, she relaxed, the finger dropped out of her mouth, and she returned to her chair; but whenever I hit on one, excitement rose until her finger was bitten. Nevertheless she became upset when I lost several rounds and began to comfort me by saying: "Next time you'll win." Seeing her unhappy face, I repeated several times that other children behaved quite differently, that they were pleased to win and unhappy only when they lost.

As we continued to play, her excitement increased. She remained considerate toward my men when she felt that I was looking at her; but as soon as she felt unobserved, she tried to take extra jumps or to push her men secretly into more favorable positions. This became more and more blatant until finally she cheated quite openly, placed her men wherever she wished, and insisted continually that it was her turn and not mine. In contrast to her former behavior, she stamped her feet now when she lost, swore at me, accused me of cheating, and even threw the men off the board and refused to continue playing. Thumb sucking stopped; so did the unhappiness about my losing. Instead, every win made her eyes sparkle with pleasure and made her boastful and triumphant about her skill.

In what follows, let us try and extract from Gerda's manifest behavior some knowledge concerning the latent working of her mind.

Our first impression was certainly that Gerda was a well-brought-up child, i.e., one who knew exactly how she was expected to behave. On the other hand, difficulties appeared at the very beginning of the game. When she allocated the color black to me, this meant in her language, which I had learned to understand on other occasions, that I, or my men, were destined to die. This frightened her, she rejected the thought and atoned for it by taking the black men herself, thereby turning the death wish back toward her own person.

I understood next why it needed my casual remark about the other children to make her less careful about attacking my men. Evidently, her wish to win was strong enough to frighten her so that, remembering what she had been taught, she turned it into its opposite and saved my men instead of killing them. But what I said seemed to indicate that I did not share these strict precepts, and if I did not mind, she suddenly did not mind either and could permit herself to use the skill at her disposal and to fulfill her wish to defeat me.

A day later, she seemed to try and avoid these conflicts by avoiding the black-colored men. But some of her good behavior had disappeared and her feelings were more obvious than before. She even sucked her thumb, as was her habit whenever she was anxious or expected to be disappointed. As I knew from other revelations in her analysis, she had taken the usual frustrations of early childhood specially to heart, particularly those connected with the cessation of breast feeding and the loss of her mother's exclusive care. Her fantasies continually returned to the happy period of her life when she was still an infant in arms. In her treatment she would play at being a baby, unable to speak or walk; or she would show me photos of herself as a curly-haired baby, describing how charming she used to look before her mother had cut her hair and longing to look that way again. It was this kind of disappointment which she re-experienced when, in her play with me, she was threatened by losing and which caused her to bite her finger. Presumably, in the past, she had meant to bite the frustrating breast; in the later situation, the aggressive oral wish appeared deflected from the object and directed against herself.

Nevertheless, in spite of some loosening of her inhibitions, she still was unable to enjoy winning. Experience had taught her that wish fulfillment tends to be followed by punishment. Therefore she required reassurance from me before the next step could be taken, though it needed no more than a minimum of it to release her aggression. Once this had happened, she spared no effort to achieve her ends. Fairness and good behavior dwindled to nothing in the face of her intention to win over me, to defend the intactness of her own forces and to destroy mine. Thumb sucking ceased, which was easy to understand since her instinctual wishes had now found in the game a much more effective outlet which had rendered it superfluous. I understood that she sucked her thumb when frustrated, that she bit it when revengeful, and that both activities ceased when other pathways were opened up to express her angry feelings.

I have presented this extract from Gerda's analysis to illustrate the usefulness of such observations for obtaining a glimpse of the inner workings in a child's personality with its conflicting passions and the mechanisms used for their control. Such observations of children at play can be made on many occasions, within and outside the analytic treatment situation. Whoever deals with children knows those who cannot bear to lose, who become depressed, cease all efforts to win or even take offense and stop playing. With girls this reaction can frequently be traced back to the frustration of their masculine wishes. Other children may show an opposite type of behavior: they may boast how well they are able to play and how quickly they are going to win, only to fail miserably when they are put to the test. Investigation proves that their boastfulness is no more than a defense to cover up a secret conviction of their utter incapacity ever to be successful.

While for adults games are no more than pleasant means of relaxation, play has a very different role in the life of children. A child at play reacts as he does in real life, experiencing all his passions, his satisfactions, his disappointments, and his conflicts. To win or lose a game means to him a very real success or defeat. It is this very confusion between fantasy and reality, play and life situations, which turns every observation of this kind into a useful piece of material for analytic investigation.

Chapter 3

THE URGE TO TELL AND THE COMPULSION TO CONFESS

Man's urge to tell others what is going on inside of him has always attracted the analyst's attention and interest. The existence of this urge to tell can be traced back to earliest infancy. The infant lets the environment know about his need for nourishment, warmth, and comfort by crying; the toddler is already able to communicate these same needs by means of words. But the child's wishes (expressed in this way) are not confined only to the life-sustaining necessities; they also comprise being loved, with all the feelings of pleasure the child derives from this. Thus the expression of a need for love would, in an extreme case, take the form of a declaration of love.

This simple situation is changed when the powerful educators introduce a distinction between permitted and forbidden needs. From then on the child will indicate only the wishes that are

Presented to the Vienna Psychoanalytic Society on December 20, 1933. First published as "Mitteilungsdrang und Geständniszwang." *Imago*, 20: 129-143, 1934; and *Zeitschrift für psychoanalytische Pädagogik*, 9:127-137, 1935. Here published in English for the first time.

33

permitted, while the prohibited ones will be excluded from communication and be hidden from the parents because the child then feels threatened with the loss of their love. Yet experience teaches us that the forbidden desires nevertheless do find expression. The child gives himself away, tells more than or something different from what he intended. He makes a parapraxia or forms symptoms and in this way, as if under a compulsion, he gives expression precisely to those wishes which his parents prohibited and which he himself now views as bad. This distorted form of expression could best be described as an involuntary confession. We know what the child intends to achieve with his normal voluntary confessions: with their aid he wishes to obtain the parents' forgiveness and thereby to assuage his self-reproaches. He seeks their assurance that in spite of his bad wishful strivings they will continue to love him; he wants at all costs to prevent the threatening danger of loss of their love.

The derivation and the aim of the child's parapraxias and symptoms, of his involuntary confessions, are not equally obvious to us. They represent less a confession than a self-betrayal. Their formation can perhaps be simply explained on the basis of the strength of the wishful impulses which prevail over the opposing forces. We note, however, the occurrence of a new element which again, for the second time, creates a new situation: the feeling of guilt or the need for punishment. Under its influence a confession becomes a compulsion to confess. This touches on a topic to which Reik (1925) has devoted a book. Reik explains man's urge to confess his sinful thoughts and actions on the basis of his wish for punishment, with the punishment serving to assuage the feelings of guilt that plague the individual who is conscious of his sinfulness.

Analytic insight permits us, then, to discern three different forms of communication: first, the simple communication of life-sustaining needs and the infant's wish to be loved; secondly, the voluntary confession of forbidden wishes to obtain the parents' forgiveness; and thirdly, the compulsion to confess which pertains to the same forbidden instinctual wishes but which, under the pressure of guilt and punishment, aims to alleviate the pangs of conscience. But a more thorough consideration of the forms and motives of these expressions leaves us with a sense of dissatisfaction. Behind all these communications seems to be hidden a certain instinctual force that cannot be explained by the interplay of prohibition, feeling of guilt, and wish for punishment. We may be able to find another element that fills this gap by carefully tracing the early infantile development of the urge to tell, to communicate.

These communications begin, as we have seen, in infancy with the first cry of hunger and the screaming that should indicate every disturbance of the infant's physical well-being as well as the absence of pleasurable experiences to which he has become accustomed. The next advance in communication occurs when his hands reach out for the desired objects and he cries with disappointment when such an object disappears or proves to be unobtainable. By now the child is quite able to make his wishes intelligible to the adults on whom the fulfillment or denial of his wishes depends.

The child's next developmental acquisitions, crawling and the beginnings of walking, ensure him a certain degree of independence from the adults. He is now capable of obtaining many things he wants by himself; he begins to direct his attention to all sorts of objects; looks at, touches, and examines them, and continuously widens the scope of his activities. The young child's interests change, of course, depending upon his individual characteristics and the developmental phase in which he is. He is interested in playing with water, with everything dirty; in his own body, urination and defecation; in playing with his genitals and in all the usual substitute activities. The number of objects in the environment that a two-year-old child takes interest in is already so great that they can no longer be listed in detail. All his actions, however, have a characteristic in common: the concentrated attention and complete devotion with which he pursues and carries out each newly discovered activity. These phenomena can easily be observed in every public park. Small children who for the moment are left to their own devices by the attending adults will play by themselves and are so completely absorbed in their play that the entire outside world, with the exception of this one fascinating center of their activities, has receded for them. If we look closer, we shall discover that the center of attraction is a piece of road gravel, some sand, water, dog dirt, or a bird's excrements. At the side of a street one often encounters a child who has crouched down, without the slightest concern, almost directly under a horse in order to inspect with the most intense concentration the physical proportions of this big animal.

We should not forget, however, that this independent search for pleasure represents a new situation for the young child. The infant has been, after all, completely dependent on his caretakers. His first reactions to pleasure and unpleasure was the quick and, as far as possible, complete expression of his pleasant or unpleasant sensations. The experiences of the first few months of life have taught the infant that it was not difficult to elicit in the persons who cared for him a corresponding reaction or at least an adequate response to the feelings conveyed by him. The toddler continues to be dependent on the person he loves; for this reason he wants to share his new interests, even those he has discovered independently, with that person. The child frequently uses his first words to draw an adult's attention to one of his newly found interests. His joyful excitement about this discovery is so great that he cannot keep it to himself. He wants to tell about it and for the time being has no reason to refrain from such a communication. His excitement can express itself in a sudden and, to the environment, often surprising sentence.

"Chicken hurt [dirt] under the bench" was the first sentence of a one-and-a half-year-old girl on vacation who among all the surprising novelties of country life obviously noticed first the ample supply of chicken droppings.

A mother reported that her two-year-old boy made his first verbal connection in conjunction with his first independently made observation. With great interest he drew her attention to dog dirt in their garden and called it "Lux's bam."

I had the same experience with a four-year-old. He calls me, points to a little heap of dirt in a corner of the room, and exclaims: "Look at that BM, that's Karl's BM." Karl is a much taller boy, undoubtedly much admired by him.

During a summer vacation a two-year-old lives in a farm house in which the only toilet is an outhouse located in the garden. She spends the greater part of the day in front of this door, carefully observes everyone who enters, and with genuine concern asks everyone who leaves, "Big job, or little job?"

All the examples, cited so far pertain to the well-known interest that the child, during the anal phase of his pregenital development, takes in his own excrements and those of others.

But these examples also disclose that the child is not satisfied with simply pursuing his interest; we are struck by the fact that he searches for someone with whom he can share his pleasures. These endeavors are by no means confined only to his anal interests. We recall the father's report on the analysis of little Hans:

> On about January 5th he came into his mother's bed in the morning, and said: "Do you know what Aunt M. said? She said: 'He *has* got a dear little thingummy.' " (Aunt M. was stopping with us four weeks ago. Once while she was watching my wife giving the boy a bath she did in fact say these words to her in a low voice. Hans had overheard them and was now trying to put them to his own uses.) [Freud, 1909, p. 23].

An analytic patient told me of a persistent conflict she had had with her mother in childhood. Her mother had insisted on her using the pot before going to sleep, and the patient maintained that at that time she was unable to urinate. She recalled such a scene during which she suddenly called out to her mother: "Mummy! I just found out something! If I tickle myself down there, then it comes." The patient further recalled how proud she had been about this discovery and how great she had imagined her mother's joy would be. The new trick would finally do away with the long and boring period of waiting for her urination. She was completely dumbfounded by her mother's violent rebuke.

At that time the little girl's communication seems not at all to have been related to a feeling of guilt. The discovery of masturbation and of the pleasurable feelings connected with it were for her a great experience, and it seemed only natural to her to let her mother participate in it.

In this illustration, too, the child's interest in masturbation that the patient recalled tells us nothing new. The only element worth noting is the child's attempt to induce her mother to take part in her newly found pleasure.

A little boy calls me over to his aquarium. "Look at the fish; look how they swim on top of each other." Each time a fish covers another, he shouts again: "Look, look!" He obviously tries to call my attention to something extra special—something that for him has a very special significance, probably in analogy to his observation of a sexual scene. Nothing in his behavior would indicate timidity or anxiety or any thought that what he pointed out to me might arouse my disapproval.

The child's wish to tell us about his experiences and discoveries persists beyond the earliest infantile years. The mother of a six-year-old girl reports that her daughter runs out of the garden, comes tearing up the stairs, bursts into her room, and shouts, breathless and in great excitement: "Mommie, mommie, come quickly, Bubi [their dog] is just getting married in the garden; come, come on." With this she turns around, abruptly leaves the room, runs down the stairs and back into the garden. It is striking that in this case the little girl's urge to tell about her observation was stronger than her curiosity. That she was capable of leaving what was probably the most exciting spectacle in her life; that in this moment she thought of her mother; and that this thought was sufficiently compelling to induce her to turn away from the spectacle and run to her mother—these circumstances present the best evidence for the strength of the instinctual force that feeds the urge to tell.

The urge to tell about sexual experiences, the wish to have the mother take part in the pleasurable experience, is what these examples have in common. At first the child uses the most simple means: he invites the adult to look and, to the extent of the vocabulary at his disposal, he verbalizes his experience. His untiring efforts obviously have the aim to convert his lonesome pleasure into a shared experience—an experience *à deux*. The child is engaged in a search for a partner. Further consideration would indicate that he thereby tends to re-establish an earlier state. After all, he felt the first sexual stirrings when his mother attended to his body care; he experienced her ministrations as pleasurable and now wants to repeat them. When the child, with his newly won independence, discovers new sources of pleasure, he naturally turns to his partner of an earlier period. He invites his mother: "Come, let us both enjoy this new pleasure, as we once shared earlier pleasures." The examples cited above are the first harmless, open and direct sexual communications by means of which the child invites participation and cooperation.

But this ideal state of affairs does not last long. The young child's natural urge to tell soon comes into conflict with educational requirements. When the child runs to the adult to tell him about his exciting discoveries, he encounters not sympathy and interest but rebuke. He learns that one should not notice such things and even less talk about them. The child feels hurt that his interesting communications are so little appreciated and withdraws from the adults to pursue his new activities by himself. He certainly does not yet give up the interests that have been criticized, such as his anal pleasures; on the contrary, he retains some of them even into adulthood; he merely learns to hide his activities from the view of the critical adults. But he does conform in his external behavior and at first attempts by every conceivable means to safeguard his parents' high opinion and love.

Yet, this cessation of sexual communications ushers in all of the child's secretiveness. The adult enters the child's room and the child quickly drops what he held in his hand or instantly begins to play with something entirely different. The adult stands outside the child's room and does not hear a sound. As soon as he opens the door, the child bursts into feverish activities which are to hide that he has just been interrupted in the silent pursuit of some secret. The adult feels that he has disturbed a pleasurable activity.

This uncommunicativeness and secretiveness are also new acquisitions of the child, but they do not succeed completely. The adult senses the child's restlessness. Although he wants to keep his secrets, he nevertheless is subject to a compulsion that despite this wish urges him to tell. The child cannot break away from his real interests. He must talk about them, must at least hint at them. It is merely the old direct route of communication that no longer can be used; he must deny his interests if he wishes to refrain from making his parents angry and from averting the danger of being punished and of losing their love.

Small children are especially fond of nonsense talk. They jabber away in some unintelligible gibberish which they want to make sound as though it were a foreign language. Possibly, they are imitating the adults, are enjoying the sound of words which do not yet have a meaning for them, and they may simply experience pleasure in the use and sound of their own voice. But if one pays closer attention to this "nonsense," one frequently can make sense out of it and suddenly understand what the child is really trying to say.

I recall such an incident with a four-year-old girl. I was out on a walk with this child leading her by the hand. While I was preoccupied with my own thoughts, the child was singing loudly beside me. At first I paid no attention to her nonsense, but her singing became increasingly louder, shriller, and more penetrating until I was finally forced to listen. I noticed that she again and again varied one and the same sentence in her song: "My tail tickles me, my tail tickles me." Apparently, it mattered very much to her to give me this piece of information about her body.

Let us compare this story with that of the patient who as a child told her mother, "When I tickle myself down there, it comes." Both children tell the same thing; they describe their newly discovered sensations of pleasure during masturbation. But while one child naïvely and trustingly told her mother about her experience, the little girl who was walking with me used an indirect form of expression. Having had some unpleasant experiences, she already knows that her mother prohibits masturbation. Perhaps she is not even fully aware of what she is singing; intoxicated with the melody and the rhythm, she probably loses sight of the meaning of the accompanying words. The urge to tell, the wish to have me share her pleasure and activity, the invitation and even seduction to take a part and be an accomplice are the same as in the first example; only the form of expression differs, the singing disguising the wish in compliance with and for the sake of external proprieties.

The same four-year-old says: "Once I put the nailbrush in my nose. Will my nose get very big one day?" With this, too, she tells about her masturbation. One could also assume that a feeling of guilt and anxiety about the dire physical consequences are beginning to establish themselves. But that is not yet all she tells us. She also betrays her knowledge of the male organ and of the hole into which it can disappear, and expresses her hope that one day she too will possess such an organ. In this sense her communication contains an invitation, an attempt at seduction, addressed to her mother, although it is disguised by guilt feelings and the fear of punishment. It is also of interest to observe that parents will react to such a communication by the child with disproportionately vehement defenses and rejection. One can assume that unconsciously they have perceived the child's unconscious intention to seduce them.

The child's inquisitiveness can also be used indirectly in the service of the urge to tell. We know that the child asks his innumerable questions because his sexual curiosity is unsatisfied. But even this explanation does not fully do justice to the existing circumstances. The child asks and asks, a continuous stream of questions, but he pays no attention to the answers, as if he had nothing to do with them. If we follow his questions without answering them as though they were associations, we realize that they lead to a theme of utmost significance in the child's life. The child wants to tell us something, wants us to guess what he has to say, but does not dare to take the direct route. Sometimes he will ask a question and, before one can possibly reply, quickly answer it himself. He demands no answer. He wants to say, "Oh, I know all that. I only want to tell you something with my questions, but I am afraid of what you will say to it." But in spite of his anxiety his questions continue; the urge to tell prevails and succeeds in giving expression to the child's important concerns. This passion for asking questions, then, is like the child's nonsense talk, merely an indirect manifestation of the sexual urge to tell.

From what has been said so far we realize that the child's urge to tell, both in its direct and in its indirect manifestations, is doomed to fail. The child will be rejected by his parents who want no part in his sexual pleasures. The child then withdraws into himself and pursues his pleasures alone. But that is not all. He does not merely withdraw his invitation for partnership and participation from the adult, he also withdraws some of his libido from the adult. It is as if he wanted to say, "If you don't want to share something nice with me, I don't want to have anything to do with you."

It is during this period that mothers begin to complain about the child's inaccessibility. They do not succeed in getting the child to answer questions, and the child seems peculiarly uninterested in everything that until then had been of vital concern to him. A mother tries, for example, to explain to her child where children come from, and she tries very hard to do it well. But she encounters such a wall of indifference in the child that she gets stuck. Or she asks the child, "Would you like me to tell you where children come from?" and receives the prompt reply, "Oh, no. I'm not in the least interested in that." The mother knows very well that the child does not speak the truth. In fact, he behaves like a rejected lover who wants to have nothing to do with the object of his love and disappointment. Parents are often quite amazed and disappointed to find that this attitude of the child's persists throughout the entire latency period.

I here want to refer to a comment Bernfeld made in his discussion of Buxbaum's paper on lying (1933). Bernfeld pointed especially to the educator's emotional attitude to children's lies. He senses that by lying the children remove themselves from his sphere of authority and become inaccessible. The background of this attitude can perhaps be further illuminated by examining it from the viewpoint of the child's urge to tell. A child who lies feels rejected by the adult; the lie is the opposite of the invitation to be a partner and accomplice; it interrupts the intimate contact between child and adults. The child who no longer tells the truth to the adults also is no longer dependent on the adults for love. His lying is his revenge for not having succeeded, with the aid of truth, to win the adult as a partner. Concealment and secretiveness do, of course, have the same function as lying.

During the early period of development, the child's urge to tell manifests itself in relation to his immediate family members. During puberty it is transferred to objects in the more extended environment. We know that the adolescent takes himself and his interests very seriously. He searches for someone like-minded in whom he can confide his ideas and theories about himself and the world. He longs for a comrade with whom he can engage in lengthy philosophical discourse, who shows understanding for all his subjective and objective problems, and who will not belittle or ridicule his grandiose ideas for improving the world. But most of all he searches for someone with whom he can talk about himself, who will not become tired of listening to the description of his fascinating, unfathomable, and complicated feelings. He is ready to confide his most intimate thoughts and to reveal the secrets that so passionately excite him. He develops a new and astonishing propensity for being ruthlessly frank about himself. His friend should know him, understand him, and share the truth with him.

But his mood suddenly changes, and his philosophizing turns into silly nonsense talk, laughing and giggling—which, mutually shared, are enjoyed no less.

These two types of behavior in adolescent friendships remind us, on the one hand, of the direct and frank communications of the young child who wants to tell about and share his wonderful discoveries, and on the other hand of the nonsense talk of the child who in a later phase communicates his thoughts indirectly. In this respect, as in so many others, the similarity in the emotional attitude during early childhood and puberty is striking. Both young child and adolescent use the same means of communication; and in both developmental phases the instinctual background remains entirely the same: the lonely pursuit of pleasure is abandoned in order to search for a partner.

This similarity becomes even more striking when we consider how frequently the philosophizing or the silly nonsense talk are abruptly replaced by direct sexual activities, i.e., mutual masturbation. Parenthetically, philosophizing and nonsense talk continue to play a role in later life in the early stages of falling in love; moreover, nonsense talk and joking are counted among the forepleasure activities of normal sexual intercourse.

With regard to the development of the sexual urge to tell from

early infancy to puberty, we can conclude that a definite intention motivates the child's communications, both in their direct
and frank and in their indirect and disguised forms. The child
utilizes the communication of his sexual concerns and activities
in order to attract another person's interest in him. We might
say that by boasting about them he wants to seduce us.

But with this insight we begin to realize that the underlying
mechanism represents nothing new; we are on familiar ground.
The instinctual force that finds expression in the child's urge
to tell is nothing other than exhibitionism—exhibitionism that
has the aim of showing off his body, his genitals. As we know,
the exhibitionistic act is always an attempt to seduce. The exhibitionist needs a partner, one who is ready to let himself be
seduced to join in the pleasure of looking at the genital. Under
the influence of the urge to tell, the child behaves in the same
manner, the only difference being that instead of displaying his
genitals he displays his sexual interests and activities. By confessing his sexual sins he exhibits in order to seduce.

When verbal communications accompany the exhibitionistic
act, they have of course always been recognized as such. Persons
who have succeeded in accommodating their exhibitionism in
their language behavior take a special pleasure in their verbal
facility, in well-chosen, striking, and surprising turns of speech,
but require for their enjoyment at least one person who listens
to them with rapt attention. They behave in this area like an
exhibitionist who, instead of showing off his naked body, be-
decks it with especially beautiful, colorful, and striking clothes
in order to attract the other's eyes. The nonsense talk and the
silly joking, on the other hand, resemble the skills of a clown,
who by his clowning succeeds in becoming the center of attention. Showing off the body and showing off with words combine
in the exhibitionism of the actor in whose skills word and gesture mutually support each other. The close relationship between these behaviors becomes even more apparent if we look at
these phenomena from the viewpoint of the repression of ex-

hibitionism and the resulting inhibitions of speech. In stage
fright, for example, we can clearly discern both elements: the
fear of speaking and the fear of revealing oneself; that is to say,
the fear of being heard and looked at. As a result the individual
becomes reserved, shy, and inconspicuous. But the very same
persons, in their secret fantasies, dream of being great orators
or actors who are admired and applauded by incredibly huge
audiences.

Having followed the manifestations of the urge to tell in normal human development, I now turn to its utilization in the
neuroses of children and adults, where the same mechanisms
can be viewed in abnormal exaggeration.

In our seminar on child analysis Annie Angel [Katan] reported on the case of a ten-year-old girl. This patient began her
analysis by enumerating her misdeeds: she was a thief, a liar,
she rode the trolley without paying her fare. Her description
gave one the clear impression that she was immensely proud of
her heroic exploits. During the session she was exceedingly
unruly, threw paper, damaged the furniture, and gleefully slid
down the backs of chairs. She was quite good at gymnastics and
once offered to demonstrate to the analyst some of her recently
learned feats. When the analyst consented, the child instantly
and with lightning speed began to undress herself before she
could be stopped. One day the child arrived at the analytic hour
carrying a huge bag which she threw at the analyst's feet, shouting: "Look at all the things I have stolen." This child's behavior
clearly reveals two trends: she boasts, on the one hand, about
her athletic feats and, on the other, about her misdeeds. The
exhibitionism in her behavior was obvious to all the participants
in the seminar, but not its motives. From the vantage point of
the urge to tell one would have to say: she exhibits the stolen
items as she exhibits her body in order to seduce the analyst.

The second example, also from the seminar on child analysis,
was reported by Berta Bornstein in 1933. The patient was an
eleven-year-old girl whose dissocial behavior was definitely

compulsive. Her need to gossip with the servants as well as other people outside the home constantly created havoc; she stole small objects and occasionally also money. But instead of concealing her misdeeds, she felt compelled again and again to tell her mother, who each time became highly agitated. Clearly, she could not control her urge to confess.

Our first thought is that the girl acts under the influence of guilt feelings and the need for punishment. But the astonishing factor in this process is that the mother reacts to the child as though the confessions concerned not simple misdeeds that could easily be forgiven or responded to with appropriate punishment. The mother reacts with vehement defenses as though she were warding off a sexual approach. The child exhibits her sins in front of the mother as though she were saying, "Look how bad I am. And I know that you are no better. Couldn't we be bad together?" The mother's unconscious reacts as if she had understood the attempted seduction and must reject it.

Another illustration was provided by Edith Jackson. The patient was a seventeen-year-old girl who came for analysis because of a homosexual relationship with a girl of the same age. The patient related that one day she felt compelled to tell a recently married relative about her homosexual affair. There was no external reason for this confession. The patient was astonished and frightened when this young woman responded with an unequivocally homosexual approach to her. Obviously, the young woman had correctly interpreted the confession as a sexual invitation.

Another example derives from the history of a male patient, who as a young man formed a friendship with an older colleague. At a certain point in the course of this relationship, which was of extraordinary significance in this patient's life, he suddenly felt compelled to confess something to his older friend. Some time ago he had had an affair with a girl, in the course of which he had engaged in perverse activities. He believed he owed his friend this confession, felt duty-bound to tell his friend everything about himself and not to make himself out better than he was. He hoped his intimacy and complete frankness would further strengthen the bond of their friendship. But the result did not correspond to his expectations: instead of drawing closer together, the two men became estranged. The older man did not quite know what to do with this unwelcome confession, while the young man felt deeply hurt and rejected. The unconscious content of his confession was apparently an attempt to seduce his friend to engage in the same perverse activities. But the older man did not understand and denied the young man the instinctual gratification he had expected as a response.

And now a final illustration. Several years ago a young woman with whom I was acquainted told me about a strange incident in her life, which I believe I understand only now.

My friend had a cousin with whom she had a warm, genuinely sisterly relationship in her childhood. One day, several years after her marriage, she suddenly felt compelled to make him her confidant and confess to him that she had started an extramarital relationship with a young man whom her cousin knew well. The effect of this confession was overwhelming. Her cousin immediately made sexual advances to her, was beside himself when she rebuked him, began to mistreat and beat her, and finally in a sudden fit of rage attempted to rape her. She just managed to run out of the room, while he broke down and immediately had to be hospitalized. But the effect which this scene had on my friend was also unexpected. Once it was over, she felt compelled to tell everyone at hand about the course of this event in the most minute detail. Her urge to talk was so unbearable and so uncontrollable that after twenty-four hours she finally persuaded a physician to induce sleep and silence with the help of a morphine injection. But the urge to talk about this event persisted, though in a milder form, throughout a prolonged period of her life.

There is no doubt in my mind now that the cousin interpreted her confession as a sexual invitation, whereas she was left with the urge to repeat over and over again, in relation to others, the confession of her invitation directed to her cousin.

It is to be expected that the urge to tell which we have so far followed in its normal development and in its neurotic exaggerations also plays an especially significant role in analysis, in which telling and confessing naturally form an integral part. In his work the analyst struggles with all those forces that prevent the unconscious material from becoming conscious. As an aid in his endeavors he can count on the natural tendencies of unconscious strivings to break through to consciousness. But apart from this tendency he finds other aids in the patient himself: the patient is motivated by a conscious wish to be cured which stems from his insight into his illness; in the stage of positive transference the patient wants to support the analyst's efforts in order to gain his love and approval; finally, the analytic situation provides ample opportunities to gratify the patient's compulsion to confess and his need for punishment.

Thus, the urge to tell that has been described in this chapter appears to be capable of becoming a positive carrier of the analytic cure. Making repressed sexual material conscious can simultaneously gratify the patient's exhibitionistic needs. "Let us look at these bad things together; let us share them," may at times become a patient's motivation for analysis.

This tendency can be observed most clearly in the initial hours of an analytic treatment. We know that patients frequently reveal the deepest content of their neuroses in the very first analytic hours. In his first dreams and associations the patient often brings us the most important material, though he does not of course recognize it or appreciate its significance. We are accustomed to explain these occurrences by assuming that at this initial stage the patient is not yet warned, does not yet know about the means of understanding and interpreting that are at the analyst's disposal, and so is still unaware of the dangers entailed in the revelation of his unconscious. Naturally, at this time the patient brings not only unconscious but also conscious material. He senses, or may already have been informed by others, that his illness is somehow connected with his sexuality; as a consequence he makes every attempt to confess all the sexual sins of which he is conscious. This accumulation of conscious and unconscious sexual material then leads to exhibitionism that will be used in the service of seducing the analyst.

The repression of material that occurs very soon after the first interpretation perhaps needs no longer to be understood solely on the basis of the anxiety that the patient, now warned of the dangers of analysis, experiences. The patient, after all, also experienced a rejection: his confession, his invitation to partnership, has received no response. Therefore, precisely like one who has been rejected, he again withdraws from the analyst with all his secrets and uses the disappointment he repeated with the analyst to reinforce his repressions.

But he succeeds as little as he did in childhood in finally relinquishing his wish for shared sexual activities. We find this wish again, e.g., in the patient's demand for hypnosis. "Just ask me questions, I'll answer all of them." "If only you would hypnotize me, so I could say everything without knowing what I'm saying." We know that the patient's wish to be hypnotized is a wish to be sexually overwhelmed. In this context the idea of hypnosis represents an attempt to hold the analyst responsible for the confession, that is to say, for the exhibitionism. When the analyst forces the patient to reveal his sexuality, he becomes the seducer rather than the seduced.

We can similarly understand the behavior of acting-out patients who feel compelled to talk about details of their analyses to persons in the outside world. These patients act like the homosexual patient who felt compelled to disclose the secret of her homosexual activities to her recently married relative. The exhibitionism has merely been displaced from the analyst to the outside world.

I hope that in this essay I have succeeded in convincingly

describing man's urge to tell and in delineating it from the compulsion to confess which is familiar to us from Reik's work. On the basis of the foregoing considerations it appears to me that the urge to tell, especially when it is traced back to its early beginnings, represents a positive striving. It is not in the service of unpleasure or masochistic gratifications, but functions as a means of attracting, winning, and seducing a partner. A manifestation of sexual strivings in the service of the pleasure principle, it aims at a positive pleasure gain. The compulsion to confess derives from the pressure of guilt feelings and the need for punishment. Its aim is, on the one hand, to alleviate conscience, and, on the other, to gain masochistic gratifications by accepting the punishment.

Chapter 4

EMPATHY BETWEEN INFANT AND MOTHER

In "Child Analysis and the Mother" (Chapter 1), I have attempted to describe the strength of maternal influence on the child, and to demonstrate how far the child's problems are distorted and obscured by the impact of the mother's conscious and unconscious affective reactions. Since then, this empathy between mother and child has continued to engage my interest, and the present paper is devoted to the same problem.

To begin with, I wish to emphasize that what concerns me here is not the development of the infant's observational abilities as such. The latter is a wider subject and one which has been dealt with intensively and extensively by academic psychologists. But while they deal primarily with the development of the intellect and only secondarily with the affective side of life, I reverse the order, refer in the first place to the affects, and secondarily to the intellectual side merely for the purposes of illustration.

The infant is, above all, a receiver of stimuli; from a certain age onward, he begins to assimilate what he receives; i.e., he

First published as "Die Einfühlung des Kleinkindes in die Mutter." *Imago*, 21:429-444, 1935. The English translation is reprinted from *Journal of the American Psychoanalytic Association*, 15:764-780, 1967.

begins to observe, an activity which is, of course, not restricted to vision but spreads equally over the whole of the sense apparatus. Some of his observations come to the notice of the parents, who react to them either with encouragement or the reverse; most of them remain unnoticed and, as such, the child's own private affair.

It may be justified to assume that, from early on, the infant directs attention to the varying expressions on the mother's face and reacts to them with pleasure or unpleasure, according to their nature. He carries on with these observations on his own, collecting his own experiences, and drawing his own conclusions from them, which he stores up for future use. In this manner, all unknowingly, he acquires valuable knowledge. One specific facial expression of the mother, for example, means to him that some pleasurable event is in the offing. Another expression signifies that the mother is in a hurry; whatever she has to accomplish for the child will be done quickly so that she can leave. Yet another means that the mother is preoccupied and even the most tempting smile of the child will remain unanswered. Out of these and similar experiences, the infant constructs his own inner world in which he reigns supreme, a world which is constantly enriched by new experiences of his mother's expressions and attitudes.

This fabric built from residues of external stimulation becomes more elaborate as the infant is able to extend his observation to the more complicated affective reactions shown by the mother. His ability to observe, though present from infancy, increases from month to month and may reach a peak at certain times. In general, it keeps pace with those other capacities of the child which are under parental control, i.e., which are accelerated or kept in check by parental praise or criticism. At times, the child's capacity for empathy may be advanced far beyond his other achievements, as the parents notice with astonishment. To them, this secret knowledge possessed by the child remains something extraordinary, unexplained, almost supernatural. A mother, for example, who feels distressed for some reason, will be surprised by the child suddenly appearing at her side with the question: "Sad?" The child has guessed the mothers' mood without being told about it. Or the child may bring a toy to the mother, in an effort to comfort her. There are other instances when the child's ability to guess is less pleasing to the adult world. Mother or nurse may be in a hurry, for example, because of an outing. Just then the child will be especially difficult to handle, sensing beforehand that he will be left behind. Another time the mother may feel depressed and, seemingly without cause, the child begins to whine and to resist feeding or sleep; he shows in his behavior that he has sensed the mother's mood and become infected by it. This intuition of the child resembles what we find in animals. He observes and understands and, without communicating his observations, he uses them as a basis for his own behavior.

So far as the infant is concerned, it seems that this type of experience, which he acquires independently, is valued more highly by him than what he is taught by the adult world. On the one hand, it is not limited or fixed; new impressions arrive, blot out, alter, or increase the content. These observations concern realities, in contrast to the precepts communicated by adults, which are often no more than suppositions, prejudices, or even pious lies. The infant learns thus to live in two different worlds simultaneously: in a "real" world of his own, shared with nobody, in which words are superfluous; and in another, adult, world, in which this kind of observation plays a minor part, in which secondhand experience is handed down to him by the parents, and in which words are added to the images of things and to the facts.

The gradual building up of this second set of experiences is not difficult to follow. Here, too, the child learns gradually, for example, that fire burns and that falls are painful. But teaching, as it comes from the mother, is of a peculiar nature. She may point to the burning stove and add the word "hot." However, next day, when the stove is not burning, she may repeat her action and word since her motive is to warn the child off the stove whatever its condition at the moment. The child, already much too observant to confuse a hot with a cold stove, is not deceived, of course, but he is puzzled. He receives the impression that the mother's words do not always coincide with reality, an impression which is confirmed repeatedly.

There may be an occasion when the mother has a visitor. The child observes this person with interest, notices a pimple on his nose, and remarks on it. This creates an awkward situation which makes the mother angry and from which the child will draw the conclusion that certain facts, though observed, must not be mentioned. Or the child, to his amazement, overhears the mother falsifying facts when making excuses for social convenience, a situation which is far beyond the child's conception. This teaches him gradually to assess the adult world as a mixture of truth and falsehood, very different from his own inner world. He begins to compare the picture of the world as offered by the parents with his own and cannot help feeling that the latter is clearer, more intelligible, and reliable. But here he is in conflict. Owing to his own love for the parents and his great need to be loved by them, he feels forced to adapt to their world, and he succeeds in this endeavor, even though much has to be sacrificed for it. So far the child was a strong believer in the "facts" he observed and also took it for granted that the parental figures were part of this real world of experience which he had constructed for himself, reliable, secure, immutable, and above all predictable whatever the occasion. Such expectations on the child's part invariably meet with disappointments. The child observes the parents and concludes that their behavior is unreliable, that they are changeable, often untruthful, and guided by motives which are alien and beyond his understanding.

But before the parents' reversal and distortion of "facts" have come to the child's knowledge, other experiences have crowded in on him. He has learned that even the parents' facial expressions of emotion are not always what they seem to be. This is confusing since essentially the area of the emotions in the world outside is nearest to what goes on in the child himself, and is therefore easiest to follow and to understand. There are occasions when the mother smiles and the child feels nevertheless that her friendly expression is no more than a covering for irritation, anger, anxiety. If observation started for the infant with scrutinizing the mother's face and deriving pleasure or unpleasure from her expressions, he has to understand now that the mother's real feelings and their expression do not always coincide. The mother may, some day, tend the child as she always does, and still the child may sense that she does so against an inner resistance. Or the mother may be in a state of anxiety which she denies so as not to affect the child; still he will sense that she is anxious. The mother may try to show herself full of affection for the child in spite of the fact that this offspring is, in truth, unwanted and a disturbance in her life. She does everything in her power not to let the child feel the true state of affairs. Nevertheless, the child will experience her affection as false.

Gradually, after understanding the adult's feelings directed to himself, the child also comes to understand those which the adults near him experience for each other. Granted that at times these feelings may concern the person of the child as well. For example, the parents may be united in fearing for the child's health or safety; or they may be at cross-purposes with each other, with the child at the center of their quarrel. The child observes this, his own emotions aroused by theirs, and he has difficulty in deciding whose side to be on. On the other hand, often enough the parents' quarrels concern extraneous matters. In this case, the child is left out and has occasion to observe that adults hide their real feelings not only from him, but also from one another. They may speak to each other, but their words disguise instead of revealing their feelings. The mother may do her utmost to hide her love, her anxiety, her feelings of pleasure or jealousy not only from the child, but also from the adult world. She tries to deceive the father as well, she may act coolly and with indifference, for instance, while feeling the opposite. Or mother and father, while feeling alike, may hide this from all other people; or the father may show his feelings freely in the presence of strangers and only hide them from the mother, etc.

Even when faced with observations of this kind, the small child with his heightened susceptibility manages to collect experiences and to draw conclusions from them. Here, as with reference to his own person, he senses deceit and falsehood without understanding the reasons for them; but his desire to understand grows in proportion to the mass of impressions he receives. To interpret what happens in the adult world he has to fall back on his own inner world of "facts." This means that he observes the insincerity of adults with great acuteness and that he begins to take it for granted that the adults' feelings and actions do not necessarily come from the same source. The resultant uncertainty is accepted by him as a new "fact."

As time passes, the inner situation of a child who assimilates these facts without comprehending them becomes more and more complex and the gulf increases between his own "factual" world and that of the parents. While the child is not too confused, and while his relations with the parents remain fairly stable, he will attempt to satisfy his curiosity by collecting and storing an ever-increasing number of observations. But there is a limit to these attempts, and this will be reached when sexual riddles take the center of the stage and the child feels threatened by his own passions and the concomitant jealousies, frustrations, and anxieties. Here, the straightforward path, taken so far, becomes too dangerous and the child turns to safer methods of conflict solution. His ability to observe accurately becomes inhibited and he begins to repress or distort past experience. In short, he drops his former observant attitude in favor of one or the other of the defense mechanisms which are at the disposal of human beings for the purpose of warding off danger.

What has been said so far can therefore be summarized in a single hypothesis: namely, that the child's ability to observe is more penetrating and more far-reaching than had been thought so far. If, formerly, we believed in a surprising telepathic gift in the young child, this is explained much more simply by the acuteness of his observations,[1] his attentiveness to the world around him, the logic of his conclusions, and the correctness of the reactions based on them. There is nothing uncanny in all this, and infantile nature has become more intelligible to us in one particular respect. But this is by no means the end of our investigation. On the contrary, the attempt to solve one problem has brought us face to face with a further, even more difficult one.

If we return once more to the infant's first year of life and compare it with the beginning of life in the animal world: what, in fact, are the similarities between them? Our answer is that both human and animal young pass through a period of learning in which they exercise their sense organs, develop their abilities; they receive stimulation, are perceptive and instinctive; they learn to grasp complexities and to draw conclusions. So much for the similarities. The differences between the two situations appear when we begin to measure the distance between the young and the mature creature. The animal mother, in the course of her life, has gone further and further in perfecting the use of her sensory apparatus, and her ability to receive and interpret stimuli arriving from the environment are much more intense than they were in the first months of life. Here, the line of development takes a straightforward course. In contrast to this, the human mother, in the course of her life, has *lost* much of the intuition and perceptiveness which she possessed as a child; what is left are no more than fragments of the original capacities.

[1] Similar attempts to explain telepathic manifestations were made in a discussion in the Vienna Psychoanalytic Society following a review given by Grete [Lehner] Bibring of Freud's "Dreams and Occultism" on May 3, 1933. See also Paul Schilder's review (1934) of a paper by Hollós (1933).

Their place has been taken by other abilities which a process of education has promoted and which are meant to serve adaptation to the customs and laws governing an adult human community.

Thus, while animal young and human young resemble each other in many respects, the mothers of both species do not do so, and the task of adapting to the mother is a completely different one in the two instances. The young animal is an instinctive being whose instinctive interests are shared with the mother animal. Through watching the mother's behavior the young animal learns to distinguish between situations which are for her—and therefore also for him—either pleasurable or fear-arousing. He lives in an uncomplicated world without contradictions in which his growth proceeds in a straightforward line. In contrast to this, contradictions abound in the world of the human infant. There are the puzzling changes in the mother's attitudes, as described above; the lack of coherence between her feelings and her facial expressions; the fact that the parents demand from the child what they do not carry out themselves. The infant is ready to imitate the parents, but there are many instances when imitation does not serve the purpose. As a consequence, the infant becomes involved in conflict and fails to extract sense from his observations. An animal mother, under the impact of fear, will either attack or run away, and the young animal at her side will not only perceive her behavior but share it. The human mother under the same conditions will try above all to hide her fear so as not to pass it on to the infant, whether she hides it only from the child or denies it also in herself. Therefore, the occasions are rare when emotions are shown to the children undisguised. So far as their conscious efforts go, parents usually try to keep children in the dark about their real feelings, unsuccessful as they may be in these attempts.

To return once more to the earliest mother-infant relationship. So far as the need for care and nourishment is concerned, the infant is wholly dependent on the mother. In the ensuing close contact between them, the mother is the first external source of stimulation; she is responsible for arousing pleasure and causing frustration; and she becomes the target for the infant's earliest positive and negative affects. Inevitably her predilections, or their repressions, will give direction to the infant's experiences. A mother, for example, who enjoys kissing, may smother the infant with kisses which the latter will enjoy in turn. Another mother may enjoy the game of mouthing the infant's hands and feet; this will also arouse pleasurable sensations in the child. Or a mother may be inclined to resort to frequent enemas which, again, will excite another part of the infant's body. In short, and as is well known to the psychoanalyst, the mother's oral and anal inclinations are powerful influences on the child. On the other hand, her influence also makes itself felt when she merely has the impulse to act in one of these ways, but is prevented from doing so by inhibitions, shame, or better knowledge.

Whenever the latter happens, her own restraint has further repercussions. The mother who refrains from kissing the infant will also prevent other adults from doing it, or will react with disgust if this happens against her wishes. She may also be inhibited in kissing so far as her relations with her husband are concerned, and this does not remain unnoticed by the infant for whom this particular expression of affection thereby acquires a negative connotation. The same is true for the other bodily areas to which reference has been made. If the mother refrains from playing with the infant's limbs, she will nevertheless continue to be attracted by them and betray this in a number of abortive mouthing movements. The infant will sense that his limbs are important objects which excite the mother's orality. Mothers who have learned not to give enemas are usually unable to hide their preoccupation with the child's digestive tract. They are overanxious when elimination is irregular, and they pay excessive attention to the child's diet. Whatever happens, the infant cannot fail to notice how highly significant his excrements are in the mother's eyes.

It has to be added here that where the mother tries to abstain from acting out her impulses, the restrictions which are imposed on them will occasionally break down. Such breakthroughs are loaded with affect and therefore important to the child, the more so if they happen rarely.

What follows are a number of further examples which I was able to collect.

One mother, among those observed, suffered from an excessive fear of infection. Consequently, she strove to protect her child in every way from dangerous germs; she paid special attention to washing and to avoidance of contact with specific objects and persons. In the beginning the infant enjoyed the stimulation connected with the washing procedures, but soon the restrictions and prohibitions imposed on him made themselves felt in an unpleasant way. Above all, the protective measures taken by the mother constantly directed the child's attention in a specific manner. The mother's neurotic anxiety in this matter became a vital factor in the child's development.

Another mother, who was unusually jealous and domineering in character, habitually took the center of the stage at all times. She smothered the child with affection and enjoyed his complete dependence on her. On the other hand, she found it intolerable if the child paid attention to anybody else; she became irritable and angry with him on such occasions, and eager to separate him again from his new love object. Naturally, the child sensed this. Partly he enjoyed being such an important person for the mother and appreciated the attention paid to him; partly he felt unpleasantly restricted in his choice of love objects. Again, we shall not be surprised to find that the character of the mother played an important role in determining the growth of the child.

Another mother had depressive episodes during which she withdrew all interest from the child and remained concentrated on her own problems. During such times, the child felt unhappy, out of touch with and out of reach of the mother. Whenever the mother recovered from her bouts of depression, her affections returned to the child. But the child remained affected by the intermittent character of the mother's relationship to him.

Initially, we should have expected the child to react with hostility and rejection to these anxieties, jealousies, or mood swings on the part of the mother. Experience showed that this is not the case. One mother, suffering from anxiety states, reported that on days when she was most anxious, her little boy was apt to play with especially dangerous tools or to run to her complaining of the most harmless scratches as if they were major injuries. Also, at such times, he spoke incessantly of illnesses and accidents. Granted that such a mother may exaggerate innocent remarks, it remains a fact that the child does not attempt to withdraw from her excessive care, but, on the contrary, plays into her fears.

Likewise, the jealous mother reported that her child could not do enough in favoring other people in her presence, kissing and hugging the nurse or her friend in a provocative manner. Evidently, by demonstrating his affection for these others, he attempted to increase the mother's jealousies. The periodically depressed mother reported that her child excelled in naughtiness, irritableness, and provoking behavior whenever she felt worst, a change in the child noticed not only by her but confirmed by all other members of the household. According to this mother, it felt as if the child had every intention of increasing her depression. This happened so regularly that the mother had learned to use the child's reaction as the first indication of the recurrence of her depression, even if at the time she had not yet become aware of it herself.

Experiences such as these show the extent to which the personality of the mother becomes a decisive factor in the development of the child's personality. Doubtless, the largest part is played in this by those traits in the mother which are highly affect-laden either because of their manifest importance in her libidinal life or because of the effort at repression: here, the mother's unconscious is no less vital for the child than what happens in her consciousness.

What has happened is that, all along the line of development, the child has followed where the mother has led him. This began with the pleasurable stimulation of those parts of his body which fitted in with her predilections or disinclinations, the mother "seducing" the infant where she felt attracted, or attracting his attention through her very efforts at repression. After responding to the mother's seductive actions or their opposites, the child on his part then makes every effort to seduce the mother, for this purpose employing the ways and means which are charged with affect by her, and reacts to whichever impulse dominates her at the moment. This interaction between mother and child creates a bond of intimacy as well as the semblance of far-reaching similarity between them. The mother's character, her neurosis, her obsessions, anxieties, symptoms, in short, her affects as well as her repressions have passed from mother to child with lightning speed and power.

This shows us that it is perceptiveness which enables the child to explore the mother's surface as well as her depth, and that it is the conscious and unconscious reactions of the mother which betray her central problems in positive or negative ways to the child. While direct observations teaches the child what happens in the mother's consciousness, perception of her defenses and abstentions leads indirectly to conclusions about the unconscious part of her personality. Understanding this, we do not maintain, as we did before, that the child's unconscious has made contact with the unconscious of the mother. We say instead that the child is an acute observer of all those overt reactions of the mother which betray what happens in the depth of her mind. The child draws conclusions from what he has observed and bases actions on these inferences.

Remarkable as these capacities of the child are, they are

limited so far as duration is concerned; i.e., they diminish and are lost as another capacity, that of adaptation to the adult world, takes over.

As mentioned above, from a certain age onward knowledge of the observed facts is repressed from the child's consciousness to avoid danger. The more serious the conflicts which the parents display to the child, the more energetic are his efforts to deny them. As we know, the child has his own ways and means of guessing the mother's unconscious wishes. On the other hand, guessing is not restricted to these, and also extends to the mother's dislike and criticism of his prying. Further, it is disappointing to the child to discover that he is not always the central figure in her emotional life.

Gradually the child learns to expect that his treasured observations are not welcomed by the parents. Consequently, he begins to keep them to himself and in the further course of events to experience them as a hindrance to adaptation and to cease making them. Finally, lack of exercise and repression do away with this particular capacity altogether, and what had been collected so eagerly is blotted out from his mind. A child in the latency period usually presents a picture which is the opposite from the earlier one: instead of keen attention and acute perception, there is a remarkable lack of interest in external events, often to a degree which arouses criticism from the adults who begin to feel that countermeasures are indicated. It is interesting to note, for example, that some progressive schools have found it necessary to introduce into their program exercises to sharpen perception.

In those rare instances where mother and child are analyzed simultaneously, it becomes possible to explore in detail the origin of the child's empathy with the mother. His apparently intuitive understanding for the mother's unconscious can be traced back to earliest observations and conclusions drawn from them, i.e., to repressed impressions which are lifted once more into consciousness as a result of analytic work. An illustration of this was supplied by Berta Bornstein (1934) from her analyses of a mother-child couple. I quote what follows from her own report.

The patient, a girl of twelve, was tied to her mother by feelings of intense hate and was aggressively demanding toward her in her behavior. In talking to the mother she had developed the habit of using the mother's own turns of speech and of issuing commands and prohibitions as if she were the mother dealing with an infant. She never carried out the mother's demands. Identification with her was restricted to her overt attitudes.

A central fantasy of the child remained unintelligible for a long time until the mother's analysis threw some light on it. This fantasy, in the form of a *pseudologia phantastica*, contained the following items: that she was born in England into an aristocratic family, was brought up strictly, and as a motherless child.

While some of these items were open to interpretation such as the noble birth, the strict upbringing, the absence of a mother, others were not, for example, the alleged English nationality. There was no explanation why this detail was adhered to stubbornly in the *pseudologia,* and the child was unable to add anything which would lead to its explanation. This is where the mother's history came in helpfully. The mother, it emerged, at the end of her oedipal period had formed a strong masochistically tinted attachment to an English governess and had warded off his masochistic tie from childhood onward, in fact, up to the time of her analysis. Both the tie to the English governess as well as the struggle against it were largely repressed.

The mother gave every assurance that this governess, who had spoiled her childhood, had never been mentioned in conversation with the children, in fact, that the existence of such a person in the mother's childhood home was totally unknown to them.

The question then arose as to how our small patient succeeded in identifying with the mother's unconscious. Therefore, the analysis of the mother was explored to find the means by which the mother might have betrayed the ideas which troubled her unconsciously in a manner unknown to herself but revealing to the child who in turn perceived them without being conscious of this. Once found, the indications given turned out to be anything but subtle. The mother who treated her children with the utmost severity wished for and emphasized simultaneously their independence and liberty, both measures being a means of overcoming her attachment to the English governess. As at the same time she felt guilty about rejecting this mother figure, on the one hand, she emphasized her rejection of an English upbringing; on the other, she felt the need to justify this attitude in her own mind; so before sending her children to the park, for example, she would say: "Go by yourselves, do as you like, no need for an English governess." The child, knowing only too well that too many excuses add up to self-accusation, could not but sense the mother's inner insecurity. Thus it seemed to her that the mother acted against her own inclinations when she sent the children out unprotected by a governess. What the child experienced as the mother's vulnerable spot became the point of attack where the girl's criticism of the mother and disappointment in her could be acted out. The result was a reproach against the mother, worded approximately as follows: "Shame on you for not employing an English governess who can protect your children against the dangers of the street." Accusation and reproach on a deeper layer also formed the basis for her defensive identification with the mother; by using this mechanism, thereby appropriating the mother's wish as her own, she did away with the parent who had disappointed and neglected her (as she did in the fantasy of being a motherless, English child). The mother similarly had used her attachment to the governess to free herself of her own mother. Whenever our young patient identified with somebody, she produced in herself a caricature of the object of identification and betrayed through her exaggerations the hostile attitudes which had given rise to the identification. The mother, she argued, wanted to have an English governess; therefore she had to have one as well. But, as usual, she had to improve on the occasion, she had to become not only a child under the care of an English woman, but an English lady herself. (In fact, this was the model for the accent which she adopted in talking to the mother at times.)

I take as another illustration some facts from the analysis of an eight-year-old girl, in treatment with me. This little girl had sudden outbursts of aggression in her analytic sessions. At such times, the otherwise friendly, equable child changed into a destructive imp who tried to wreck the room, who threatened me by throwing vases or plates, and began to use her working tools such as knives and scissors as if they were weapons.

The child's mother showed herself extremely worried and repeatedly expressed the fear of her little girl developing into a sadistic adult. During one of her talks with me, this mother began to report on her own past. Her childhood had been extremely unhappy and she had witnessed terrible quarrels between her parents. Worse than that, she herself had been tormented by aggressive and sadistic impulses which she had tried to fight without ever confiding in anybody. She had been unable at that time to pick up scissors or knives without wishing to hurt somebody with them. Nevertheless, she had never done so and self-control had been successful. After adolescence, the compulsive ideas ceased to plague her.

After this revelation by the mother, the child's apparently senseless behavior appeared in a new light. The idea is not too far-fetched that she sensed the mother's aggressive impulses and acted them out as if they were her own.

In this particular case, the interaction between mother and child could be traced a step further. The mother related, on another occasion, how excited the girl had been after reading in a storybook about a fatal poison, and how she had come running to say: "Now I have learned how people can be killed." To this the mother had reacted with fear and anger, admonishing the child that it was wrong to think such thoughts; that, anyway, no prescriptions for killing were needed; nothing was easier, any simple tool could serve the purpose. Nevertheless, it was quite forbidden to have such wishes or to think such thoughts.

In reviewing this example, we see a mother who has led a lifelong struggle against her own severely aggressive impulses.

Although she managed to control them, she feared constantly that the compulsive ideas might return and again trouble her. Under the impact of this fear, the mother could not fail to watch her child from the beginning for any signs of aggression and to become distressed at the slightest indication of it. The child, she felt, had to be spared the unhappinesses which she herself had suffered. The little girl, on the other hand, was by no means oblivious of where the mother's fears lay. Her aggressive acts increased as if she intended to provoke the mother, and her final remark that at last she had learned how to kill betrayed her knowledge of the mother's fears. The mother's answer, in turn, revealed her own ambivalence: that she considered it so easy to kill could not fail to be meaningful for the child. We have every right to assume that what happened here had happened many times before and that in this and similar ways the child had succeeded gradually in obtaining insight into the mother's conflicts.

Before concluding this paper, I want to emphasize my conviction that the interactions described above do not exhaust the possible sources of empathy between mother and child. There are other elements as well which remain unexplained, and other situations where even the most detailed examination fails to furnish links between the mental processes of the mother-child couple. Whenever an affect or an idea appears simultaneously in the two partners, one gains the impression that the process in question is a telepathic one, but this has yet to be proved. As seen above, the sensory apparatus of the infant is highly receptive to stimuli arriving from the mother. It is not impossible that this receptivity exceeds by far what we imagine it to be at present. However that may be, the fact remains that in their unconscious mother and child are frequently occupied with the same problem at the same time. Instances of this are known to many people and I can add to them from personal experience. I myself underwent analysis simultaneously with my children. More than once I was struck by the fact that sometimes the subject which played a major role in my analysis at the same time dominated the analysis of one of the children. There was, though, one important difference between the two processes. Whatever was displaced from me onto the child appeared out of context in his treatment, as if it were a foreign body not linked with the general sequence of material. Coincidences of this kind were not rare, and the links which could be traced were on the whole more obvious with the sons than with the daughters. I break off here since I am at a loss to find an explanation. But I cannot help feeling that the next step in understanding the problem of mother-infant empathy should lead in this direction.

CONCLUSION

It is my contention that young children have a greater capacity for observation than had been thought previously; that they observe the direct expressions of affect as well as the efforts to deny emotion; that they are especially receptive to indications of those repressed impulses on which the mother's character is based, are seduced by them, and use them in turn to seduce the mother; that these capacities are lost as the child matures, develops, and adapts to the environment. In short, empathy between infant and mother, mysterious and almost uncanny as it used to appear formerly, is here shown as lodged to a large degree in the acuteness of the child's perception.

This assumption, if accepted as fact, diminishes the relevance of two other possible explanations of the phenomenon of empathy: telepathy and heredity.

So far as we believe in a telepathic link between mother and child, we attribute to the unconscious mind of one individual the ability to develop intuitive understanding for the unconscious contents in another.

An explanation based on the facts of heredity presumes an innate similarity between mother and child, with certain character traits, etc., being passed on directly from the mother to the child. A strong belief in such possibilities is shared by many parents. It lies at the basis of many of their fears for their children, their worries about defects of their own being handed on to them, and their guilt feelings for many of the children's unwelcome impulses and attitudes.

Compared with our helplessness and ignorance when faced with hereditary or telepathic explanations, we feel on safe and familiar ground when it is demonstrated, as in this paper, that empathy between infant and mother can be based on an early phase of acute and lively observations, perceptiveness, and receptivity in the infant and child.

Chapter 5

PROBLEMS CONFRONTING THE PSYCHOANALYTIC EDUCATOR

In recent years we were able to introduce an increasing number of teachers to psychoanalytic thinking. They as well as other workers in the field of early education were encouraged by us to undertake a personal analysis and at the same time to attend courses in psychoanalytic theory. We arranged a seminar for the discussion of cases that presented special difficulties in the nursery school or classroom and in this way helped to apply the basic principles of psychoanalysis to the practical problems in the teacher's daily work. It was our hope that, working in this manner, the teachers themselves would contribute to the establishment and gradual extension of a system of upbringing which deserved the name of psychoanalytic pedagogy.

Our hopes were fulfilled insofar as our students became much more familiar with the children under their care than they had

Contribution to the Symposium on "Revision der psychoanalytischen Pädagogik." This paper was first published as "Probleme des psychoanalytischen Erziehers." *Zeitschrift für psychoanalytische Pädagogik*, 11: 91-97, 1937. The English translation is here published for the first time.

been before entering our course of instruction. They have learned carefully to observe the different reactions of the children,
and in many instances can correctly identify the underlying
cause of a child's behavior. Naturally, it was not easy for the
teachers to acquire this new understanding: they first had to
learn to observe patiently, to collect data and facts about individual children, and to interpret what they observed. Everyone
who works in the field of psychoanalytic pedagogy knows that
each one of us have learned by trial and error, has adopted certain methods, experimented with them, and often dropped them
again in disappointment until he was finally able to adapt himself to this new way of working. All these enducators have
convinced themselves of the correctness of psychoanalytic
teachings, having had the opportunity to verify the tenets of
psychoanalytic child psychology by means of their own observations in their work. But this does not prevent an individual
teacher from carrying her subjective inclinations and interests
over into her objective work; e.g., seeing in a child, more clearly
than other things, what the teacher experienced in her own
analysis; or neglecting certain observations and methods in
favor of others more suited to her individual personality or
talents. Different educators utilize psychoanalytic teachings in
such different ways that it is tempting to distinguish various
groups according to the method by which they apply psycho-
analysis to education.

There is one type of teacher, for example, who is above all
frightened by the encounter with psychoanalysis. For them, the
newly acquired knowledge seems to turn the education of the
child into an almost insoluble task. They suddenly recognize
the tremendous impact which their prohibitions have on the
child and the severity of the inner conflict which they thus create in him. They feel incapable of assuming an active part in
this process and, at first, simply do not know how to cope with
the responsibilities imposed on them. Finally, they withdraw
from the most difficult part of their work, and avoid paying

close attention to the child's intrapsychic conflicts because they do not yet know how to help the child solve these conflicts. Instead, they prefer to confine their activities to making the child's life in kindergarten and school as pleasant as possible: that is to say, they diminish their demands on the child in order not to contribute to an intensification of the child's conflicts.

Another type of teacher finds a different way out of the same situation. These teachers are not at all averse to looking straight at the difficulties presented by the children in their care. But then, they believe in interpretation as a panacea for all difficulties. They assume that having succeeded in grasping a particular child's problem and having communicated their hunches to the child, all conflicts and difficulties will disappear. These teachers have an especially keen eye for the child's unconscious; they are adept at quickly and correctly translating the child's symbolic actions and at grasping the unconscious material depicted in the child's drawings. But having correctly understood this material, they will immediately interpret it to the child and forget completely about the consequences that such interpretations must have. They are then quite surprised when the child, on the basis of such an interpretation, develops a stormy transference reaction to the teacher, or when the child uses the interpretation he received in school to apply it in a provocative way at home; above all, these teachers are disappointed when the child, without persistent work directed to his resistances, simply does not know what to do with the interpretation given so freely. But this is not to say that teachers should not interpret at all.

Teachers in yet another group by no means content themselves with these sudden and almost accidental insights into the unconscious of the child. It is their ambition to understand the child's personality completely in all its aspects. Not only do they observe the child's conscious and unconscious reactions in school; they also want to study the details of the child's behavior at home. To complete their picture of the child, they need to know about his family milieu, his parents, and his entire previous development. These teachers focus primarily on the child's parents. They are particularly adept at unearthing the hidden interactions between mother and child and view it as part of their task to force a better understanding of the child on the mother. They go even further than that. They perceive correctly that a major share of the child's difficulties is rooted in the influences that the mother exerts or even in the unconscious conflicts of the mother that dominate her attitude to the child. In order to obtain better conditions for the child at home, these teachers delve deeply into this background of the child's developmental difficulties, which can in fact be found only in the mother's life. Their attempt to send the mother for analysis is the last logical step if one follows this approach. But in general the educator has little success with the trouble she took over the mother. What she perceived was correct. But this does not prevent extraordinarily difficult relations between teacher and mother from arising. And to cope with or utilize these, the teacher would need more insight or more authority than her position allows her.

These three types of psychoanalytic educators demonstrate that the introduction of psychoanalytic knowledge has on the one hand vastly increased the scope of the educator's opportunities; on the other hand, it has simultaneously increased her difficulties in finding her bearings in this greatly extended field of work. The analytic consultant must never lose sight of the dangers confronting the analytically trained teacher: on the one hand, from her personally motivated interests and, on the other, from those inherent in handling unconscious material.

But the acquisition of psychoanalytic knowledge creates new difficulties for the teacher not merely in the way she discharges her educational work. In addition, she is in fact confronted with new objective problems in her kindergarten and school groups and must deal with these issues.

Before her psychoanalytic training the nursery or elementary school teacher must constantly keep two goals in mind. On the one hand, she must impart a certain amount of didactic knowledge to the children, i.e., instruct them; on the other hand, she wants to bring the children in her group to a certain level of age-appropriate social behavior and interaction. After her analytic training the task of understanding the individual child and his problems appears to her to be of at least equal importance.

There are indeed situations in which the teacher's varied tasks mutually support each other. The teacher may, for example, know how to remove a child's inhibition so that he can then reach the previously unobtainable educational goal of the class. Furthermore, each individual child, regardless of whether he is normal or abnormal and regardless of whether or not he requires her special psychological help and attention, provides the teacher with a rich source of psychological material which in turn spurs her general interest in her classwork.

In other instances, the teacher's different tasks come into conflict with each other. As Edith Buxbaum (1936) and Hans Zulliger (1926, 1935) have shown in their work applying psychoanalysis to group education, the formation of children's groups is by no means only an advantage for the education of the individual child. The claims made on the teacher by the individual child are frequently in direct opposition to the requirements of group instruction. The teacher who is faced with such a conflict between the needs of the individual and the needs of the group will at one time decide in favor of one of her goals and at the next time for another.

It is also true, of course, that the existence of the group does make the teacher's task of instruction decidedly easier. She needs to have a certain standard or level toward which she ideally hopes to work and, no matter how different the individual children are, this standard or level is contained in the concept of a normal and active community of children. The ideal image of such a community then not only becomes the goal for the class as a whole, but simultaneously also guides her work with the individual children. A teacher's work with the individual children in her group can be fruitful only if the following conditions are met: when the individual child has gained insight into his vulnerabilities and difficulties and has mastered them with the help of analytic aid, then he can take his measure and compare himself with others in the group. The group represents the community to which he should belong and at the same time vividly keeps in his view the goals with which he should identify.

What I have described up to now by no means exhausts the teacher's new problems. We know that in the analytically oriented schools with which we are familiar a new problem has arisen: there is a very important difference between the needs of children who come from an analytically enlightened home and those whose parents know nothing about analysis and its applications to the understanding of the child. The two groups of children have entirely different developmental histories, have been brought up in entirely different atmospheres, and consequently demand entirely different educational procedures if one wants to do justice to their real requirements.

My foregoing description of the teacher's educational work was concerned primarily with the child coming from an analytically uninformed environment. Insight into the personality of the child, into his inner world and conflicts, should in these cases serve primarily to counteract and undo some of the consequences of the early and strict upbringing, to alleviate the anxieties arising from excessive restrictions on instinctual drives, thereby enabling the child to adapt to the demands of his environment in a better and less conflictful way. At the same time we want to guide the parents toward a better understanding of the child's attitudes and problems and induce them to change their educational measures so that, in cooperation with the school, they can ensure better conditions for the child's further development.

But the children coming from a so-called analytically enlightened environment already show everything that in the other cases we so laboriously attempt to achieve. The child's reactions arising from his different complexes not only are known to the parents; the child, too, is informed about them, having been given innumerable interpretations. He has, as far as possible, been spared overly strict prohibitions and traumatic restrictions. He has learned to trust the adults, to verbalize his fantasies and anxieties, because he has become accustomed to finding understanding for them. Whenever difficulties arose—and they inevitably do so in the course of an individual's development— the parents met them with sympathy and solicitude and offers of help. Such parents are of course well aware of the influences which their personalities exert on the child and have gone to great pains to control their own affects in the hope of thereby sparing the child the imposition of additional conflicts.

When such a child enters kindergarten or school, he naturally anticipates meeting the same understanding as he has come to know in his parents. The parents on their part expect that their methods of upbringing have prepared the child well for his first encounter with external reality. It is only natural that they seek to find a school that will make neither overly strict nor cruel reality demands on the child. They seek to obtain the most favorable circumstances for the child, hope that the analyzed teacher is capable of genuinely understanding their child, and are quite prepared to tell the teacher about every detail of the child's developmental history that they deem necessary for such understanding.

But the analyzed teachers, even those who may have become quite adept at handling the other children, are at a loss when they encounter these analytically raised children. They know that the child is sent to school to bring him into contact with the external world outside his parental home. Evidently, the child needs the challenges and demands that such a real community makes on the individual. The teacher knows that in these cases it makes very little sense once again to fulfill a need that has already been fulfilled: such a child needs no interpretations of his actions and no new confidante for his secrets. He is in school above all to receive stimulation for new achievements. Owing to the understanding upbringing they have had, however, it is precisely these children who are especially oversensitive, who are not readily inclined to accept restrictions, who in particular can scarcely tolerate any criticism or admonition, and who frequently experience inconsiderate and unkind behavior on the part of their agemates as a profound rejection. Thus they must first negotiate a particularly long and difficult path before they can adapt to the ordinary demands of school and attain a good level of performance.

The teacher's task in relation to these children is again a very special one. What these protected children have so far not been able to gain—their lack of resilience—must now be made up within the community and with the help of the teacher. Here, then, in addition to the usual goals of education—for work and appropriate behavior—there is a new air: the gradual accommodation to the demands of external reality, and these demands are no longer attuned to the special needs of the individual.

But even with the consideration of the needs of the group and the altogether different needs of different individuals, the list of the tasks confronting the psychoanalytically trained teacher is still incomplete. Each such group contains children who present difficulties that are beyond the competence of even the best-intentioned teacher. The disturbances of these children exceed the usual developmental difficulties. These are the neuroses of childhood that can be cured only by therapeutic child analysis. But it would be wrong for the teacher, reasoning that she lacks competence in this area, to withdraw from these children. It is precisely these children whose entire subsequent fate is often determined by a teacher's analytic or nonanalytic attitude. With such cases the teacher has the task of tactfully contacting the parents to ascertain the extent to which they are aware of the child's pathological behavior and, where necessary, to bring to their attention the child's abnormality by comparing him to normal children; and to impress upon the parents, carefully, considerately, but nevertheless quite firmly, that whatever help the home or the school can offer in this respect is merely a stopgap measure, and in this way gradually convince them of the child's need for treatment.

But even this work with the parents presents only one side of the teacher's task. The child, too, must learn to recognize his symptoms and disturbances as such and at the same time should be told that there exists help for such seemingly insoluble problems. The understanding that he here meets for the first time should simultaneously prepare him for the understanding that the child analyst is ready to bring to his neurotic conflicts. The teacher here has the opportunity of really preparing the child for his analysis, of giving him insight into the fact of his illness and thereby also arousing his wish to be cured, both of which constitute necessary prerequisites for carrying out an analysis.

As child analysts we know that the acknowledgment of the illness and the appropriate attitude to the analytic task usually require weeks and even months when they are brought about in the introductory phase within a child's analysis. The same work could with far greater advantage be performed outside the analysis. It is true, however, that to achieve this, the analytic educator would have to assume as his last and most extreme educational task the role of educating the child for analysis.

Chapter 6

FANTASY AND REALITY IN A CHILD'S ANALYSIS

When analyzing children in the latency period, we find that their conscious fantasies provide us with excellent material for interpretation. At that age, the defense organization of the ego has developed sufficiently to inhibit the free acting out of unconscious trends either in play or in the transference, while at the same time their expression in verbal form is not yet as natural to the child as it will be later in preadolescence or in adolescence. What the child indulges in instead are daydreams, so-called "continuous stories," fairy-talelike short fantasies, i.e., products of the imagination, so far as this side of the child's life has not been interfered with by neurotic inhibitions. Since the latent content of these daydreams remains hidden from the child, they are told to the analyst as freely as the nightly dreams.

Nevertheless, analysts need to be warned not to apply the same interpretative techniques to these daydreams as they use for night dreams. Even though daydreams are also subject to primary process thinking and show evidence of displacement,

First published as "Phantasie und Wirklichkeit in einer Kinderanalyse." *Internationale Zeitschrift für Psychoanalyse*, 24:292-303, 1939. The English translation, by Anna Freud, is here published for the first time.

condensation, representation by the opposite, symbolization, etc., the role of the secondary process in them is a very different one. There may be large parts in them which are lifted wholesale from favorite books or fairy tales. Where these are concerned, only the connection with the original theme of the source is relevant for interpretation while any free association to the borrowed details proves misleading. As regards the wish-fulfilling function of the daydream, this is revealed most clearly if we investigate not a single specimen but—in contrast to ordinary dream interpretation—look at a whole series of them. We see then that they are motivated by one and the same instinctual wish which finds thinly disguised expression, using fairly monotonously almost identical methods of structuralization, building up of expectation, and final climax of excitement.

So far as daydreaming during the period of analysis is concerned, its occurrence can be pinpointed and interpreted as we do with night dreams. In both instances we are led back to a repressed unconscious wish joining forces with a day residue. But, according to my experience, there is with the child patient a further element which needs to be considered. Based on an unconscious empathy with the most important love object, i.e., the mother, children seem to be able to receive clues from her as to the content of her fantasy life and to incorporate these with their own. What results are shared daydreams between mother and child, a fact of which both partners ordinarily remain oblivious.[1]

What follows are extracts from the analysis of a six-year-old girl so far as they can serve to illustrate the above. Needless to say, the treatment of this child has revealed more than will be quoted here, and as a description of her case and her recovery the account to be given is fragmentary and incomplete.

Joan entered analysis in a state of mourning after separation from a much-loved aunt. This depression, which had already

[1] See also Grete Bibring's report on dreams and the occult (1933); and Chapter 4, which contains further references to the literature.

lasted a year, was apt to give way occasionally to rages against
her mother whom she accused, quite legitimately, of having
caused the aunt's, i.e., her sister's departure. Besides this the
parents worried about Joan's withdrawal into a fantasy world.
She imagined herself as a princess, demanded dresses appropriate for a princess as well as all the other advantages belonging to that status. In view of her very modest financial circumstances, the mother was at her wit's end. She said, despairingly,
that she did not know her own child anymore.

When I first met Joan, I was struck by her unusually attractive
appearance. She was small for her age, with delicate features
and coloring, graceful, distinguished, and poetic in her verbal
expression. She was dressed very prettily, in sharp contrast to
her mother, whose plump body was clothed poorly and shabbily.
Her father was shorter in stature, otherwise resembling the
mother's appearance.)

During the first weeks of analysis, while her mother was
absent, Joan did not mention her fantasy of being a princess.
Not until the day of the mother's return did she demand suddenly to copy pictures of princesses from a certain book of fairy
tales. She said: "Look, how beautiful they are! What beautiful
dresses they have! They do not need to do a thing, only to sit
and look beautiful. They look haughty and they have to be
served. When they drop something, they do not need to pick it
up; they simply call somebody to pick it up for them."

Her fantasy of being a princess was acted out in other ways
as well, especially in repetitive behavior toward the end of the
analytic session. There was in my consulting room a clock
which struck when the hour was full. Two or three minutes
before this happened, Joan would start on some important theme.
As she said herself: "I want to ask you something before the
clock strikes." And then: "I cannot wait to know what I shall
get for my birthday"; or "Tell me about being rich or poor"; or
"I wish my father were a king." Then, with the striking of the
hour and before I had time to answer, she jumped up, ran to

the door, waved good-bye to me, and disappeared. Obviously, she was reproducing the scene in the fairy tale when Cinderella has to leave in the middle of the ball, as well as other tales in which the striking of the hour initiates some frightening event.

There was no difficulty for the analysis here to uncover the links between Joan's fantasy of being a princess and the reality demands which the poverty-stricken mother had to make on the child. Since a princess can have whatever she desires, is served, etc., Joan became a princess, at least in her fantasy. But at the same time she could not quite escape the pressures from the environment: as soon as the clock struck, reality returned, presenting its unwelcome demands.

The mother then informed me that a similar division between fantasy and reality had taken place earlier in Joan's life. As a young child Joan had been a bad eater and, to encourage her to eat, her aunt used to read fairy tales to her. The mother had resented this attitude of her sister who, according to her feelings, had spoiled the child by giving in to her too much, gave her too many presents, sewed pretty dresses for her, etc. For this reason she was relieved rather than sorry when her sister decided on emigration to one of the colonies. The mother also related that Joan had reacted with refusal of food to her next pregnancy. This had been so bad that she had to send the child to the same aunt, in the country. There, the symptom disappeared, only to reappear when, after the birth of the little brother, she returned home.

I concluded from Joan's analytic material, combined with the mother's tale, that the following had happened: in Joan's imagination the image of her mother had been split into a good and a bad part, the good mother being represented first by the aunt and in the transference by me. It was the role of the good mother to feed her and to supply her with beautiful dresses; that of the bad mother to discriminate against her and to neglect her for the sake of the new rival. The affection offered by the aunt served to compensate her for the disappointing behavior of the mother. That it was the aunt who introduced her to the fairy tales may have paved the way to her own use of such fantasies for coping with her frustrations.

I was interested to see that the mother's constant battle with Joan's fantasy life was no more than the conscious half of the picture; unconsciously, she was in collusion with the child's imagination. The harder and more exacting her own life with its economic pressures, the more she enjoyed her little daughter's charming appearance. She was proud of the way everybody admired the child and she made every effort to ensure this admiration by the way she dressed her. Besides being pretty, Joan was intelligent and impressed people by her clever remarks and her refined speech. The mother colluded in this respect as well and even managed to arrange for piano lessons for the child, to acquire the loan of a piano, and to find room for it in her crowded living quarters. On the other hand, this positive involvement was apt to give way suddenly to the opposite, negative one. She would then criticize bitterly what she herself had promoted, would scold the child for her refined manner, and complain that Joan kept aloof from all the chores which she, as the mother, had to carry out herself.

Similar to Joan, the mother also transferred her attitudes to the analytic situation. On the one hand, she admired my room, my flowers, and my furniture, and was pleased that Joan could find with me the beautiful surroundings of her fantasies. On the other hand, she also felt enraged by the difference of this from her own environment. "Of course, this is why Joan likes to come here! And that is the reason why she behaves so terribly the rest of the day. She compares our life with the one here and it makes her more discontented than ever." Obviously, by now I had been cast in the role of the hated sister who spoiled the child. But, no less obviously, she had revealed that, so far as her own unconscious inclinations were concerned, the princess fantasy was by no means as alien or as disliked as professed in consciousness. If she could not be a princess herself, at least she could be the mother of one, a role which she was not willing to concede either to the aunt or to the analyst. I felt that the mother's object relationships were at least as ambivalent as Joan's, nor was she any better adapted to the difficult real circumstances of her life.

As Joan's analysis proceeded, different elements entered into her fantasy of being a princess, were incorporated with it, and finally replaced it. But these new fantasies, too, proved fairly transparent.

Joan reported that she wished for three kinds of lessons: gymnastic, swimming, and music, i.e., piano. She said: "When I was still in my mother's stomach, I thought it was a hall for gymnastics and I did physical exercises. I jumped and skipped and turned somersaults. Once I jumped so high that I got into the tube for food and that made her feel sick." She demonstrated how the mother had spit up, thereby inadvertently spitting at me. "When my brother was in my mother's stomach, he just ate and ate until everything was emptied out." "I wish I could go swimming. Once, when I was only one year old, I went swimming with my father. He put a belt around me and threw me in the water and I went under. The swimming instructor who stood next to my father jumped in. He did not know that I was in the water and he stood on my face. His toes were in my nostrils and it hurt very much. His ankle came into my mouth, so I bit him very hard and he went quickly up again. My father was also in the water. He swam above me and I was in the water under him."

This fantasy as a whole could be understood as a symbolic representation of the unborn child's experiences *in utero;* the swimming pool standing for the amniotic fluid; the antics and piano playing for the movements of the fetus; the high jump for oral birth. These purely symbolic elements were added to real memories. Joan had undoubtedly made her observations during the mother's pregnancy, especially of morning sickness, and these individually acquired memory traces served to reinforce the symbolic factors. When the particular item about feeling sick appeared, her aggression was aroused and she spat at me, transferring the anger felt toward the pregnant mother. This was followed closely by the expression of her jealousy toward the little brother as the bad child who empties out the mother,[2] again a symbolic representation connected with memories of seeing him fed at the breast and her own oral envy connected with such observations. Her fantasies then proceeded from pregnancy and birth to symbolic representation of sadistic intercourse via the man who was imagined to overpower her, throw her into the water, jump on her face and push his toes into her nostrils. Impregnation appeared, symbolized by one individual swimming on top of the other as it happens in the fish world. The female's aggressive feelings toward the male organ were expressed by the idea of biting the man's ankle, thereby causing pain.

The child's communications in the analytic hour were complemented further by the mother's reports which explained where Joan's detailed information about sexual matters were derived from. The mother had the following to say about her pregnancy with Joan: "Even when I carried her, she had her rages with me already. She used to jump around inside me until I was quite sore. Her brother was different. He was so quiet in the womb that I worried sometimes whether he was alive." Since the mother was proud of having enlightened her children about sexual matters at an early age, we may assume that Joan had frequently been confronted with this curious description of her intrauterine existence. As regards the mother's involvement in the child's fantasies, the foregoing report revealed some important items. Obviously, Joan had been an unwelcome child whose conception had been resented and whose alleged rages in the womb had to be understood as due to the projection of the mother's own aggression toward the unborn infant.

[2] See Melanie Klein (1932).

As the analysis proceeded further, Joan turned from mere fantasy to active play with the toys I offered. She played with two dolls which she named Gretel and Hansi. She herself played the role of the mother while I had to be Kate, a servant girl. The children were supposed to be ill and to have to stay apart from each other, but Hansi tried over and over again to return to the sister's bed. The mother, finding him there, slapped him and almost smothered him with her own body. Then the mother tried to cure the children by putting many pillows on them to make them perspire. The children screamed until finally the mother promised to give them sweets or other good things.

What this fantasy offered was again a combination of real experiences with symbolic representations of intercourse. In reality, the children had frequently been ill and were separated from each other on such occasions. Other real elements were their attempts to get together again; the mother's nursing and punishing them. But then, the same items were also used symbolically, the mother's smothering the brother with her body representing her intercourse with him, the same process also being played out in a more innocent manner by substituting pillows for the human body.

From then onward, the two dolls remained the main actors. They died since they were so naughty. The mother went out into the street to look for other and better children. She found two, brought them home, and named them as before. They had an aunt who was very nice to them, gave them sweets, and read to them. The fantasy developed from there, using material derived from Joan's relationship to her aunt and from the quarrels between aunt and mother.

In a further development of Joan's play, both children were attacked by wild animals. The children were very frightened, but the mother reassured them, saying that it was not so bad and that they had to be brave. So the children were brave, but it did not help; the wild animals attacked them nevertheless and scratched their faces. The mother tried repeatedly to hold the animals off.

When interpreting this fantasy, I linked it with the earlier one of being ill and nursed. In Joan's imagination the mother separated the children from each other, as in reality Joan wanted to separate the parents. Brother and sister played the role of father and mother and, therefore, had to be kept separate and punished by the mother. The latter wanted to keep the little brother for herself, to "smother" him, as Joan, in reality, wanted to keep one of the parents for herself.

In a next fantasy the two children were described to be thirty years old and to begin working. They were engaged by a king, the boy as cook and the girl as personal maid. Gretel served the king so well that he fell in love with her and proposed marriage. But unexpectedly, the names of bride and groom changed from Gretel and the king to that of Joan and her brother Arthur and remained so from then onward. Joan asked whether it mattered that they were siblings, whether it was all right for siblings to marry. She added: "When they are married, they will kiss the whole time and will only eat good things."

When arranging for the wedding, she did not get beyond the preparations. Bride and groom had to have beautiful dresses made by us, a house had to be built and furnished. This was dragged out for weeks, Joan insisting every day before leaving that "tomorrow they will really marry."

Her thoughts were concerned next with the wedding trip. The children wanted the mother to accompany them. Since she was already seventy-five years old, they did not expect her to disturb them much. Joan was already thirty-one, but the mother always forgot this and treated her like a little child, which made her very angry.

From being a prince and princess, the two dolls advanced to

being king and queen. Their clothing became more and more magnificent, they were equipped each with a crown. Nevertheless, the wedding ceremony was postponed from day to day. While this happened Joan received a real invitation to a dress-up party and was unable to make up her mind whether to appear dressed as a cook or as a princess.

I thought that this last-mentioned fantasy brought advances in Joan's analytic material. What emerged clearly was her ambivalent attitude toward her mother, i.e., her positive tie, which was responsible for letting the mother share the wedding trip, as well as the negative feelings expressed in her objections to the mother's nagging. The theme of rich versus poor re-emerged, but with some significant differences. She now seemed doubtful where in the social scale she belonged in reality. She also acknowledged for the first time via the change of names that the people she was concerned with were herself and her brother, and not figures out of fairy tales ("Is it all right for siblings to marry?")

Finally, she succeeded in staging the wedding ceremony. The dolls were married in a synagogue, in the presence of many guests. There were prayers, songs, and a festive meal. Afterward Joan wanted to bathe the dolls but stopped herself, saying: "No, they can do that later." She conducted the newly married pair to the newly furnished house, put them to bed immediately, and, placing the boy doll on the girl, asked her: "How is it? Does it hurt?" Next day, on arrival, she immediately hurried to the dolls, asking the female whether the male doll had lain on her all through the night.

There were further changes in the fantasy. King and queen sat on the throne watching two people (represented by a dog and a cow) who quarreled in front of them. As Joan explained, they "do that" with each other. The king, feeling quite helpless, asked an angel behind him what he should do. The angel advised that both of them should be put in prison and given a hundred strokes. Another time the king was angry with his queen and

turned his back on her. She minded that and asked to be forgiven. But the king hid away from her, finally turning once
more to the angel for advice.

There were several elements here which were easy to interpret.
The introduction of dog and cow pointed to the possibility of
coitus observations made on animals. The introduction of the
angel as advisor to the king pointed to me who, as the analyst,
had to advise the mother how to deal with Joan's angry thoughts.
Obviously, Joan still devised cruel punishments for sexual misdeeds and also minded very much whenever the mother was dis-
pleased with her.

Next, the dolls were demoted to the status of ordinary people,
a married couple. The man kicked the woman's stomach and
hurt her with a nail protruding from the toecap of his shoe.
Joan lifted the woman up, saying: "Look, she is bleeding from
her stomach where the man kicked her. We have to change the
furniture around. They must not share a room while she is bleeding." Another time she drew my attention to the fact that the
woman doll was not wearing drawers. She bent the doll forward
and said: "Look, the wind has lifted her skirt. Now she has to
wear a belt and bandage." "Once I saw my mother when she
bent over."

I was struck by the increasing lack of distortion in this fantasy. She had, by now, given up the displacement of her thoughts
to eminent figures such as king and queen and was talking about
ordinary men and women. She was, furthermore, able to communicate her own sexual theories ("the man kicking the woman's
stomach with a nail") as well as her observations of the woman's
menstruation with the conclusions drawn from them.

Next, the girl doll was described to live alone, like a hermit.
But here she corrected herself: No, not quite alone, her mother
lived with her. Her mother did everything for her, sewing, cooking, looking after the house. Gretel, the doll, had very simple

dresses now, she did not care anymore about being dressed beautifully. But in winter she put on warm clothing and went out to the lake to break ice. Soon her feet froze, but her mother followed her, discovered how cold she was, took her home, put her to bed, and gave her hot tea to drink. The girl was very weak, but it did not matter since the mother was very strong. She was almost as old as the mother since she had been born eight days after the mother's wedding.

There was, here, a complete change so far as Joan's wishes were concerned. She no longer wished to be a princess and to be dressed as such. Instead, she admitted that her real wish was for the mother's care and love. The only remaining distortion referred to their ages. By bringing these nearer to each other, she lessened the dangers inherent in the relationship between child and mother.

Some important elements missing in the above fantasy were supplied later. The mother had no interest in her son, she did not even want to see him. The son was king and had driven his sister from the castle after twice kicking her stomach and slapping her face. Gretel said she would not return to him even if he needed a wife and even if she were chosen from among others. She was fed up with men. "The king can find another wife, easy enough." The king had been deserted by all his servants except for a single one. He had also lost his money. He only needed to look at pearls, for them to disappear.

It was the function of this fantasy to deal with her sibling rivalry. While removing the brother as a rival in relation to the mother, she retained him as a sexual object (who slapped and kicked her in her face and stomach). Her exaggerated efforts to leave him and her insistence that she would never return to him could be taken as an indication of the opposite attitude: that she was unable to discard him, i.e., that she herself was the remaining faithful retainer. Evidently, her negative relationship to her brother referred only to the triangular situation with the

mother; so far as he as a person was concerned, he remained a
love object.

Joan concluded the whole series of fantasies with the following daydream. She invented a peasant family, father, mother,
two children, a cow and a dog. They owned a nice cottage and
fertile fields. But the children were very naughty, destroying
everything, house, furniture, produce, ect., beating the distressed
and helpless parents. Beating the children was no good since
they beat back worse. The parents took the children to the forest
to lose them there, but they found their way back. They threw
them into the river, but the children climbed out again. To this
Joan added: "I often thought that I should like to jump into the
river when I felt so unhappy, with the devil in me. What can
one do to get rid of such a devil? I liked my aunt, but Mother
always quarreled with her. I hate Mother."

After this was said, her fantasy was reversed. Joan became
the grandmother who invited the naughty children into her
house, feeling sure that she could deal with them. She took them
home and allowed them to come into her bed and they changed
and became good and quiet. Their change was like a miracle;
suddenly they were the nicest children that ever lived, considerate, helpful, working for the grandmother from morning to
night. When the parents visited, they could not believe their
own eyes and hardly recognized that these were their children.
Even after their return home, they remained as good as they had
been with the grandmother. As Joan said: "That was easy. The
devil had left them."

This last and most elaborate daydream contained many elements which revealed the changes that had taken place in Joan
herself. The naughty children represented her own behavior
under the domination of her "devil," the good children her
changed ways after the devil had been conquered. What she felt
to be devilish was her hate for her mother, derived partly from
oedipal and partly from sibling rivalry. Her ambivalence toward

the mother could not be solved and led to the split between a good and a bad mother figure. In reality, the aunt had become the good mother, in the daydream it was the grandmother. The recovery of the children was atypical example of straightforward wish fulfillment with almost no distortion added.[3] Obviously, Joan imagined that the children had turned bad because the bad mother frustrated them too much and that they turned good as soon as the good mother, in the guise of the grandmother, allowed them into her bed. The devil, i.e., their aggression, was appeased for all time by the satisfactions offered to them. Joan's main motive, her battle for love, care, and bodily pleasures offered by the mother, was no longer subject to repression and had been set free to enter into her conscious life.

What has been left out in the above are the links between this series of daydreams and the wider context of the child's analysis. As a patient, Joan produced no nightly dreams and therefore her daydreams had to serve as an alternative source of material, the rest of it being supplied by her behavior, her attitudes in the transference, her spontaneous communications, her drawings, her free play, etc. All this was no different from any other child's analysis.

On the other hand, her particular daydreams, with their gradual modifications, allowed for some special insight into the unfolding of themes and problems during a child's analysis, the sequence being roughly as follows: retreat from frustrating reality while mourning the departure of the aunt (the fantasy of being a princess); impregnation, womb, and birth theories (the fantasy of the swimming bath); sibling rivalry and jealousy of the brother in relation to the mother (the fantasy of the children being ill); primaly scene and coitus observations on animals (fantasy of the wedding); the analyst as superego, condemning sexuality (fantasy of kings and angel); the problem of men-

---

[3] As in the case of Little Hans (Freud, 1909).

struation and its cause (fantasy of the "ordinary" couple); removal of the brother and sole possession of the mother (fantasy of the hermit and the deserted king); cure by maternal love (fantasy of the peasant family).

Nevertheless, her daydreams also lacked some of the elements which had proved pathogenic for Joan's development, one of these being her penis envy. In reality, this was as significant for her jealousy of her brother as her rivalry for the mother's love and attention. But while the latter dominated several of the daydreams, her envy of his masculinity appeared openly only in the one when the king had lost his money and merely needed to look at pearls for them to disappear. In Joan's poetic language this could only signify his complete castration. On the other hand, her penis envy also appeared in its own particular disguise which had already been promoted by the aunt, a disguise employed by many women whose masculine wishes are expressed via the wish for feminine beauty and adornment. With Joan, this led to the wish for princely clothing as a substitute for the penis and thus to her compulsive vanity with its battle with the mother for the supply of the right dresses. Since this root of her hate for the mother was more severely repressed than the jealousy of father and brother, it was also less available for the manufacture of daydreams which, after all, as psychic structures, belong to the conscious rather than to the unconscious realm of life.

Chapter 7

PRECURSORS OF SOME PSYCHOANALYTIC IDEAS ABOUT CHILDREN IN THE SIXTEENTH AND SEVENTEENTH CENTURIES

The twentieth century will probably be recognized as the one in which great advance has been made in the understanding of children. All kinds of child care reform have been introduced, based on investigations and scientific research. Facilities have been obtained to set up modern institutions of all types, schools, child guidance clinics, reform schools, hospital clinics, and hospitals for children. Teachers have to undergo a long training, doctors a specialized training in pediatrics, and parents are given the opportunity to get professional advice, help, and guidance in all spheres of child care. Often such advice, as how to behave toward their children and how to handle them, is even thrust unasked upon parents. Child psychology is the backbone of all these modern attempts of child care.

Reprinted from *The Psychoanalytic Study of the Child*, 6:244-254. New York: International Universities Press, 1951.

It is therefore surprising to find, in looking over the literature on education and pediatrics of the former centuries, that even in the sixteenth century some of the present-day twentieth century problems were discussed and considered; and that what is adopted only now as being psychologically sound was then, in the sixteenth and seventeenth centuries, encouraged by the leading educators and medical men of that time without the psychological knowledge and understanding of this modern age.

Breast feeding has been a problem much discussed over the centuries. Even during the last fifty years, whether an infant is better off at the mother's breast, given breast milk from another mother, or bottle-fed, has been a controversial subject among obstetricians and pediatricians. While some doctors favored the mothers nursing their infants, many were of the opinion that by prescribing formulas (which secured practically the same nutritive value as mother's milk), they had the feeding situations much more under their control. In this way they avoided the irregularities of quantity and quality caused by breast feeding. Nurses, too, from their observations and close contact with the mothers and babies, felt that the infants were better off when the feedings could be regulated. They noticed that every worry and disturbance of the mother affected her milk and therefore the infant, and so were glad to substitute a bottle for the breast. The mothers themselves were divided, some preferring not to nurse their infants for practical reasons, e.g., so that they could continue working, or not be tied to the infant; so that they would not lose their figure; or because of some other fear of the nursing situation. Other mothers preferred to nurse their infants; they enjoyed the nursing situation, the closeness of the tie, and felt it was the natural thing to do. These mothers wishing to breast-feed their infants were surprised when they were not encouraged to do so either by the doctor or by the nurse, but that at the first difficulty in the nursing situation they were discouraged from further attempts and the infant was immediately put on a formula.

It was only gradually that, through the teachings of psycho-analysis and the understanding of psychoanalytic theories, the significance of the oral zone for the development of the child was realized, in the first place with regard to the feeding situa-tion. Not only is the taking in of nourishment pleasurable, but the mouthing and playing with the nipple and biting are experi-enced as a pleasurable sensation. These first experiences in enjoyment are valuable for the child's later feeding habits as well as general development. Analysis showed how these earliest oral pleasures point the way for the child to the first concentra-tion of feeling on an object in the external world, namely, the mother who provides these pleasures. When the mother does not breast-feed the child herself, one of the bridges is lacking which leads from bodily gratification to object relationship. The close bodily contact between mother and child, the mother's feeding, handling, and loving care of the infant are therefore of the utmost importance for the child's well-being and growth. Separation from the mother had all kinds of impoverishing con-sequences, even in the first days and weeks of life. This early close mother-child relationship is the kernel on which all other relationships are built.

One of the modern experiments is the Rooming-in at Grace–New Haven Community Hospital, pioneered by Dr. Edith B. Jackson. The doctors and nurses give these mothers every en-couragement to breast-feed their babies; when difficulties arise in the feeding situation, they try to help the mothers overcome them. The novelty of this experiment, however, lies in the "roming-in," that is, the mothers keep their infants in the room with them, instead of in a separated nursery as is customary.[1] In this way the infants, from their first hours of life, are never separated from their mothers, the closeness of the mother-child relationship, with all its emotional factors, is recognized as most important for the infant's present welfare as well as future

[1] Similar views are expressed and applied, though not on the basis of psychoanalytic considerations, by Prof. Sir James Spence.

development. The mothers are encouraged to take notice of their infants, to handle and to care for them. Thus the infants get their own mothers' unhindered attention instead of the impersonal attention of the nurses. And under the care and guidance of the doctors and nurses, the mothers gain confidence and assurance in the handling of their infants, which also reacts favorably on the infants.

Jackson rightly points out that in the beginning of the century increased knowledge and control in the fields of bacteriology and nutrition made for rigid schedules and impersonal hospital routine. This affected the point of view of doctors and nurses in the handling of their patients in and out of hospitals. The advantage of formula feeding as against breast feeding was a natural consequence of this trend.

What is surprising, however, is to find a similar controvery in the sixteenth and seventeenth centuries, not over breast feeding as against bottle feeding, but in respect of mothers who nursed their own infants as against mothers who gave them over to other women to be nursed. It was the custom in those days for women of the well-to-do classes to have wet nurses, or in some countries, England and France, to farm out their infants.

From the diary of John Evelyn, born 1620, we have a description of his early days:

> I was now (in regard to my mother's weakness, or rather customs of quality) put to nurse to one Peter, a neighbour's wife and tenant, of good, comely, brown, wholesome complexion, in a most sweet place towards the hills, flanked with wood and refreshed with streams, the affection to which kind of solitude I sucked in with my very milk. [It appears that he was kept in this foster-home for fifteen months.]

In the memoirs of the Verney family (1647), Margaret Verney is mentioned as sending her boy of three weeks with his wet nurse to Claydon, the nurse's home. They travel on horseback. The mother writes to her husband who worries about the trip on horseback for the baby: "Truly I think it will be a very good way, for the child will not endure to be long out of one's arms."

The death rate of even these supposedly better cared-for infants was great and the death rate of infants of the wet nurses themselves was appalling. Some doctors and educators took up the fight against this practice and tried to influence mothers to nurse their own babies. Tradition, custom, and superstition were so strong that these enlightened educators made little headway at this time.

As the following examples show, doctors pointed out to mothers the possibility of the nurse substituting one infant for the other; the danger of the nurse infecting the infant with some illness of hers; the fear that some bad character trait of the nurse might be sucked in with the milk, as was commonly believed. It does not seem astonishing that doctors tried to make the mothers aware of these dangers, but it is surprising to find that they mention such psychological reasons as the necessity of breast feeding the infant for the sake of the mother-child relationship; the nursing situation as a pleasure rather than a duty; and that nursing was advantageous for the mother as well as for the child. The nervousness of the mother affecting her milk was also mentioned.

Comenius (1592–1670) counseled mothers to nurse their own children.

Jacques Guilleneaux wrote a book on the nursing of children, translated into English 1612, in which he gave reasons why a child should not be delivered to another woman to nurse:

(1) Danger of substitution.
(2) "That the natural affection which should be betwixt mother and child by this means is diminished."
(3) "It may be feared that some bad condition or inhibition may be derived from the nurse into the child."
(4) Fear to communicate some imperfection of her body into the child. Guilleneaux said further:

I would have you imitate Blanche of Castile sometime Queen of France, who nursed the King St. Lewis, her sonne her owne self. . . . A great Ladie of the Court gave him sucke to still him and make him quiet, which coming to the Queenes eare she presently took the child and thrust her finger so far downe into his throat that she made him vomit all the milke he had suckt of the said Ladie, being very angry that any woman should give her child sucke but her selfe.

Claude Guillet (1656) of Leyden, in *Callipaediae*, translated into English by the Poet Laureate Nicholas Rowe, abused in verse the mothers who did not nurse their babies.

> Say therefore are not those absurdly vain
> Who cause their Children's Fate and then complain;
> Who with a hopeful beauteous offspring blest
> Forget themselves, and hire unwholsom Breasts;
> And to some common Wretch commit the care,
> Of Infant Celia or the future Heir;
> Besides Desiases and unnumbered Ills
> That latent Spread and flow in Milky Rills
> That from bad teats and putrid Channels pass
> And Taint the Blood and mingle with the Mass,
> The noxious Food conveys a greater Curse
> And gives the meaner Passions of the Nurse.

William Cadogan (1748) urged mothers to nurse their children:

I am quite at a loss to account for the practice of sending infants out of doors to be suckled or dry nursed by another woman, who has not so much understanding, nor can have so much affection for it as the parents: and how it comes to pass that people of good sense and easy circumstances will not give themselves the pains to watch over the health and welfare of their children. . . . The ancient custom of exposing them to wild beasts or drowning them would certainly be a much quicker and more humane way of dispatching them.

Hugh Smith, a doctor, gave advice to mothers in a series of letters (1767). In Letter VII he wrote that for mothers to suckle their children would prove to be a pleasure rather than a fatigue, and in Letter V gave arguments in favor of suckling as well for the mother's sake as the child's and the evils apprehended in delivering children to the care of foster nurses.

In *Levana* (1807) Richter writes: "As regards the physical empoisonment of the milk by mental excitement, I should prefer the nurse to the lady. . . . A lady, whom a false stitch of her maid, like the sting of a tarantula, sets into an armed dance, may poison it 3 or 4 times a day."

Artists as well as poets have over the ages pictured the nursing scene as representing the highest conception of mother love and the nursing baby as showing blissful contentment. What has happened to the maternal instinct and the natural pleasure of the mother in feeding her infant, that she is willing to give up nursing her child? Even her maternal possessiveness is lacking, for she gives up the closest possible relationship to others, or abandons it in favor of a substitute type of feeding. She apparently struggles little against tradition, custom, or the changeable advice of doctors.

It would be possible to attempt tentative answers to these questions, but far more interesting to probe into the deeper layers of the mind through the analysis of mothers, thus gaining greater understanding of the unconscious conflicts, wishes, and anxieties symbolized in the nursing situation. A first attempt of this kind has been made by M. P. Middlemore in her book *The Nursing Couple* (1941).

FEEDING

In modern times, the feeding of children has been much under discussion owing to the greater knowledge of food values as well as to the increased number of feeding problems among children. Clara M. Davis in 1928 started an experiment in an orthopedic ward of a children's hospital in Chicago, where she gave children the opportunity of selecting their own food and of eating as much or as little as they pleased. She also laid little stress on manners. Davis (1930, 1935a, 1935b) carried this experiment still further by supplying infants with a variety of formula feedings, allowing the babies to taste and enjoy or taste and reject what was offered to them. This experiment proved that children selected balanced diets over a period of time and ate with pleasure as much as they required to keep them well nourished.

Psychoanalysis has pointed out that the natural craving of a child for food and the satisfaction he acquires in eating should not be disturbed. For a child to take in nourishment against his will or without pleasure can lead to certain eating difficulties. Forcing him to eat a prescribed diet or certain quantities of food at fixed times and in an established manner is a way of spoiling the appetite and is conducive to forming feeding fads and habits.

Except for prescribed diets little is found in the literature of former times about children's feeding habits. Stress is put on children's manners, love of sweets, and prevention of greed and gluttony. A few doctors and educators show a certain astonishment that children are not allowed to follow the dictate of nature and eat what they enjoy.

Locke (1693) was swayed by what he considered a child should or should not eat, and he was afraid of evoking a child's greed. For instance meat was supposed to be harmful while bread was essential for a child. He thought that a child learns to eat what is good for him through custom. But of bread he says: "If he be not hungry, 'tis not fit he should eat." And:

> That you will not teach him to eat more nor oftener than nature requires. I do not think that all people's appetite are alike; some have naturally stronger and some weaker stomachs. By this I think, that many are made gourmands and gluttons by custom, that were not so by nature.
>
> Concerning the timing of meals I should think it best, that as much as it can be conveniently avoided, they should not be kept constantly to an hour: for when custom has fix'd his eating to certain stated periods, his stomach will expect victuals at the usual hour, and grow peevish if he passes it; either fretting itself

into a troublesome excess, or flagging into a downright want of appetite.

Locke, it seems, realized that if you upset the enjoyment of eating, disturbances occur.

Cadogan (1748), in a letter to one of the Governors of the Foundling Hospital, writes:

> In the business of nursing, as well as physick, art is destructive if it does not exactly copy this original. When a child is first born, there seems to be no provision at all made for it; for the mother's milk seldom comes till the third day, so that according to nature, a child could be left a day and a half, or two days, without any food; to me, a very sufficient proof that it wants none.

And about feedings:

> I would prevail, therefore, that the child be not awakened out of its sleep to be fed, as is commonly done.

Richter's *Levana* also mentions the timing of food:

> As early as possible determine the hours of eating, and consequently the times for sleep; only observing that in the first years the intervals must be more frequent and shorter than afterwards. The stomach is such a creature of habit, such a time keeper, that if, when hungry, we delay its usual period of gratification for a few hours, it does nothing but reject food.

The feeding problems of the past apparently had to do with the fear of children overeating, overindulging themselves, while the present-day problems are concerned rather with children's lack of appetite and undereating, resulting in undernourishment.

ILLNESS

What has come last and with the greatest resistance in this century has been the acceptance of more modern methods of treating children who are ill. Until a short time ago the physical symptoms took precedence and excluded everything else. Doctors and nurses did not take any notice of the child's usual existence, his parents, his environment, his habits; they concentrated on the child's illness, everything else was a hindrance to them. The illness was their concern and the cure of the children their sole responsibility. It is only very recently that, owing to the analytic findings concerning the connection between the child's emotional life and his physical well-being, an effort has come to be made not to forget the child while one treats the illness. The child's relationship to his parents, his daily life, wishes, habits, idiosyncrasies are all taken into account as well as his illness. Attempts are made to avoid separating the child from his mother during the illness; or, if this is unavoidable, to prepare the child for the separation. That emotional factors can aggravate an illness, or even produce one, is now a recognized fact. Operations, painful and unpleasant treatments, even changed surroundings are recognized as potentially traumatic events in the child's life. To choose, if possible, a favorable period in the child's development, and to prepare the child for such events as tonsillectomy and circumcision is considered a method of lessening the shocks.

The problem of children separated from their mothers has been in recent years, and still is, under constant observation. The enforced separations of the wartime evacuations have shown up the danger to children's development. The operation in the Hampstead Nurseries of the system of allowing parents' visits at all times, whenever they could manage it, has shown how the children reacted to long and short separations and to no separations (see Burlingham and A. Freud, 1942, 1944). The results of an investigation into the effects of hospitalization on children are described by Bowlby et al. (1952).[2]

B. W. Maclennan in an article, "Non-Medical Care of Clinically Ill Children in Hospital" (1949), urges that the closest

[2] See also James Robertson (1958).

cooperation should be maintained between medical staff and parents and that parents should be encouraged to visit. He stresses the need of a child for at least one adult with whom he can feel secure; if he is especially ill and removed to a room alone for the sake of quietness, he needs a special nurse or the mother. Maclennan suggests dividing the wards into families; the family consisting of doctor, sister, or staff nurse, and one or two junior nurses to be allocated to a small group of children.

All these suggestions are directed to giving the child a sense of security and confidence.

In a preliminary report on "Observations on the Emotional Reactions of Children to Tonsillectomy and Adenoidectomy," Lucie Jessner and Samuel Kaplan (1949) stress the importance of preparing the child for the operation by the mother, or preferably by some trained person, before hospitalization. They also recommend that in the hospital "unnecessary frightening sights and sounds be avoided wherever possible."

These are efforts to save the child emotional shocks.

A proposed experiment in the home care of seriously ill children, sponsored by Dr. F. S. W. Brimblecombe in connection with the Paediatric Unit of St. Mary's Hospital Medical School, is now under consideration. A mobile hospital team would be formed with doctors, nurses, and an ambulance with diagnostic and therapeutic equipment, in connection with the parent hospital. The cooperation of the general practitioner connected with the case and the social services of the district would be essential. The choice of case would depend on the home conditions and the personality and intelligence of the parents. Children of under five are contemplated, and especially cases of breast-fed infants. But all cases except certain fever cases could be cared for. This unit would then serve the ill child at home, giving him practically all the services he would have in a hospital. In this way the child would not have to be removed from his normal surroundings and especially from the care of his mother. The mother would feel secure that she was doing the best for her child by having the guidance and supervision of the doctors and nurses.

In 1947 the Montefiore Hospital in New York started a home care service of this kind for children with rheumatism. It is not, however, expressly stated on what psychological considerations this work is based.

Nearly identical action was taken, though not on psychoanalytic principles, by Professor Sir James Spence. Professor Spence has suggested and carried out new reforms in children's hospitals in Newcastle-upon-Tyne. His insight into childhood, the child's need as well as the parents', has been the foundation of his reforms. Mothers and infants are kept together in maternity hospitals. A small number of mothers can remain with their children and care for them when seriously ill under the supervision of the trained staff.

Professor Spence suggests that in the children's department there should be small units of five to eight beds, and rooms for two children and single rooms. He does not believe in isolating medical and surgical cases, but suggests that children should be in wards according to age, temperament, and nature of their illness. Each unit should contain a treatment room in which all dressings, lumbar punctures, and other painful manipulations can be carried out, and where anesthesia will be frequently used. There should be a full-time worker in the unit, who should have a room near it.

Professor Spence has been carrying on a home care service for children with tuberculosis for several years. Children are brought for treatments to the outpatients' department of the hospital and returned the same day by ambulance. Professor Spence's Department of Child Health runs a scheme of home care for premature infants. In connection with this scheme, Dr. F. J. W. Miller, Professor Spence's chief assistant, who runs this service, stresses the fact that home care has a good psychological effect on the family.

If analysts and others today point out the harm done to the child whose emotional life is neglected during illness and stress the need for security in familiar surroundings with the mother close at hand to make it possible for the child to cope with pain, therapeutic measures, in the past commonsense and an open mind have led medical and other authors to make similar suggestions.

The following advice is given in Richter's *Levana* as to the care of children who are ill.

> The heat of fever can only be allayed by what the child fancies. . . . I will give yet one other piece of good advice, the very best, to women: that is, when a child is really ill to do nothing whatever—especially nothing new—not to change or moderate temperature—to give him what he wishes to eat or drink—to say nothing if he fast for a few days.

When a child cries during an illness: "In the second kind of crying, . . . that caused by illness, the gentle, soothing mother's voice is in its right place—namely, by the sick bed."

Richter also points out the harm that fear as such can create. He tries to counteract the superstition that the sickness of the mother is repeated in the child.

> And it is for this very reason that superstitions, fancies about marks, misbirths and similar things ought to be so much guarded against; not because what is dreaded brings the fulfilment, but because it, along with those evils which are produced by alarm before a thing occurs and undue anxiety after it has happened, weakens the body, and brings for the sufferer years of trouble.

Dr. M. Brouzet (1754), in a section of a book dealing with the leanness of children, mentions that jealousy is among the causes of poor nutrition in infants.

> When it is suspected that this leanness is owing to the infant's pining, we should discover what it is that makes him

pine and we shall generally perceive that greater fondness is shown to some other infant in the house than to him, and on this account he is filled with jealousy. We cannot conceive the sensibility of an infant in this respect: he conceals his uneasiness within his own heart and keeps it an impenetrable secret; we must guess at his pain. The only means of discovery is to show less fondness to his brother or sister to whom there has been shown a great deal.

We should then carefully observe his eyes and we shall soon know if his disorder proceeds from jealousy: for if it does, he will no sooner perceive this change than his looks will become serene and he will appear less melancholy and thoughtful than usual. . . . That infants are capable of jealousy is a point that cannot be doubled, they are so even while at the breast. "I have seen," says M. Austin, "an infant jealous that could not pronounce a single word, and with a pale look and angry eye already look at another infant that sucked with him."

In 1722 George Armstrong started the first dispensary in England for children. An institution for the inpatient treatment of children was also suggested, but not adopted as it was considered impracticable. George Armstrong gave the following reasons for the impossibility of carrying out such a project. "But a very little reflection will clearly convince any thinking person that such a scheme as this can never be executed. If you take away a sick child from its parents or nurse, you break its heart immediately; and if there must be a nurse to each child what kind of a hospital must there be to contain any number of them?"

No analyst who, with the help of the analytic technique, has explored the hidden emotions in the child's mind could find a stronger or more appropriate expression than this of Armstrong's for the depth of emotion experienced by the infant who is deprived of his most important love object during the miseries of a bodily illness.

Chapter 8

PRESENT TRENDS IN HANDLING THE MOTHER-CHILD RELATIONSHIP DURING THE THERAPEUTIC PROCESS

There is a certain type of question which is brought up for discussion in my child analysis seminar with practically every case. Could not this child have been helped simply by guiding the mother? How far would a child guidance clinic have solved this problem for the child? Would not group therapy for the child, or for the mother, or for both, be indicated here? Would not the mother be more efficiently helped by someone who is not her child's analyst?

These questions are all the result of the times, the attempts to help the child through preventive methods, through more intelligent early handling, through meeting the child's problems at a stage earlier than the one when the child is sent to analysis.

Reprinted from *The Psychoanalytic Study of the Child*, 6:31-37. New York: International Universities Press, 1951.

The trend is now toward including the whole family in an effort to solve the child's problems, toward extending the therapy into ever-wider fields, toward grouping the children and mothers. This is done in part to increase the numbers helped, but in part also because group therapy is considered to have a therapeutic value in itself.

These present-day trends are bound to affect child analysis. They have already succeeded in eliminating certain cases from analysis, especially many of the younger children; child guidance clinics are able to sort out cases and refer those for analysis which need more intensive treatment. There remains, however, a large group of cases which at present can be helped only through analysis. The persistent question raised in my seminar, whether the mother might not be more efficiently helped by someone who is not her child's analyst, is a proof that the interrelationship of the mother and the analyst remains a most difficult problem during the child's analysis.

Until the child can make himself partly independent of the mother, that is, until he has reached latency, the mother's behavior toward a child and the home atmosphere she creates are all-important for the success or failure of the analysis.

Managing the mother poses many problems: how far the analyst should take the mother with him through the intricacies of her child's analysis; what interpretations which have already been given to the child should be repeated to her, what interpretations should be withheld, the dosage and timing of these interpretations; how to keep the transference of the mother in a state favorable for the analysis—i.e., on the one hand not too weak, on the other hand to prevent it from overwhelming the whole analysis. All these questions pose most difficult tasks for the analyst, as I have previously attempted to show (see Chapter 1).

Sending the mother into analysis herself has often proved necessary when the mother's neurosis overwhelmed the child, so that the child could not be made independent of her, or when the mother had an unconscious fantasy which the child had taken over from her. But there are many cases where the mothers are not so seriously implicated, where such a drastic measure as her own analysis is unnecessary. It is then that the suggestion is made that the mother be advised by a psychiatric social worker, that is, by someone who is not personally concerned with the relationship of the mother to the child's analyst. This attempt to reduce or eliminate the transference relationship of the mother to the child's analyst is a natural consequence of the difficulties I have previously enumerated.

The rationalized advantages given for separating the mother from the child's analyst and giving her an adviser of her own are many: that the child's difficulties are connected with the mother's difficulties; that the mother is in need of treatment so as to understand and master her own problems, which come from her own childhood, and therefore affect her treatment of her child. The mother will bring to her adviser the daily problems which she has to meet in connection with her child, and these problems will be worked through with her. In this way jealousy of the child's analyst will be reduced and the mother need no longer be envious that her child is getting all the attention and help when she is in great need of it as well.

I would like to counter these arguments by putting a question of my own: is it really an advantage to separate the mother from the child's analyst in this way? What are we really doing? We are trying to give the mother, who is the child's main love object as well as his superego, insight into her own problems as far as they act on the child, so that she can change her behavior toward the child. At the same time we are trying to reduce the child's dependence on the mother's neurosis and to strengthen his own ego, so that the child can develop in a more normal way and not revert to the same symptom formations or regressive activities and fantasies.

The method used in treating the mother in a child guidance clinic is to give her explanations of her behavior, leading her back to an awareness of her own childhood problems, and some interpretation of preconscious material. She is also made conscious of the superficial reasons for her child's behavior in relation to her own behavior. She is told of the various stages of her child's instinctual development and the mechanisms of defense her child uses. The child's analyst keeps in touch with the mother's adviser and tells her about the stage the child has reached in his analysis, and the analyst in turn gets information about the mother.

This all sounds very satisfactory. Following the mother's lead, however, it often happens that the mother will bring in material which takes us far away from the child's problems into all sorts of other intimate problems and other relationships which may only reawaken conflicts and which cannot be dealt with. This situation must produce disappointment for her. The explanations and interpretations given to her concerning herself as well as the child are preconscious. They often do not affect the mother; she still has to behave as she has done before, since the interpretations do not touch her actions, which are unconsciously determined, or her fantasies, which are unconscious. The result must be that she is aware of her behavior, but unable to change, and therefore is now troubled by a feeling of uncertainty and guilt.

Let us now study the situation of the analyst who analyzes the child and accepts the added responsibility of the mother as well.

The analyst is aware of all the difficulties which the situation presents: the added transference relationship of the mother to the analyst which he must use and deal with throughout the whole of the child's analysis. But there are certain advantages for the analyst if he keeps the situation completely in his own hands. It is possible for him to make good use of various opportunities that turn up in the course of the treatment: a glimpse of the mother when she accompanies her child to his session can give him some hint of the mood of the day, a kind of barometer of the child's state; a remark the mother lets fall to the analyst or to the child can be a helpful suggestion he can use in the session or make a mental note of for later use. At the end of the session the analyst may be thankful for the opportunity of seeing mother and child reunited; he may use the occasion to make a remark helpful to one or to both. Another opportunity might be the telephone calls of the mother, telling of daily happenings which could bring the analyst valuable information. In this way the analyst can become a reservoir of material collected not only from the child's sessions but also from these casual encounters with the mother. Then there are the interviews the analyst can arrange with the mother. He can use them to enlarge or to correct the observations he has already made; to gain information about the child, his life at home, and his reactions to all kinds of situations. He can use them to give the mother the opportunity to bring her own observations; to encourage the mother to ask questions about her child's behavior, activities, fantasy life, and her own reactions to them; and, above all, to allow the mother to express her worries about the analysis itself.

These are all rather self-evident opportunities for the analyst to make use of. But there are others which are more subtle. Berta Bornstein, in her paper "Emotional Barriers in the Understanding of Young Children" (1948), states that "The contact with the parents should not go beyond such mild and supportive psychotherapy. The analyst should not apply the genetic and dynamic aspects [of her understanding in] discussions with parents regarding the meaning of their conflicts with their children." But is that really possible?

It seems to me that even when one is trying to avoid giving the mother dynamic interpretations, the mother still receives them. When the analyst gives the child interpretations of a deeper kind, this material is bound to affect the mother. Even when the analyst does not explain these to the mother and does not connect (to the mother's conflicts) these interpretations given in relation to the child's instinctual life, the interpretations given to the child affect the mother as a kind of wild analysis. It is in answer to this secondhand analytic procedure that the mother reactivates her own childhood, and as a consequence brings memories of her own childhood experiences. All that the analyst can do in his interviews with the mother is to tone down these dynamic reactions which have been called forth by the child's analysis. This he does by superficially analyzing the preconscious material as well as by giving advice on how to handle the child to enable her to cope with the child's behavior problems at home.

When the mother brings to the interviews intimate material from her own life, although this may bring with it difficulties in the transference relationship, it may also contain valuable clues for the understanding of the child's neurosis. As a rule, it is possible for the analyst to keep this transference within bounds if he is not seduced into analyzing the mother, but can keep his objective interest focused on the child and his problems. The mother will usually fall in with the analyst's wishes, sensing very soon that the material the analyst accepts and values has always some connection with her child and his problems. The mother's narcissistic hurt at not receiving full analytic attention will be compensated for when she feels that she is allowed to cooperate in the work of the analyst to help her child.

We must now ask ourselves whether the analyst benefits more from separating the mother from the child's analysis, thus avoiding the disturbances the mother creates, or whether the analyst gains more by accepting these disturbances in the hope that he may be able to make subtle connections between mother and child which would otherwise be lost and in this way gain a greater understanding of the child.

My activity as supervising analyst gives me the opportunity to compare what happens to mothers under both conditions. I hope, in the future, to be able to illustrate this with more detailed material. For the present I would like to bring one example of a mother's reactions during the time she was in advisory treatment with a child analyst working in a child guidance clinic and compare them with her reactions when the same child was in analytic treatment a year later.

Bobby N. was a two-and-a-half-year-old boy who had feeding difficulties and was still wetting and dirtying himself; he could not talk properly for his age, and he bit his mother. The mother was a simple woman, somewhat slow in understanding, but unusually cooperative. The case appeared to be ideally suited for mother guidance. The therapist gave the usual advice to the mother: to pay less attention to his feeding and habit training. He soon ate better and was dry, and after two months he no longer soiled himself.

Another of Bobby's difficulties was that he clung to his mother, and he could not stand separation from her. (At the age of two years he had been separated from her when she had had to undergo an operation.) The mother was told not to try and separate from him until he gave indications of wanting to do so on his own. When she had to go to the hospital for an examination, she was advised to prepare him for the few hours' separation long in advance. She did this so well that Bobby let her go without difficulty. At the hospital she was urged to remain for a treatment, but she refused, remembering what the therapist had told her as well as the promise she had made to Bobby that she would return soon.

The therapist found out that the mother would not let Bobby touch his penis. She helped him to urinate and insisted on washing his penis and pushing back the foreskin whenever she saw any secretion there. The therapist explained to the mother the harmlessness of Bobby's touching his penis and at another time the fear she gave Bobby in cleaning his penis. The therapist called in a doctor who happened to be there, and he corroborated what she had just said. The mother apparently understood. Once, when Bobby refused to have his feet washed (this was an identification with her as she had an eczema of her leg), she told him that she was not going to lose her leg. His speech improved after these interpretations of his castration fears.

The therapist advised the mother to let Bobby sleep in a room of his own; he had always slept with his parents. This she did, and Bobby adjusted to this change without difficulty and slept better.

The mother began spontaneously to tell the therapist about her own childhood. Her mother had died of cancer when she was six years old. Her father told her that she had killed her mother because she had bitten her breast. Her father used to beat her mother and herself.

In spite of the fact that Bobby's mother was as helpful to the therapist as any mother could be, cooperating in every way, following the therapist's educational advice with understanding and resulting improvement, Bobby now became worse again. He could not sleep, and he developed a new symptom of breaking away from his mother into the street, running right into the tr'affic. The manner in which he did this was dangerous and appeared obsessional. Bobby was therefore sent into analysis.

Bobby's analysis at three and a half years of age was a most fascinating one and gave the impression of being successful. The mother was as cooperative with the analyst as she had been with the therapist. However, little educational advice was given to her until toward the end of the analysis. The analytic material developed from one problem to the next and was played out in fantasies. Each phase of the analysis covered many weeks. The longest one was occupied with uncovering a primal scene in the fullest detail. Frequently, while Bobby was engaged in fantasy play, he would call his mother to come into the therapy room. And the mother was able to make apt remarks to the analyst, showing her understanding of what was going on.

When Bobby's analysis was reported in my seminar, his former therapist was deeply shocked to find that the interpretations and advice she had given the mother over a period of a whole year had apparently been obliterated from the mother's memory after Bobby left the treatment. It was to be expected that the same material that the mother had worked over with Bobby would also come up in his analysis; but the mother behaved as if she had never been told how to treat Bobby with his habit training or with his food. As an example of something very difficult to understand, the mother told the analyst that when she gave Bobby his bath, he struggled, apparently in fear of having his penis cleaned. When the analyst told her that it was not necessary to clean his penis so often and then reminded her of the occasion when the therapist had called in the doctor and he had said the same thing, she could not remember it at all.

The one thing the mother had kept to was to have Bobby sleep in a room of his own.

The mother now began to tell the analyst about herself. The analyst had suggested to the mother that she occasionally have a quiet time with Bobby, show him a picture book, for instance, or read aloud to him. She responded by saying that she did not want Bobby to become a bookworm like the analyst, and then said that she could not stand Bobby's success when she was such a failure herself. She had to get on by herself, why should Bobby have it better? She had won a scholarship but because of lack of money had not been able to make use of it.

Bobby's running into the street had stopped, but he re-created the same situation in the hour. It was quite clear that Bobby ran away to provoke his mother to come and catch him. The mother was told of his mechanism and when she did not respond anymore to his provocation, he stopped provoking her. The mother then told the analyst, "I don't tease Bobby anymore, but I can scarcely resist doing so."

CONCLUSION

This is all the material necessary to show how the mother reacted first toward her adviser and then toward her child's analyst. In both cases the mother was most cooperative. The extent of her cooperation was shown in the incident when she refused to remain in the hospital and returned home rather than break her promise to Bobby.

One would think that since the mother had succeeded in establishing habit training with the help of the therapist, she would continue to treat Bobby as she had learned to do when the trouble recurred during the analysis.

We can ask ourselves: was the transference a different one to the therapist and to the analyst? And if so, was the difference due to their personalities? That may be so in some cases, but I do not believe that it was the case in this instance. To me it seems that the different reactions of the mother in the two situations can be traced back to the different forms of treatment to which she reacted. In the advisory treatment no material was touched that did not belong to the conscious and preconscious layers. She reacted to this with material from her own conscious and preconscious mind. In Bobby's analysis the interpretation of the analyst naturally reached further down to the child's unconscious, and this again had repercussions on the mother. Repressed rivalry and penis envy, to which she had formed reaction formations, were stirred up in her and betrayed themselves in her attitude to her child's analyst and brought to the foreground awareness of her rivalry and competition with the child, of which she had been oblivious. It was the working through of these feelings which finally relieved the mother and enabled her to deal with the child differently on the basis of a beneficial change in her own personality.

When faced with material of this kind we cannot help being impressed by the difference in the effectiveness of the latter approach so far as the mother is concerned. To realize that one has spent a fruitless year advising a mother is rather a shock to an analytic worker and should be taken as a warning. A careful comparison of our ways of dealing with mothers and of their reactions may lead us in time to a better clarification and classification of our approaches to the parents.[1]

---

[1] For further developments in this direction, see Chapter 10.

Chapter 9

NOTES ON PROBLEMS
OF MOTOR RESTRAINT
DURING ILLNESS

According to some of our theoretical assumptions expounded recently by Hartmann, Kris, Loewenstein (1949), the muscular apparatus is more essential for the discharge of aggressive than of libidinal tension. In spite of this particularly close tie between aggression and motility, it seems plausible that on the libidinal side too, an essential though less spectacular flow of discharge takes place constantly by way of muscular movement, creating a similarly close link between libidinal tensions and motility. Instances where muscular movement is particularly prominent or particularly inhibited provide us with the opportunity to test as well as to illustrate this theory.

MUSCULAR MOVEMENT AS GENERAL DISCHARGE
OF INSTINCTUAL ENERGY

The most impressive example of muscular movement used for the discharge of instinctual energy is provided by the infant in

Reprinted from *Drives, Affects, Behavior*, edited by Rudolph M. Loewenstein. New York: International Universities Press, 1953, pp. 169-175.

119

his second year, especially in the short period after independent movement has been established and before verbal expression is achieved. During this time when speech is not yet available for discharge, a variety of emotions, libidinal as well as aggressive, are expressed in movements. Impatience, anger, rage, as well as pleasurable anticipation, bursts of affection, jealousy, feelings of frustrations, each finds its outlet in specific movements of the head, the arms, hands, legs, in short the whole body.[1] (See, for instance, the characteristic bouncing up and down or beating movements with the hands for pleasurable anticipation; kicking with the feet in rage.) Muscular activities such as walking, crawling, running, jumping, climbing, continually discharge the tensions created by the violent and urgent impulses which dominate this stage. In frustration, and under the impact of conflicting emotions, muscular activity becomes diffuse; spread over the whole body, i.e., undirected and chaotic, it reaches its climax in the so-called temper tantrum of the child.

On the other hand, in this period of life the infant indulges in more motor activity than his ego can control and employ sensibly. Therefore he lays himself open to continual thwarting of his movements by the environment, for the sake of his own safety as well as for the safeguarding of surrounding objects. Such bodily restraint which blocks his main avenue of expression leaves large amounts of tension undischarged. Infants are known to react to this state in two ways. Where restraint is sudden and unexpected, they answer with a paroxysm of aggression with increased attempts at motor discharge; where restraint is a chronic feature in the child's life, i.e., where infants are never given sufficient scope for moving, it is an observed fact that the restraint of muscular movement has an adverse, inhibiting effect on the emotions which are prevented from finding motor expression, with the result that these children appear duller and more apathetic (other circumstances remaining equal).

[1] See Ernst Kris (1939) on facial expression as a reduction of body movement.

CHILD PATIENTS UNDER MOTOR RESTRAINT

The same close connection between the mode and freedom of discharge and the fate of the affects waiting for discharge seems to be apparent in older children whose muscular movements are restrained forcibly for reasons of orthopedic treatment. Thesi Bergmann, in her paper "Observation of Children's Reactions to Motor Restraint" (1945), describes patients from two to sixteen years of age who, in the course of orthopedic treatment showed two stages in their reaction to the enforced restrictions. In the first stage the children are immobilized in their plaster casts. They are then found to be docile and apparently content, the abnormality of their situation being expressed mainly by regressions to more infantile modes of satisfaction and behavior. In the second stage the children are relieved of their casts and permitted to begin moving about. But this partial freedom of movement does not act as a relief for tensions. On the contrary, the children are then especially difficult to handle; they are overactive, hard to keep within bounds, easily fly into rages and throw temper tantrums.

The same pattern of behavior is reported, for example, of a latency child, a boy who came to analysis because of aggressive outbursts against his parents and strangers and of destructiveness toward objects after he had been in a plaster cast for many months. The mother reported that during the period of enforced immobility, the child had been gentle, considerate, and especially easy to handle, but that he had broken out in wild uncontrolled behavior after the cast had been removed.

David M. Levy (1944) and others have reported similar cases of enforced restrictions with the same behavior patterns as aftereffect.

So far no explanation of this incongruity of behavior has been stated explicitly, although the interpretation suggests itself easily that in the second, uncontrolled period these children work off the emotions, anxieties, and frustrations which were dammed up in them during the immobilized state. Still, this does not answer the question why other modes of outlet such as speech were not used during immobilization, nor why the children showed no manifest signs of rising tension in this phase. This is where the analogy with infant behavior may be helpful. It seems possible that the full restraint of mobility to which the child has to submit develops within his ego into a restraint of affect, i.e., a massive repression of emotion which reduces manifest tension. This control of emotion cannot be kept up except during complete immobilization. The partial lifting of motor retrictions leads to a breakthrough of the repressed feelings, makes tensions unbearable, so that outlets in muscular movement, aggressive speech, and general uncontrolled behavior have to be found.

MECHANICAL VERSUS VOLUNTARY RESTRAINT

Another type of motor restraint can be studied in patients with heart disease or tuberculosis on whom no mechanical restrictions are imposed but who, on medical advice, have to immobilize themselves more or less in bed in order to be cured. This means that their ego has to supply the restraining action, which in the case of the aforementioned patients was supplied by the apparatus (plaster cast) or by the environment. The normal impulse to move and to discharge tensions through the musculature is opposed in their case by another impulse acting in the opposite direction (the wish to be safe, to improve, to be cured), represented in the mind by the fear of the consequences of movement. This creates a state similar to that known from the dreams of inhibited movement, where a wish to perform a certain movement is opposed by the counterwish not to do so, a conflict which results in the dream in a feeling of complete paralysis. Similar sensations of paralysis are reported by adult patients under the conditions of complete bed rest.

In an article on tuberculosis, called "A Patient's Point of View" in the *Nursing Times* of March 22, 1952, the following remarks written by a patient were included under the heading, "Working off Emotion":

> Quite often, in my own case, I found that while I was following some quiet occupation such as reading, I would suddenly have a feeling of being "bottled up" inside. Only by violent exercise such as kicking and stretching was I able to overcome this feeling, which I can only describe as having a mental origin and a physical effect. It was like being bound hand and foot and wanting desperately to move. The phenomenon continued throughout the illness and was present not only when lying still in bed, but on occasions when I was writing or doing occupational therapy. This, I think, proves that lack of exercise and lying still in bed are not the only factors that contribute to this feeling. I believe this to have been a kind of stagnant emotion which some light exercise would have relieved.

Another tuberculosis patient was greatly disturbed by states of bodily sensations after several months of bed rest. She lay quietly in bed, apparently content and at peace, when she would be overcome by unbearable feelings of tension. She felt as if her arms and legs were actually engaged in violent and uncontrollable muscular motions of beating, striking, and kicking. The sensations, though felt as violent activity, had, of course, no reducing effect on the existing tension. These sensations went on for hours and continued off and on for several days. They could be described best as an imaginary temper tantrum. However, there were no accompanying emotions of annoyance, anger, and rage toward anyone or anything, merely a concentration of attention on the bodily feelings. There was no thought content which could be brought to consciousness, except attempts at interpretation such as: "This must mean that I am impatient, or tired of lying in bed, or of being ill." These states recurred sev-

eral times during this period of illness and again to a much
lesser degree several years later during a relapse of the same
disease after several months of complete rest.

That a busy and active person when forced to give up all
normal occupations, interests, and physical activities becomes
disturbed and irritated, does not need explanation. The situation
warrants emotional outbreaks. What is astonishing with these
two patients is that although they are aware of tension and of
the need to express violent emotions by means of muscular
activity, they remain in ignorance of the nature of their emotions. The first patient merely feels "bottled up" inside, "bound
hand and foot" and "unable to move."[2] In his interpretation of
the state he hints at a "mental origin" of his bodily feelings and
expresses the view that lack of exercise and lying in bed cannot
be the only factors to create so much stagnant emotion; but he
never refers explicitly to the general complex of annoyance, frustration, anxiety, fear of death, etc., which seem to be the inevitable reactions to an illness of this kind.

The second patient responds to the identical feelings of tension not by action, but by muscular sensations of movement
only, the imaginary movements increasing in violence since no
release of tension is achieved. In her case, too, none of the
accompanying affects become conscious. The strength of the
counterimpulse (not to move, not to endanger herself) can be
deduced only from its inhibitory effect which reduces outlet
in motility to a mere imaginary activity.

The reactions of both patients may be compared with those of
the children in plaster casts, their changes of mood corresponding to the presence or lifting of the mechanical restraint. So long
as they achieve immobility, they inhibit their emotions together
with their actions; any reappearing wishes to move coincide
with returning waves of chaotic and usually unrecognized emotions.

_____

[2] As in the inhibition dreams mentioned above.

REGRESSIONS UNDER MOTOR RESTRAINT

AUTOMATIC MOVEMENTS

Certain types of tics in animals as, for instance, the head shaking of chicks or the weaving of horses are considered a result of confinement to limited quarters. With infants, the well-known rhythmical movements such as rocking and head knocking, which have a place among the autoerotic and autoaggressive activities of early life, are known to increase when the children are confined too much to their prams or cribs. According to David M. Levy (1944), tics are often found in hyperactive children as a means of warding off forbidden motor impulses. This last observation would be valid for the state of the patient under the voluntary restriction of bed rest who similarly has to ward off his dangerous and therefore forbidden motor impulses. It would be worthwhile to observe such patients for the emergence of "nondangerous" ticlike, automatic movements of those parts of the body which escape restriction, such as the drumming of tunes, biting or pulling of lips or hair, etc. Compulsive activities of this nature which are usually dismissed as expressions of mere "boredom" may well be qualitatively reduced and displaced substitutes for the normal ways of motor discharge of affect.

PASSIVE EXPERIENCES

Another substitute for active muscular movement is provided by the passive handling of the patient's body by others. This attention given to the body by the mother or nurse gives rise to a variety of sensations, exciting, pleasurable as well as painful ones. These pleasures revive the experiences between mother and child in the earliest stages of life; while they are regressively enjoyed by some child patients, they are violently opposed by others. When adult patients under motor restriction are handled by the nurse, their childhood memories of pleasurable handling, feeding, etc., are also revived. As adjusted personalities with well-stabilized defense mechanisms, they have less to fear from this reactivation of former passive pleasures. Only when unconscious passive trends are kept under precarious and labile ego control, the patients will feel threatened by whatever bodily care is given and, instead of accepting it as a substitute pleasure and relief, will develop violent, paranoid reactions against the nursing personnel.

VICARIOUS PLEASURE IN THE MOVEMENT OF OTHERS

Another substitute for the pleasure and relief offered by muscular activity of the individual's own body is the pleasure in observing the movement of others. Before they reach the stage of independent movement, infants often spend their waking hours in watching and contemplating anything that moves, whether it is the changing facial expression of the mother, the moving of a shadow, a leaf that falls or waves in a breeze, that is, whatever passes in their line of vision. Anything that catches the attention of the infant by its motion is a source of attraction and produces a delighted concentration. This pleasure is not lost after independent movement has been acquired. The child who has learned to walk and will move about constantly in his second year of life is equally attracted by the toys which move, particularly wheels, carts, etc. In the years to follow he is fascinated by the mechanical toys with independent motion such as trains, engines, toy cars, or their counterparts in the adult world. (For the boy the mysterious independent movement of the mechanical toy probably symbolizes the mysterious independent action of his own genital.) From then onward interest in the watching of moving objects outside seems to keep pace with the pleasure in muscular movement.

In adult patients under voluntary restraint, the enjoyment of watching moving objects reacquires many of the characteristics of the baby stage. Following with the eyes the nurse who is occupied in the room; watching the moving of a curtain, the swinging of a lamp or of a spider web, the swaying of trees outside the window; observing the birds—flying by or the fish swimming around in an aquarium—all these can be pleasurable preoccupations over many hours and days. For many patients this is the only welcome and relieving antidote to the constant preoccupation and concentration with their own immobilized and ill body.

CONCLUSION

There is, probably, no illness where revolt against (voluntary) motor restraint plays a greater part or leads to more disastrous consequences than tuberculosis. The conflicts between the fantastic, unrealistic wishes and plans for activity that crop up in the patients' mind and their decision to obey doctor's orders and lie still remind one of the continual struggles of the two-year-old against all measures which restrict his freedom. As the illness develops, and with it the fear of ever-increasing or renewed restrictions, the state of mind of the patient resembles increasingly the blind paroxysm of the toddler under the impact of frustration. It would be interesting to know whether the so-called "elation" of the tuberculosis patient, his dangerous periods of activity which sometimes prove fatal, does not similarly represent a "blind" struggle, a denial of the worsening disease and its requirements. The "last fling" of the tuberculosis patient would then represent the immediate and impatient motor wish fulfillment regardless of consequences which is well known to us as appropriate to the instinctually stormy second year of life.

Chapter 10

SIMULTANEOUS ANALYSIS
OF MOTHER AND CHILD

INTRODUCTION AND PREHISTORY

The case of Bobby N. was referred to in Chapter 8. It is one of those cases on which much effort by psychiatrists, analysts, child guidance workers, etc., is spent, often with the disappointing result that the child falls back into his former abnormalities after the contact with and effort of the respective workers have been withdrawn. Though there seems to exist in the child a good potentiality for improvement or even complete recovery, another force seems to be at work which constantly counteracts the therapeutic efforts which are made. Analysts have recognized for some time that this force emanates from the mother, usually in spite of the mother's conscious efforts to cooperate in treatment. In child guidance work where dealings with the mother are of necessity of a more superficial nature, her pathogenic influence on the child is ascribed mostly to her hostile feelings toward him, i.e., her rejection, or to her seductive behavior, or

This paper, written in cooperation with Alice Goldberger and André Lussier, is reprinted from *The Psychoanalytic Study of the Child*, 10:165-186. New York: International Universities Press, 1955.

to the abnormalities of her own object relationships, or to her psychotic traits. It seems to us that nothing short of an analysis of the mother can reveal in detail which influences are at work and what the more intimate relations are between her unconscious fantasies and attitudes and her child's disturbance.

BOBBY IN CHILD GUIDANCE TREATMENT

Bobby was first brought to a child guidance clinic (Hornsey Infant Welfare Centre) at the age of two and a half, his symptoms then being feeding difficulties, wetting and soiling, retardation of speech, biting attacks on the mother, and clinging to her. The case was assigned to Miss Ruth Thomas, then the visiting psychologist.

The mother attended for the period of one year, once weekly. She seemed a simple woman, somewhat slow in understanding, but cooperative. She followed the advice given with regard to the handling of feeding and habit training and the child improved. His eating increased, and wetting and soiling disappeared after two months. In connection with Bobby's separation anxieties, the mother was instructed not to expose him to shocks. She showed her understanding of this by preparing Bobby well for a half day's separation from her when she had to go to the hospital for an examination. When urged there to remain for treatment she refused, remembering her promise to Bobby to return on the same day and Miss Thomas's advice. She cooperated equally well where Bobby's castration fears were concerned. The only point where she proved adamant was in her allegedly hygienic attitude toward handling and cleaning his penis.

In spite of the mother's helpfulness, Miss Thomas distrusted the stability of the improvement, and when Bobby developed the new symptom of breaking away from his mother to run into the street traffic, she advised child analysis.

BOBBY'S FIRST ANALYSIS

At this time, at the age of three and a half, Bobby was taken in analysis by Dr. Martin James, then an analyst in training at the London Institute of Psycho-Analysis. Again the mother cooperated to the fullest extent to which her own difficulties

permitted. The analytic material developed in an orderly fashion by means of fantasy play, a primal scene being uncovered
finally at the end of the first year. Again the child improved.
The analysis was broken off when the analyst had to leave
London. It was a striking point in Dr. James's observation
that the mother had forgotten whatever interpretations and
advice she had been given during the first child guidance
treatment.

Dr. James managed to keep contact in occasional interviews
to watch the child's progress. When the situation deteriorated
once more, Bobby was referred to the Hampstead Child-
Therapy Clinic where, for the reasons mentioned above, his
case was selected for inclusion in our project of Simultaneous
Analysis of Mother and Child.

BOBBY AND HIS MOTHER IN ANALYSIS

The analysis of Bobby, aged four years and ten months, and
his mother now became the concern of a team of workers.
The mother's analysis was undertaken by Dr. André Lussier
of Montreal, Canada, then in training at the Institute of Psycho-
Analysis in London. The analysis of Bobby was carried out by
Miss Alice Goldberger, an analytic child therapist trained in
the Hampstead Child-Therapy Course. For the purpose of
keeping the analytic work of the two therapists independent
and uninfluenced by the material of the other partner, Dr.
Lussier and Miss Goldberger were instructed not to communicate with each other. Instead, both reported their material to
me at weekly intervals for purposes of integration. The analytic material is therefore theirs, my part being that of supervising or controlling analyst. I have received permission from
both to use it in the communication which follows.

FEEDING PROBLEMS

THE CHILD'S BEHAVIOR

As in every child's analysis, the first account of the early feeding
problems was given by the mother; in Bobby's case it was only
to be expected that her reports might be even more colored by
her own disturbances than happens usually. Her first description

of Bobby was that of a perfect baby. It took some time until she remembered that she herself did not have enough milk, that accordingly there was difficulty in breast feeding, and that the child had to be weaned at the age of twelve weeks. As regards his own activity in the feeding process, she described that he would not grasp a rusk to chew, that she had to hold it for him, that he would not attempt to hold a spoon to feed himself. According to her, this passive attitude toward food had outlasted babyhood and persisted up to the time she brought him to analysis. When he was four and a half, she would still sit beside him at mealtimes, feed him like a baby, and urge him to eat more than he wanted to take voluntarily. By that time he had acquired many food fads and would ask her for special dishes which he would then refuse.

According to the mother, Bobby's feeding difficulties had reached a peak at the age of one year when he suffered from a severe attack of diarrhea, retained no food, cried, whined, and hardly slept. This condition seems to have lasted for eight months when he was finally put on a strict diet, which she kept up for six months. When Bobby was two years old, the mother had to go to the hospital and Bobby was sent to a residential nursery. According to the mother, he fell ill there and returned severely constipated. The mother blames his further difficulties on this time of separation. When Bobby went to school, the mother distrusted his eating the school meals and insisted on having him home to feed.

In contrast to this behavior with the mother, his father reported that Bobby ate well when with him. The same was reported from school when the teacher finally insisted on his remaining for meals. In his sessions with the therapist Bobby would show greed for food, would demand quantities of drinks, and eat by himself without any difficulty when given food. There seemed to be no doubt that his attitude to eating varied with his moods. Periodically he had states of depression when he felt unloved and unworthy of love. Once, when he had been moved to a lower form in school and had fallen into such a mood, he told his therapist that he ate too much, but that he felt all the time as if he were starving. In this and similar sessions he demanded not only food but other signs of affection. It was characteristic of his oral greed that he could not bear frustration at such times, but had to have his wishes fulfilled immediately or fall into a panic.

This evidence given by the father and the teacher as well as Bobby's behavior in the analytic session showed that he was able to have a normal or even increased appetite with perfect ability to be active in feeding himself. His abnormal behavior in the feeding situation was reserved for the mother, whom he controlled and tortured by his passivity and his refusal to eat. She reacted to this by taking the active part and forcing food on him.

Seen from the point of view of this child's analysis, we would say that, through his behavior, Bobby forced the mother to react toward him as she did. Seen from the aspect of the mother's analysis, as will be shown below, Bobby's behavior takes on a different connotation. There is, in the mother's analytic material, ample evidence that in handling the child's feeding situation she was herself under the domination of powerful unconscious fantasies which determined her attitude. In this light the child's behavior will be seen as a reaction to the mother's provocation.

MATERIAL FROM THE MOTHER'S ANALYSIS

The Mother as an Unwanted Child

Bobby's mother had been told in childhood that she had been unwanted and that her mother, when pregnant with her, had taken quantities of pills in order to abort. When she grew older she was not considered normal, but queer, odd, strange. It is this image of herself as a child which she projected later onto Bobby in forming the idea that he could not be normal either. In spite of his having been a healthy baby she could not trust herself to have produced a normal child. This particular remnant from her own childhood created a need in her to have an abnormal, queer child herself.

Analytic Material Underlying the Difficulties of Breast Feeding

In the mother's analysis the simple fact told to the child's therapist that she had insufficient milk to feed Bobby proved to overlay a very different state of affairs. Actually, her milk had not been insufficient; it had flowed freely, but always dried up as soon as she put the child to the breast. The fantasy material which she revealed was the following. She had learned early (before the age of five) that she had been breast-fed herself, but that her mother developed cancer of the breast soon thereafter. The mother died of this cancer before Mrs. N. was six years old. The child conceived the idea, which persisted for ever after, that the mother's illness was due to injury which she as a suckling infant had done to the breast. She took this as a confirmation that she was born a bad child and that her fate was to destroy the people she loved. The idea that she had killed her mother became conscious, remained in her mind, and served as reinforcement of her masochistic inclinations.

These partly conscious, partly unconscious fantasies were not the only barrier to breast feeding. There was, further, the idea in Mrs. N.'s mind that breast feeding was disgusting and degrading, fit only for animals such as cows. Analysis traced this back to observations of cows being milked or suckled by the calf and the equation of breast and penis. Nursing Bobby, therefore, became for her the act of permitting him to commit fellatio with her.

There was the further idea in her unconscious that by taking her milk Bobby would empty her out, Mrs. N. equating being empty with a state of deep depression. The feeling of emptiness was connected in her mind with hunger, i.e., the lack of food which she had experienced before as well as after her own mother's death. Mrs. N.'s family had been poor; they had often gone hungry, and her mother at the time of her illness had become a bad manager, failing to provide proper nourishment for her children. When Mrs. N. was taken to the hospital once as a child because of skin trouble, malnutrition had been diagnosed. For Mrs. N. as well as for Bobby food and love, being unloved or starved, were synonymous.

So far as Mrs. N.'s conscious intentions were concerned, she had meant to give Bobby a better childhood than she had had herself. Where she had been hungry, she wanted to satisfy him; where she had been empty, she meant to keep him full and loved. But her unconscious fantasies and anxieties prevented her from realizing this aim. Her defenses against being given a cancer by him (as she had given to her mother), her defenses against fellatio fantasies, and the warding off of emptiness and depression stopped her milk from flowing for the child and forced her into making him repeat her own experiences of deprivation. What Bobby actually experienced was her withdrawal from him, her refusal of satisfying nourishment, i.e., her rejection.

Further Material Concerning Feeding

At a later period of her analysis Mrs. N. was deeply concerned with her guilt feelings toward Bobby, not only for having deprived him of her milk but also for failing to feed him properly at the succeeding stages. She blamed herself for the attack of severe diarrhea at the age of one which she ascribed to giving him meat that was not fresh and insufficiently cooked by her. According to her, he was ill for months without interruption, and it seems that during this time she tried unsuccessfully to convince several doctors of the severity of his state and of her own part in it. Finally, she found one doctor onto whom she could project her own feelings of self-accusation. She felt that after examining the child this doctor looked at her accusingly as if he wanted to condemn and kill her for neglect. These self-accusations were projected equally onto Bobby himself. She was convinced that he blamed her and that from the beginning of the diarrhea he ceased to smile at her.

During the illness, and on doctor's advice for four months thereafter, she kept Bobby on a strict diet, evidently on a starvation diet. During day and night the child continued to cry and shout "dinner, dinner." According to Mrs. N., she never slept during that period, spending the night by the child's bed. Mrs. N. felt certain that in some magical way her thoughts had produced his illness and with it the child's further abnormality, greed, impatience, and aggressive behavior toward her.

It was possible in her analysis to trace back the story of the uncooked food to the period in Mrs. N.'s life when her own mother had become incapacitated by illness and ceased to cook. The analysis unearthed Mrs. N.'s fantasies of revenge, her death wishes against her mother, and the memory of spiteful and hurtful acts committed against her. There seems no doubt that it is this hostile attitude toward her own mother which affected her relationship to Bobby and induced in him a behavior which tyrannized and controlled her in return. The suffering caused in her by Bobby's naughtiness and uncontrollable behavior served to assuage the unconscious guilt which stemmed from the relationship to her own mother.

ANAL PROBLEMS

THE CHILD'S BEHAVIOR

The mother's description of Bobby's anal problems was as dramatic as that of the oral ones. Here too she described an initial easy phase with training from birth, with few soiled napkins after the age of eight months. Trouble began with the diarrhea at twelve and a half months when she gave up potting, and with the severe constipation after his return from the nursery when he would hold back his motions for four to five days. Her description of his anal behavior sounded most odd. When unable to hold back defecation any longer, he would stand at a window, look out and dirty his trousers in this position unless his mother took off the trousers beforehand. In the nursery he had learned to run on tiptoe, and from his mother he had picked up songs. He used both in a curious ritual which was still in force in the beginning of his second analysis. When he could no longer hold back his motions, he would rush up to his mother, order everybody out of the room and, without trousers, wearing soft slippers and a vest only, he would run on tiptoe around the room, the mother singing a special song: "Tiptoe through the tulips." He then hung on to his mother, crouched down and she had to catch the feces in the pot. This ritual had to be repeated many times until, in small portions, he had finished. The mother had to empty the pot for every separate piece of feces. He did not look at his feces.

Bobby never used the lavatory, feared even to enter it. He was afraid to pull the chain or watch the water rushing down. Connected with his anal messiness was a general untidiness and messiness which provoked the mother in the highest degree. His anal obstinacy also revealed itself in his firm refusals to do whatever she demanded of him. On such occasions he would fly into uncontrollable tempers. This revolt against the mother was all the more exhausting for her as he was extremely clinging and refused to let her out of his sight.

THE CHILD'S ANALYTIC MATERIAL

In contrast to the oral symptoms, Bobby's stubbornness, obstinacy, and ambivalence were transferred fully to the analytic session and his relationship with the therapist. His strict early habit training coupled with the later inability to hold back his feces at the time of the diarrhea had left him with a feeling that he could not accomplish anything. The mother played on this conviction by assuring him constantly that there was nothing he could do right and by treating him like a baby. He expressed this in the analytic hour by refusing to undertake any play activity; he was convinced before starting that he would fail.

He soon revealed two major anxieties which dominated his behavior in feeding and in defecation: the fear of emptiness and the fear of being full. On the one hand, emptiness, i.e., the idea of being starved, unloved, deprived of all good things inside, made him greedy. It also made him retain his feces since he felt empty and deprived of good body contents when they left his inside. On the other hand, the content of his bowels was called bad by his mother and regarded by Bobby himself as such. The more he ate, the more it would accumulate in him and, due to constipation, turn him into something altogether bad. Therefore he had to refrain from eating and had to try and defecate to keep empty.

This preoccupation with the inside of his body, based on the alternating events of diarrhea and constipation in his infancy, was expressed in his analytic hours in a symbolic play, the symbol owing its existence to an actual event. At the age of four Bobby had been in an Underground train when it was held up in a tunnel for half an hour. He was much impressed and badly frightened by this incident. Following it he played in the analysis that he himself was the Underground train and in this identification rushed about the room excitedly producing noise and, as he called it, "stink." Still in the role of the train, he would get painfully stuck in the tunnel, frightening himself and his imaginary passengers. When he was not playing this game, he drew Underground trains, scribbled over them, called them dirty, and remarked, "The Underground has a funny bottom." There was no doubt about Bobby's identification with the train, nor of the identification of his intestines with the tunnels where the dirty, stinking, bad body contents were arrested.

Other meanings of his body contents and the act of defecation filled many other analytic sessions. His excrements were "good," precious, because his mother stressed their value so highly. Bowel movements signified the loss of this precious substance which was accompanied by a feeling of his whole inside getting emptied, running out. In defense against this feeling of loss, he invented a dolls' play in which the doll (representing himself) was put on the pot, the pot afterward having to be placed either on his own or the doll's head in an attempt to pour back the precious content into the body. Sometimes the doll's hat was used in the same manner in the place of the pot.

In another symbolic play Bobby represented his fear of falling into the lavatory and being washed away, as the feces were. In this play his dolls were pushed into the lavatory head first. He accepted the therapist's interpretation of this action by saying: "You didn't know, it is me. It is Bobby, I." Another symbolic game served to dramatize Bobby's fantasies of anal birth. This was staged with teddy bears, the baby teddy being born out of the father teddy's anus. It was also acted out with dolls which either fell or were pushed by him to drown; then he lifted them out of the water and they were born. At other times he himself took the role of the baby, threw himself on the floor (calling it water), and urged the therapist to bend over him and slowly to lift him out of the water through a narrow gap between the table and the wall. He made it quite clear that the feces, too, were babies who were drowned and who had to be reborn. His wish for reassurance that babies could be reborn determined some of his defecation ritual, namely, the need to pass his feces in small pieces, and to have each piece thrown separately into the lavatory. By keeping his anal babies separate, he proved to himself that he was not empty and that he could produce a multitude of children. Other games of falling and losing, although closely connected with the anal ones, had a phallic meaning. He opened a paper lantern and called it full; he folded and closed it and called it empty or dead, asking anxiously whether he too would have to die. This was accompanied by his falling down on the floor, stretching himself to his full length or holding a broom on his head and falling down with it. Here the falling was equated not only with the losing of the feces in the lavatory but with the "falling down" (limpness) of the erect penis, which Bobby represents here by his whole body. Falling, losing, emptiness were connected in his mind with death.

THE MOTHER'S ANALYTIC MATERIAL

Constipation

With Mrs. N. constipation was a lifelong symptom beginning very early during her mother's lifetime when she forced her mother to remain with her during defecation and wait for her to perform. To keep her feces inside came to represent the only means of getting attention and not feeling lonely. They became highly valued, a very precious possession. The analysis demonstrated that the emptying of her bowels was the signal of emotional emptiness and subsequent depression. She remembered vividly that as long as she had been constipated and obstinate, there was human presence around her, there was pressure, there was a high degree of attention paid to her for what she had inside; but as soon as she had complied with the demands of the mother, there was no fuss made anymore about her, nobody around, no pressure, just the feeling of emptiness inside and outside, the feeling of loneliness. The strongest imprint in her feelings was the connection between the losing of feces and the losing of attention, with the simultaneous equation of keeping the feces inside and keeping hold of the mother.

Since the mother was already ill at this time, she was made to understand that her behavior would tire her and make her die. Thus her constipation assumed a double meaning. On the one hand, it served as a reassurance that her mother was at her side, that is, not dead; on the other hand, it was an expression of her death wishes against her mother, a means of killing her. It was this ambivalence toward the mother which turned Mrs. N. into a clinging child who could not be separated from her mother even for a few minutes and whose hand had to be held continually. The mother tried to cure her constipation by means of enemas which were experienced by her as a sexual attack and resulted in permanent sadomasochistic fantasies and attitudes.

At this time Mrs. N. also projected the fantasy of her own dirty inside onto the mother. In the last phase of her life the

latter appeared to the child to lose her mind, to become negligent
and forgetful, the state of the whole house becoming one of
dreadful disorderliness and dirtiness. According to Mrs. N., her
mother accumulated possessions and secured all sorts of food,
rotting fruits, sweets, etc., in her drawers where they were found
after her death. The horror with which the patient described the
emptying of these drawers after her mother's death showed convincingly that these places represented to her the dirty inside of
her mother's body. Later she developed a phobic attitude toward
her own drawers which represented her own dirty inside. Any
preoccupation with these drawers assumed the significance of
anal masturbation. This attitude continued until the mother's
death, the constipation now (in addition to her behavior at the
breast) being used as a basis for her guilt feelings. Several years
after the mother's death at the age of nine she was sent to a
hospital where her constipation was again treated by means of
enemas.

Anal Birth Fantasies

When Mrs. N. became pregnant with Bobby this ended for
her, for the time being, the dread of emptiness and brought back
the happy feeling of keeping the mother alive within her. This
led to the wish to prolong her pregnancy indefinitely, and she
actually succeeded in delaying delivery. She experienced the
birth of the child as a loss of the feces which the outside world
wanted her to give up and reacted to it with a deep and frightening feeling of emptiness, severe depression, and suicidal thoughts.
She refused to defecate for two weeks after the birth and when
forced by necessity to do so, she had the terrifying fantasy that
she was actually defecating a baby.

On the other hand, her feces as well as the baby inside her
also represented the penis which she had desired to possess all
her life. From this aspect pregnancy was for her the denial of
castration, and the birth of the child the repeated loss of the
penis to which she reacted with depression.

Anal Union

When we compare the anal histories of Bobby and his mother, we are struck by the many similarities in behavior and fantasy content. Both Bobby and Mrs. N. as a child used their toilet training to secure their mothers' presence and attention and fought out a struggle with the mother over it, which assumed sadomasochistic proportions. With both, these struggles resulted in a hostile attitude and death wishes against the mother, which in their turn were superseded by compulsive clinging. With both, this led to the symptom of constipation and subsequent treatments, enemas, etc.

It is of interest to note that there is no similarity of external life circumstances to which this almost identical pathological result can be ascribed. On the contrary, Bobby and his mother developed under completely different family circumstances. Bobby was an only child on whom his mother's attention was lavished excessively from the beginning; Mrs. N. was the youngest of many children and had to fight for her mother's attention which was withdrawn from her increasingly when her mother fell ill. Her mother's deterioration and her early death were powerful pathogenic factors in Mrs. N.'s development and psychopathology.

It is open to speculation by which paths the mother's fantasies concerning the equation of body content and the mother image reached Bobby. We may assume that he developed a heightened sensitivity for the mother's excitement when she handled him on the pot. While she waited for him to pass his motions, she identified with him and projected onto him her own early wishes connected with her own mother. She had to remain with him as she had forced her mother to remain with her during defecation. As she had enjoyed the presence of her mother outside as well as inside on these occasions, she felt a special union with her own child when performing the same services for him. Bobby responded with his anal ritual to his mother's

sexualized attitude toward his bowel movements. Under the light
of analysis, this ritual assumed the aspect of a *folie à deux*. As
described before, the ritual consisted of tiptoeing round the
room, standing by the window while making the mother sing
and hold the pot under him. The song chosen is a love song and
the complete wording of the refrain in question is the following:

> Tiptoe to the window, by the window,
> That is where I'll be, Come tiptoe thro' the tulips with me.

Bobby's act of defecation thus becomes a moment of perfect loving union between the two partners.

Projection of Separation Anxiety

Another symptom connected with the child's anal behavior,
namely, separation anxiety, does not seem to be as evenly distributed between mother and child. In overt behavior Bobby
clung to his mother as she had clung to hers. On the other hand,
it soon became evident that, as with eating, Bobby was well able
to behave differently when not under his mother's direct influence. He enjoyed his independence when he was with his father,
with his analyst, in school, and he reacted well to a separation
from the mother when the Clinic helped to find a summer holiday place for him. It was the mother who, for two reasons,
could not allow Bobby to enjoy such independence. Her feeling
of freedom when she was without him was felt by her as a
proof of her hate for her child and her death wishes against
him. When the child showed pleasure in being without her, he
symbolized for her her own mother who had withdrawn from
her. To blind herself to her inability to part from Bobby, she
projected her feelings onto him, felt the separation anxiety to be
his, and provoked its manifest expression in every way. When
mother and child met again after separation, the anal scene was
taken up immediately. Thus, when the mother fetched Bobby
from the holiday home after the vacation, he informed her im-

mediately that he had had no motion during the whole fortnight, which of course was not true.

Projection of Body Processes

There was another striking incident in the mother's history which gave evidence of the identification of her own body processes with the child's. During Bobby's period of diarrhea at twelve months the mother suffered simultaneously from what she described as an "accumulation of stuff in the fallopian tubes" (according to the medical report, an organic effect of permanent constipation). On the day when Bobby was pronounced cured of his diarrhea, she went to the hospital herself for an examination and remained for an immediate operation. To her mind this was a necessary general clean-up of her dirty inside. She experienced the operation as a mixed anal and oedipal event. In her description, her feelings when entering the operating room were those of a young girl going to her wedding; she was all excited. After the operation her interpretation of the event changed. She felt that something had been taken away from her by force and, in her own words, that she "would never know what it was." The fantasies concerning this operation linked the anal deprivation by means of enemas with a phallic deprivation (being deprived of a penis). There was also the contrasting unconscious fantasy that the doctors left something hard and stiff inside her, which assumed the alternating significance of penis, feces, the mother inside her. In retrospect it could be shown in the analysis that when her fantasies of fullness and emptiness ceased to be concerned with the child's body, they turned immediately to her own body where they were lived out instead.

Anal Birth

For both mother and child the act of defecation represented a symbolic birth, although in this respect there were some significant differences between their fantasies. In the mother's unconscious the size of the big feces played a special part. Especially immediately after Bobby's birth she felt her excrement to be "as big as a baby." According to the analysis, in her case the equation feces-baby had secondary significance to the equation feces-mother. Therefore the expulsion of the feces is followed by emptiness, depression, and suicidal thoughts. It is difficult to say on the evidence of Bobby's material whether or not he was affected by this part of the mother's psychopathology. His fantasies of anal birth had the quality of the normal infantile birth fantasies of the anal stage. He himself was the anal baby, identified with his own bowel content; therefore he experienced anxiety when the mother did not cherish his anal products but "drowned" them in the lavatory. As a defense against his fear of being thrown away and drowned by the mother he developed the compulsive play dealing with the rebirth (the lifting out of the water) of himself, his dolls, his teddy bears. This is perhaps the point where the material of mother and child is furthest apart. Where the child experienced anxiety, the mother developed states of depression.

OEDIPAL PHASE: PHALLIC STRIVINGS AND SYMPTOMS

MOTHER'S DESCRIPTION OF BOBBY'S BEHAVIOR

The mother's complaint about Bobby's behavior in the oedipal phase was no less dramatic than that concerning earlier attitudes. As mentioned before, she described that he could do nothing for himself and forced her to do everything for him; that he would stand by limply to let her dress him, to the extent that she had to push his arms into the sleeves of his clothes; that he said continually, "I can't do it, you do it."

According to her, this passive behavior alternated with his controlling her, his insistence that she had to do as he ordered, accompanied by temper tantrums when she kept him waiting or did not do as he required of her.

She described him as extremely provocative. When she wanted

him to be quiet, he made a great deal of noise, shouted and screamed. He would run aimlessly around the room, crashing into the walls. One of his favorite games consisted of running from one wall to the other with a toy bus held in front of him, imitating the noise of an engine.

He was "rude" to her, lifted her skirts, and showed her his penis. By this she would be provoked to the degree of hitting him.

His provocations included dangerous actions by which he frightened her, such as jumping down from great heights. This behavior reached its climax in the symptom which led to his referral, namely, his tearing himself from her in the street when he would run in front of cars and buses.

Finally, she complained about his difficulties in falling asleep and his night terrors from which he would awake screaming. When this happened, she would go to his bed to comfort him and when unsuccessful take him to bed with her.

THE CHILD'S MATERIAL

Passive Actions

It was possible during the child's treatment to witness his quick transformations from a manly, active child to a frightened, helpless, and passive one. These changes occurred when he caught sight of his mother at the end of the hour. When alone with the therapist, he would soon put his coat on without assistance, but if the mother arrived before he did this, he would be seen standing limp and helpless, arms hanging down by his side while the mother would attempt to dress him. At other times, of course, as reported before, his passivity was transferred into the sessions, when he became unable to play and insisted that he could do nothing for himself.

Ambivalence

Much of his material was acted out in the analytic hour with the help of doll play, the dolls being called girls, and babies, representing his mother and himself. Or he would himself take the role of the mother and act out with dolls the sadomasochistic behavior which his mother displayed in her handling of him. He tortured the dolls, asking them at the same time whether they loved him. He would, for instance, tell his favorite doll, called Mary, that she need not be afraid, that he would merely wash her hands and face. Then, disregarding his promise, he would undress her completely, push her into the water viciously, splash her, and leave her alone lying in the bath. Again he would ask her whether she loved him. Similar behavior was transferred directly onto the therapist whom he tantalized and provoked, simultaneously begging for signs of love and affection.

Castration

The dolls were used further to act out castration fears and his defense against them. Again Bobby reverted to the use of the dolls' hats which, during his anal play, had symbolized the pot. Hats took on the new role to represent the penis, or part of it, especially the father's penis with its magical power. When representing the mother's castrated genital or the castrated male, the same hats were used as receptacles. Hats were also a symbol to represent departure. To take the hats off meant that either the penis or the whole person disappeared. While acting out his fears and fantasies he would, for example, pull off the hat of the doll Mary which represented himself (castrate himself); then tear off all the hats of all the dolls or exchange the hats of the male and female dolls (change sex with his mother).

Analysis showed that he was very much aware of his mother's genital which he considered castrated. Incidents were uncovered when he had the opportunity of making observations of her body. Once she had opened the door to him to let him into her room when she had a severe hemorrhage and her nightgown was covered with blood.

Much of Bobby's peculiar behavior and symptoms could be

traced to his castration fears. In his behavior toward his own body he identified with the sadistic, castrating mother image and developed tendencies of self-injury: he would bang his head when thwarted, pick the skin of his lips, bite his nails until he drew blood. This also served as punishment for his sadistic wishes toward the mother. He developed a fear of proximity to females, refused to sit next to girls at school, and either cried on such occasions or threatened to break them up. He also threatened his mother to "break her up," castrate her. He would refuse to let her sit next to him at mealtimes. He distinguished between his father and himself as men, on the one hand, and his mother as a damaged person, on the other hand: he and his father had to have the same kind of good dinner plates, while his mother was assigned a damaged plate with the pattern worn off. His father and himself were not allowed to use a broken chair on which he made his mother sit.

Intercourse Fantasies

Bobby's oedipal jealousy was brought to the fore when Bobby's mother started her own analysis with a male analyst. This was acted out in the transference in a wild manner by Bobby throwing himself on the couch, taking a cushion between his legs, attacking the therapist with it, etc. He began to masturbate in the hour, became excited and noisy, ending up the scene by falling down, having an accident, being broken and killed. He invited his therapist to ride on a horse with him, to go alone with him to "the Silly Islands," and to drown with him. It is easy to see that Bobby's fantasies of intercourse with himself in the male role ended invariably in his own downfall, injury, humiliation, death (castration).

Defenses against Castration Fears

Bobby used a variety of mechanisms to ward off his castration fears, wishes, and fantasies. When his castration fear was too great he regressed to anal-passive behavior, which accounts for many of his character traits and behavior patterns described before.

A lesser amount of anxiety was dealt with by means of other mechanisms. As expressed in the doll's play, he would reverse the masculine and feminine roles (putting girls' hats on the boys and vice versa). When playing intercourse with the dolls he made his female doll jump on the male one. He remodeled ice-cream cones out of plasticine, saying that boys had lovely brown ones, girls nasty red ones (this last information only whispered); this was immediately altered into girls doing brown big jobs and boys red ones. The tendency to reverse was also shown by putting on his coat front to back.

He reassured himself as to the intactness of his penis on the one hand by exaggerated exhibitionism to his mother, on the other hand by taking over the activity of the erect penis with his whole body. The latter defense explained much of his restlessness, wriggling, running about, and crashing into walls. When hurling himself bodily against an obstacle he imagined himself acting out a masculine attack on the mother. He also fantasied himself into the role of the strong protective male who rescues the female from dangers.

In his transference behavior he demonstrated many of his frightening experiences turned from passive events into active ones. Pencils in a box represented the teachers of whom he was afraid and who were punished in their turn by being locked in their box. His game of being an Underground train and frightening others represented his own fear in the Underground. He took the castrating role toward the therapist, threatening to pull off her arms, legs, and nose. Most revealing were his attempts to push back her sleeves in a very rough manner. This represented what he experienced as his mother's attack on his penis when she pushed back his foreskin. In the transference he repeated the wild excitement which he felt on these occasions accompanied by the going limp in the presence of the mother. (Incidentally, his refusal to put his own arms into the sleeves of his coat was traced back to the same situation.)

As in Bobby's case, the mother's anal fixation colored her oedipal strivings. Her conscious and unconscious conflicts over defecation coincided with her penis envy which had dominated her relationship to father and brother. For her unconscious the making of big stools was to possess a penis. All her life she had had the fantasy that something was missing on her body, something had not been completed, and it would grow some day while she slept. During her oedipal phase her equation feces-penis was linked with her intense wish for a child from the father, and this formed in her unconscious the usual symbolic equivalent: feces=penis=child. The anal-phallic meaning of the child was most conspicuous during the time of pregnancy and birth. Her happiness during this period was due to the threefold symbolic meaning of the foetus as the good body content (anal), the possession of the penis (phallic), and the re-creation of the mother inside her body.

Bobby as the Mother's Penis

Fantasies about the secret possession of a penis and of its dreaded loss filled her analysis. From the moment when she had born a male child, these were projected onto Bobby and molded her relationship to him. Bobby personified for her the brother's penis which she had wanted for herself. In this role he was for her a highly exciting, erotic influence, fascinating as well as frightening. When Bobby himself was excited, she felt increasingly unable to control him, helpless and powerless. Bobby's wild antics had for her the meaning of an erection of her own. Although she felt consciously that his exhibitionistic tendencies were intolerable to her, unconsciously she provoked them and felt thoroughly overwhelmed by them. Her analysis left no doubt that Bobby's exhibitionism meant to her the realization of her own unconscious wish to have a penis which she could exhibit. No wonder that she felt powerless in helping him control himself. Although so far as Bobby was concerned, his exhibitionism originated from his need to reassure himself about his masculinity, the meaning it assumed for the mother perpetuated the symptom and gave it an important place in his relationship to his mother. By exhibiting himself to her, he established a new union between her and himself, offering his penis to her as the cherished completion of her own body.

Bobby as the Father's Penis

Bobby's masculinity also represented to the mother another and more sinister aspect of her penis envy, namely, the father's dangerous masculinity. When overwhelmed by these fantasies she felt him to be a man, a grownup, his penis becoming a threat to her, paralyzing and dominating her. According to her own description in the analysis, all Bobby had to do to dominate her was to exhibit himself. The more excited he became the more she lost control of the situation, the smaller she felt, and the bigger he seemed to her. The analysis related her dread of him to observations during the primal scene which she had made in the parents' bedroom. The sight of her father's penis had had a deep and dramatic effect of her. These experiences were revived later in her adolescence when she felt the compulsion to look at exhibitionists and when she imagined "the worst" in connection with some workmen, i.e., when she imagined them coming toward her with erected penis to seduce her. The violent feelings which were aroused in her by such memories directed themselves against the child's penis and did not remain without effect on him. We remember in this connection that Bobby could never exhibit to his mother without the scene ending in his literal and symbolic "downfall." What usually began as a love play between child and mother ended with the mother's violent rejection of the boy's masculinity.

Bobby as an Incestuous Child

It was unfortunate for Bobby that he represented for the mother not only the father's seducing masculinity but also its imaginary result. At the period when the analysis dealt with her oedipal conflicts she would talk of Bobby in the most violent manner as a filthy creature, a filthy monster who would be the shame of her life. She was disgusted by the idea of ever having wanted a child, only a degraded and depraved woman would have such a wish; she would have to pay for it by being ashamed all her life, the child being bound to be a curse for her; she would never pay enough for her guilt. The analysis traced back this guilt to a fantasy in which Bobby represented the realization of her wish to have a child from the father.

Sadistic Conception of Intercourse: "Cat and Mouse" Fantasy

Mrs. N.'s conception of intercourse was a sadomasochistic one. Her childhood was dominated by the wish to be beaten by her father, which expressed itself consciously in the usual beating fantasies. Her fear of the father was stimulated further by seeing him drunk repeatedly and by watching him on such occasions beating a horse. In her unconscious she identified with the horse, wishing to be treated likewise. Unconsciously she attributed the mother's death to the father's brutal attack on her in intercourse. Every sexual relationship was understood by her as a rape, as a sadistic attack on a defenseless woman.

In her childhood she had an obsessive conscious fantasy which represented these unconscious ideas. In this fantasy a cat took sadistic pleasure in letting a mouse hope for freedom and escape, and then to pounce on it. Her own identification alternated between the sadistic role of the cat and the masochistic one of the mouse. This "cat and mouse" fantasy was repeated in the transference relationship in which she played the role of the victim and assigned the role of sadistic attack to the analyst.

She expected the analyst to feel "like murdering her" when she provoked him. Every detail of the analytic setting became invested with sadistic meaning, such as "forcing words, speech, dreams out of her," watching her and waiting for the first occasion to abuse her. In her own words, the analyst was "a vulture watching for the occasion to pounce on me." Especially when she left the room at the end of the hour, she would expect the analyst to force her back to the couch, because she had not yet endured enough.

But this "cat and mouse" fantasy was transferred no less compulsively onto Bobby, the child and herself representing sometimes one, sometimes the other partner. At times Bobby symbolized herself in the role of helpless victim. At other times she herself was the victim, ascribing to Bobby the controlling and dominating role. She would provoke scenes with him in accordance with this fantasy and work them up until a specific intensity and peak of excitement had been reached. This done, she suddenly reversed the roles and felt very much like "murdering Bobby," like "knifing him." Scenes of this kind usually ended in a beating which she administered in a compulsive and uncontrolled manner.

This part of the mother's analysis threw light on the child's symptom of "unruliness," being "out of control." It is to be assumed that his behavior was the answer to the intense provocation emanating from the mother's conscious and unconscious fantasy.

Acting Out on the Street

Mrs. N.'s sexual excitement which was stimulated by her sadomasochistic interpretation of the analytic setting was acted out partly in the sessions themselves and partly on the street. The more her transference feelings increased, the more afraid she became of the traffic until her attitude approximated an agoraphobic one. She did not feel safe in the street anymore and felt that she could not control her movements. Lorries and buses took on a frightening aspect, waiting to hit her and to run over her. She felt as if the radiators of the oncoming big lorries were alive and human; she felt the lorries to be driverless. This material was interpreted to her as displaced erotic excitement (radiators=erect penis; fantasy of intercourse=being run over). Again she remembered the threatening men of her adolescence coming with erected penis ready to rape her.

This insecurity in the street occasionally showed itself in the analytic room as she left the session. When she stumbled and hit herself against the wall under the analyst's eye, she felt like a prostitute.

There is a definite link here between Mrs. N.'s sexualization of the traffic and the symptom of running into the traffic which had led to Bobby's referral to analysis. For mother and child, the buses were phallic symbols. What appeared as a phobic attitude in the mother appeared in the child as an almost compulsive play with the toy buses which he held in front of him when dashing himself against the walls of the room and further in the irresistible attraction which the traffic held for him. Mother and child acted, although in a different manner, under the domination of an identical fantasy.

Manipulation of Bobby's Penis

Mrs. N.'s analysis provided some information why she had been unable in the first instance to follow Miss Thomas's advice regarding the handling of the child's penis and why she had forgotten all the conversations dealing with the matter. Since then she had been repeatedly advised that pushing back the foreskin was not only superfluous but positively harmful to the child, but had never altered her behavior. In a late stage of her analysis she produced a dream which was related to this problem. There is something like a clock; she feels she has to touch it, she has to see if it functions well. In handling it she breaks it, it stops functioning properly, she feels so guilty that if anybody asks her if she has touched the clock, she will say no.

The associations to this dream and the symbolic elements led back to the idea that she had damaged herself when masturbating. Usually this creates in a child the compulsion to touch the genital, to masturbate again, to find out whether it is still intact or has stopped to function. In Mrs. N.'s case this compulsion had been transferred onto her child. Her worry about her own castrated genital had changed into a worry about the state of Bobby's penis. She felt obsessed by the idea that there was something wrong with it and she had to check up on it. The compulsion contained both sides of her ambivalence toward his penis, her wish to have it healthy and intact (as her own) with the counterwish to have it damaged and destroyed (her father's, her brother's, and her own) in retaliation. The handling of Bobby's penis thus served several purposes: it provided her with sexual excitement in a masturbating act carried out on him; it created an outlet for the aggressive and masochistic side of her penis envy; and finally it gave her control over his masculinity which she experienced as an uncontrollable force. It is not surprising that no amount of advice coming from the environment could have any influence on this particular piece of her behavior. It is equally understandable that Bobby reacted to this constant threat to his masculinity with anxiety, regression, and passivity.

SUMMARY AND CONCLUSIONS

The comparison between Mrs. N.'s and her child's psychopathology, as it emerged in their respective analyses, is not complete. There is a mass of material on both sides which has not been used in the foregoing study in which I have set myself the aim of highlighting only the most vital points of interaction.

But even within these limitations it seems possible to show that the influence of the mother's actions, her manifest attitude, her conscious and, above all, unconscious fantasies and anxieties, is neither straightforward nor uniform. The following types of interaction seemed to me the most important ones:

1. There are examples where the mother's inhibition of function, due to unconscious anxiety, has a lasting pathogenic influence on the whole life and development of the child. Such an instance is the mother's attitude to breast feeding. As described above, she repeats her own death wishes against her mother, projecting the role of attacker on Bobby who, she fears, will suck her dry, empty her out. To protect her own life she has no milk for him, and this fact turns him from a potentially happy and satisfied into a querulous and dissatisfied infant. Here her unconscious fears play the role of active pathogenic environmental agents.

2. The same is true where her fantasies of emptiness and fullness are concerned, although the outcome is different in this case. These not only determine his feeding situation, playing a large part in the mother's evaluation of his digestive upset and enforcement of the diet, they are also taken over by Bobby and thereby turned from an external agent into an internal one. It is impossible to say in which way Bobby was reached by the mother's fantasies concerning the body content and its relation to the mother image; this may have happened through observation of her attitudes or—since this seems to happen between mother and child—by direct communication between their unconscious. However that may be, the idea of the good and bad body contents becomes an integral part of Bobby's own fantasy life and determines his later feeding troubles and his constipation.

3. Where Bobby's exhibitionism is concerned, we have described the mother's influence as a secondary, not a primary, factor in his development. Bobby's exhibitionism seems to arise normally, on the one hand being determined by his phallic wishes and, on the other, strengthened by his need for reassurance against castration fears. But this typical occurrence in the child meets with the mother's overvaluation of his penis, her conflicting desires for it, and hostile impulses directed against it. What might have been a transitory phase in Bobby's life is thus

turned into a permanent symptom by the mother's response. Bobby cannot fail to notice that, to quote the mother, he need only show his penis to dominate her completely.

4. Again, Bobby responds to the mother's sexualization of the traffic. In this case the mother defends herself against the sexual threat embodied in the cars and lorries by a near-phobic attitude. Bobby reacts to the same symbolization in the opposite manner. Where the mother avoids the traffic, he tears himself from her to run right into it, i.e., by a positive fascination, and provocation of his passive masochistic attitudes.

5. Mother and child meet most intimately in the two following symptoms which amount to a *folie à deux* in the intensity in which they are enacted: the "cat and mouse" fantasy and the anal ritual. Here, Bobby enters fully into the sadomasochistic arrangement of the mother, letting himself be provoked by her and provoking her in turn until the whole scene ends in the act of her beating him (an acting out of her own beating fantasies directed toward her father). Mother and child take turns in being aggressor and victim, usually exchanging roles in the middle of the scene.

The acting out of a fantasy with the roles divided between them is more impressive still in the anal ritual when mother and child enter into the most intimate partnership, the child moving his body to the mother's singing, his defecation being timed to her cooperation.

It needs no further explanation why Mrs. N.'s difficulties with Bobby were not improved lastingly by child guidance treatment; her problems were much too deep-seated and severe to be accessible to advice and guidance. Even under analysis she proved a most difficult patient with violent mood swings which were acted out in the transference and in her home surroundings. Even where insight was achieved, improvements alternated with relapses at the slightest provocation.

In Bobby's analytic treatment it became possible to differentiate between two different ways in which he responded, on the one hand to the mother's fantasies, on the other hand to her behavior. So far as he was under the influence of her fantasy life, analysis was able to set him free by lifting his reactions to consciousness and working them through. Although originating in the mother's unconscious, this fantasy content had become his own, could be treated as such, and analysis of it was followed by the usual relief. In many instances analysis also had to deal with a second outcrop of fantasies overlaying what had been initiated by the mother. The material of the good and bad body content overlayed by the birth fantasies of the anal babies, their drowning, their being saved out of the water, etc., is a case in point. This was slow work but satisfactory since Bobby made definite advances toward normal behavior and independence of his mother. He became able to eat and defecate without her help even in her presence, he attended school without difficulty, reacted well to other children, and even enjoyed a holiday period away from his mother.

So far as his reactions to the mother's behavior, i.e., her violent acting out of her fantasies, was concerned, the outcome was less favorable. Her behavior such as the "cat and mouse" provocation and, above all, her constant handling of his genitals acted on him as permanent seductions. Such seductions served to renew continually his close tie to her and thus to outweigh the influence of analysis which worked in the opposite direction.

This last reflection may be helpful whenever we have to assess the chances of freeing a young child by analysis from the pathogenic influence of the mother's disturbance. The child who is seduced only by the mother's fantasies can be freed from this grip more effectively than another who also has to contend with manifest actions on the mother's part and therefore with the actual bodily stimulation and excitement which are aroused by them.

Chapter 11

A STUDY OF IDENTICAL TWINS: THEIR ANALYTIC MATERIAL COMPARED WITH EXISTING OBSERVATION DATA OF THEIR EARLY CHILDHOOD

The story of the development of a pair of male identical twins which follows here is based on five different pieces of evidence and their comparison with each other:

1. The detailed direct observation made in the Hampstead Nursery between their fourth month and their fourth year (Bert:

This paper, written in cooperation with Arthur T. Barron, is reprinted from *The Psychoanalytic Study of the Child*, 18:367-423. New York: International Universities Press, 1963.

Thanks for active help in this study are due to Mr. James Shields, Lecturer, Institute of Psychiatry, for providing for testing as to identity and intelligence, and for collecting and collating the information concerning the years from November 22, 1945 to 1953; to Miss Hanni Koehler, now Mrs. Benkendorf, Child Therapist in Western Reserve University, Cleveland, Department of Psychiatry, for keeping past and present contact with the twins; to Miss Nancy Proctor-Gregg for help in summarizing and organizing the available documents.

1942 to April, 1945; Bill: 1942 to September, 1945) and published in my book on *Twins* (1952) under the names of Bert and Bill.

2. An inquiry in 1953 by Mr. Shields with special regard to the twins' identical births. Mr. Shields also traced the course of their external lives from the time of their departure from the Hampstead Nursery to their appearance in the Home for Maladjusted Children run by Mr. Arthur Barron, a qualified therapist of the Hampstead Child-Therapy Course and Clinic.

3. Direct observation of their behavior in the Home for Maladjusted Children undertaken by Mr. Barron and covering the period from age twelve to thirteen and a half (1953-1955).

4. Material from their psychoanalytic treatments, with Bert from thirteen to sixteen years (1955-1958), with Bill from thirteen to fifteen years (1955-1957).

5. Some follow-up data.

Evidence gathered from these four periods in the twins' lives will be used for a number of purposes:

(a) to check predictions on their developments which were made at the time of their dismissal from the Hampstead Nurseries;

(b) to establish links between their behavior and the conscious and unconscious motivations of it, as revealed in their analyses;

(c) to compare the analytic material during adolescence with the observational data gathered during their first years of life.

DETAILED OBSERVATIONS FROM FOUR MONTHS TO FOURTH YEAR (1942-1945)

What follows here are partly direct quotations from, or summaries of such quotations distributed through, the whole of the book on *Twins* (1952)[1] or material from development charts, or observational cards beyond those actually published in the book

[1] Throughout this paper, all page references and charts refer to this book.

for reasons of abbreviation. On no point does the material given here go beyond what was collected between the years 1942-1945.

Bert and Bill were illegitimate children, "their mother a young office worker of 21. From the maternity hospital, where they were born, they were sent to an evacuated baby hostel where they stayed for their first four months with their mother. When the mother had to return to work they were admitted to the Hampstead Nurseries" (p. 17).

Bert was the firstborn, weighing 4 lbs. 13 oz.; and Bill, the secondborn, was the heavier, weighing 5 lbs. 13 oz. (Chart 11). Bert by degrees made up some of this weight.

Identical Looks

Their identical looks made it impossible to tell them apart; they were therefore continually mistaken one for the other, not only by the nurses who cared for them, but by their mother who visited them, at first daily and then once or twice weekly (Charts 11, 12, 16). To weigh them was often the only way to straighten out the confusion. "The twins were not only alike in appearance, took the same positions, and copied each other, but from the moment they arrived in the Nursery at 4 months, they were the mirror picture of each other. When they lay in their baskets, Bill on his right side, Bert on his left, Bill sucked his right hand and right thumb and Bert his left hand and left thumb; at 17 months they still sucked these same thumbs and when they masturbated, they usually did so with the opposite hand from the one they used for sucking.

"As they got older they were often found asleep in exactly the same position on their stomachs, Bert's head turned to the right, Bill's to the left, or lying on their backs, eyes covered with one arm. They would sit on the floor opposite each other with one leg tucked under their bodies; they would both stand in their cots in exactly the same position, one arm hanging over the edge of the cot. At 14 months, they would move absolutely alike when they crawled. At 15 months, they would rock in the same rhythm, holding on to the bars of the cots at the same height, head bent in the same way, their mouths usually open. At 15 months, they pushed their cars at the same time, with absolutely the same movement and with the same expression. At 17 and 19 months they would start rocking at the same moment and in the same rhythm.

"They also had the same physical marks, birthmarks over forehead and eyes, more distinct in Bill than in Bert; these disappeared in both at about 7 months. They often had the same infectious diseases at the same time, which was not surprising since they were always together. Bert generally more severely than Bill. But at 8 months, they also had a blister on their chins developing one day apart, and both developed hydrocele at 14 months, Bill's on the right side much more pronounced than Bert's, which was on the left side and of a more bluish colour. These disappeared about the same time and reappeared again several times, always together; Bert's always less distinct than Bill's disappearing completely a few weeks before Bill's when they were 20 months" (p. 24).

Relationship to Each Other

It was Bert who first took notice of Bill at 7 months, smiling at him. Soon Bill as the stronger of the two was the one who was making overtures to Bert and disturbing him so much that Bert had often to be protected (p. 19). At 8 months he was already taking away whatever Bert was holding, and at 12 months Bill was throwing him over and sitting on him. Bill was not only stronger but more active as well. He was the first to crawl and stand. Bert noticed these achievements of his brother and was cross and unhappy until he could do the same (p. 21, Chart 14).

Copying Games

"It appeared that it was Bert who started copying-games with Bill. At 14 months he clapped his hands and Bill did the same;

he banged bricks on the table; Bill followed suit. These actions were always accompanied by laughter from both children. Soon it was impossible to tell who copied whom. At 13 months both twins were lying in their cots on their backs. One would start to shout and kick and the other would watch him and laugh; then the other would take his turn to shout and kick and the first one would watch and laugh.

"At 15 months the twins provoked each other to join in these games. One would kneel suddenly and laugh; the other would then do the same and laugh too. Or from a sitting position, one would throw himself on to his back looking at the other twin, and immediately the other would copy him. Laughter was an essential element in these games. Both twins tried to find new ways of entertaining the other. It was Bill who started grimacing, making sudden jerky clownish movements, jumping from one foot to the other, standing up and throwing himself down, making funny noises and laughing uproariously. Bert would imitate him. Bill would get himself and Bert more and more excited until the game was like an orgy" (p. 24f.). Bert with his quieter ways often used these games with a purpose in mind, i.e., if Bill was unhappy to distract him, while Bill was carried away by his inner excitement. These games became more and more complicated but never stopped so long as they were in the Nursery.

The twins were so carried away by these games that they were quite oblivious of the other children; they ignored them, completely wrapped up in each other. It also was impossible for their mother, nurses, or anyone else to get their attention at such a time. They were beyond control. "Wild movements about the room, aggressive actions against adults, children and each other were generally the result of these games. Bill was more aggressive, more uncontrollable and less able to be influenced than Bert. Bert was not able to cope with Bill's aggressive actions, he became afraid of him and in the last months at the Nursery it was felt best to separate them" (p. 26).

These copying games did not further the twins' development. Bert, carried away by Bill's dominant, domineering, and erratic nature, could not develop normally. Bill got sensations of pleasure and excitement by watching Bert's responding reactions which excited him still further (p. 26).

Aggression

Aggression toward each other started at a very early age. As babies they naturally wanted to get hold of whatever the other was holding. They grabbed, hit, and screamed until one let go crying with temper and frustration. Pulling the twin down who was standing, then hitting and rolling on him was a frequent occurrence. As already mentioned, the copying games usually ended by Bill's becoming aggressive as a result of his excessive excitement. But their rivalry was the main cause for their aggression. This rivalry started as soon as they became aware of each other. In the feeding situation when one twin was fed first, the other wanted to be fed too (p. 20). This was soon followed by the wish to have whatever the twin possessed, ranging from material objects to developmental achievements. This caused a great impetus to their learning processes and seemed to contribute to both twins becoming able to do the same thing at almost the same time (p. 21ff.). In the relationship to the visiting mother the rivalry was at its height, both boys demanding impatiently and passionately to be picked up and loved at the same moment. They would hit and push away the rival so as to get to the mother and hit and bite the mother because she was not able to respond to both. As a result both twins would end up on the floor frustrated, screaming, and in a temper tantrum (Charts 17, 21).

Love Relationship

It would be a mistake to assume from the description of the twins' jealousy and rivalry of each other and the resulting aggressive acts against each other that they did not have a positive relationship as well.

From the time around their first year when the twins began to take notice of each other they showed signs of affection and at times could even be gentle with each other. They tried to touch each other's faces, hold each other's arms and legs (Chart 15). Bert would bite Bill very gently and repeat this affectionately, and he would rub up against him. Bill at 13 months rubbed himself against Bert biting him affectionately everywhere, head, arms, and legs (Chart 16). Bert would often try to comfort Bill when he cried and would try to distract him (16 months) (Chart 19). Bill would pick up toys for Bert (23 months) (Chart 24) and get a chair ready for Bert at the table when he was absent (2 years) (Chart 24). When put to bed in the shelter, their bunks separated by a partition, they would talk to each other, excluding all the other children (Chart 24). And when they were separated at 2 years 5 months and living in different houses, Bert insisted on going to see Bill before going to sleep (Chart 24).

Reaction to Separation

It was quite evident that both twins missed each other when separated. At 14 months they both showed that they were aware that the other was missing and showed pleasure when reunited. At 16 months they ignored each other when they were together again, much in the way a child reacts when reunited with a mother after separation (p. 39f.). At 17 months they learned the word "gone" at a time of separation and used it not only in connection with each other, but also for disappearing objects. With Bill the reaction to the separation was so great that he repeated the words "all gone" continually when put to bed from 10 P.M. to 3:30 A.M. At this time balls were their favorite toys, and they tried to master the situation of separation by throwing and fetching the ball, accompanying this activity with the words "ball all gone" (p. 40f.)

When separated they mistook their mirror image for the twin. Bert at 17 months enjoyed eating, watching his reflection in the mirror, and again, when separated at 2 years 3½ months, he called out "Billy" when he saw his own reflection in the mirror (p. 44).

Twins as a Team

Bert and Bill did not only enjoy their uproarious copying games together, they also turned to each other in activities where one found it impossible to do them alone. At 17 months, they were able together to move another child's cot and showed tremendous pleasure over their success (Chart 20). They also protected each other. When one twin was threatened by another child, the other twin came to his rescue. And when one twin attacked another child, the other twin would attack him as well. At 20 months when Bert hit a boy who cried and crawled away, Bill followed the boy and hit him on the head (Chart 23).

Autoerotic Activities

Both boys sucked their hands at 4 months and continued this for some time. Bert seemed to prefer sucking his left thumb and Bill his right one (Chart 11). At 11 months both played with their genitals (Chart 14); they both masturbated from then on, Bert more than Bill. They used to rock when left in their cots (Chart 17).

Bert at 13 months was crawling on the floor when he bumped his head on a table leg. This interested him, and he deliberately bumped his head again and again until he finally cried (Chart 16). Both twins then started banging their heads, Bert when cross, Bill not only when cross, but for no obvious reason (Chart 20). Bill at 18 months was banging his head so hard that it was bruised. He accompanied this head banging with shrill screams, and kept it up until exhausted (Chart 21). At 21 months he resorted to head banging when he was emotionally upset (Chart

24). At 22 months he would say "again" each time he banged his head. He hardly cried, he seemed indifferent to pain. At 2 years 5 months he still seemed insensitive to pain, whether he hurt himself or was hurt by other children. Both boys when frustrated would bite their own hands (Chart 24).

Ego Development

At 12 months their habit training was started (Chart 15) and at 2 years 4 months they were showing signs of becoming clean. At 3 years they were sometimes clean; Bill was without nappies but Bert still had his (Chart 24). Bill crawled at 11 months, Bert a few weeks later (Charts 14, 15). Bill walked at 18 months, Bert a few days later (Chart 21). Bill's first word was "ball" at 16 months, which was taken up immediately by Bert (Chart 19). Bert seemed to be more imaginative and more purposeful in the copying games (p. 25). Both boys were always considered intelligent after the second year, although from their intelligence tests they were shown to be backward from their infancy. They were tested (Buehler Tests) at 8 months and were considered 2 to 3 months retarded. Bill was slightly more advanced than Bert (Chart 12). They were tested again at 9 months and showed hardly any progress (Chart 12) and again at 2 years 4 months when they still showed three-months retardation (Chart 24).

Superego

There was practically no superego formation in either boy. There were quite often hopeful signs which were quickly destroyed by the twins' greater involvement in each other (Chart 24). They did not wish to copy adults, only each other. Bill enjoyed the qualities in Bert which caused him excitement and no adult could fulfill this role for him (p. 26). There were rare occasions when they showed a wish to make up for having hurt one of their nurses (Chart 24). It would be too much to say that they ever showed guilt for what they had done.

Mother

The mother of the twins was a gentle woman and very much in love with a married man, who made her pregnant. She stopped work before they were born and resumed work when the twins were 5 months old (p. 17). She had planned to name a baby boy Bert (Chart 13). Thus, she gave the name Bert to her firstborn twin. Both boys' middle names were her own father's name.

Although most of the time she could not tell her babies apart (Charts 11, 16, 21), she said that Bert looked like his father and gave him attributes of his father, while she thought Bill was like her (Chart 14). She used to say that she loved Bert best, but in the handling of the twins it appeared that she preferred Bill. Soon after the twins had entered the Nursery, a differentiation was noted in the way the mother handled them. She paid more attention to Bill, held him more often and longer; she fed him first (Charts 12, 13). It is true that he was the stronger, and therefore made his demands imperative. But she showed her preference in many ways, giving him the larger piece of cake, having Bill immediately changed when both were caught out in the rain (Chart 13). When Bert was in the sickroom she hurried to Bill, although Bert was crying for her. She seemed more attracted to Bill because he was the stronger, the more active and aggressive of the twins. She remarked that he was more mischievous, more like herself (Charts 13, 14).

Around the nineteenth month Bert's aggressive ways intensified and he often hurt Bill. The mother noticed this and now turned her attention to Bert, stayed longer with him when he was ill, and said that he was more a boy now (Chart 22).

It was also at this time that the mother's relationship to the father ceased. When the twins were 2 years 2 months old, the mother married another man. Her visits to the Nursery became less frequent, she became pregnant, and one month before her new baby was born, her visits ceased entirely.

Since at this date the children were moved to the country with the whole Nursery because of the increase of bombing, it was six months before their mother visited them again; by then, the aggressiveness of the twins had increased, especially Bill's, and she felt helpless when faced with both of them (foster parents' letter).

In 1945, at the end of the War, when the Nursery closed down gradually, it was decided that Bert should go home first to his mother, stepfather, and baby sister, since he was the more manageable of the twins and there was the hope that the mother might be able to deal with him (foster parents' letter).

From now on, whenever the mother visited Bill who remained in the Nursery, she had to bring along not only the baby but Bert as well. These visits were a catastrophe. Bill was overwhelmed with jealousy not only of the baby but of Bert. Bill attacked Bert viciously, and there was not a moment during these visits that the twins were not fighting. In consequence the mother decided that she could not take Bill to live at home. She tried to place him in a residential institution when the Nursery closed, but was unable to do so. Bill therefore joined the family five months after Bert had gone home, very much against her wishes. Several months later she placed both in a residential nursery. At this date Bert had been home eight months and Bill three months.

Father

Little was known about the twins' real father, except that the mother talked about him in a loving way. He was a soldier and on duty abroad (the mother's father had also been a soldier and been torpedoed in the First World War) (Chart 14).

The father kept in contact with the mother by letters, and she was very upset when an expected cable was lost in the post and did not arrive for the twins' first birthday. He visited the twins twice, the first time when they were 3 weeks old, before they were in the Hampstead Nurseries, and the second time while he was on leave and in uniform when they were 17 months old.

At this time the father remarked that Bert looked like his famliy (Chart 20).

In the charts only one observation is noted concerning the twins' reaction to a father figure: "Bert imitates his stepfather" after a visit home at age 3 years 4 months (Observation Card).

Relationship to Nurses

While the twins were in the Nursery, great efforts were made to give them nurses (mother substitutes) who were as permanent as possible. The twins shared the same nurse (Eva) from 4 months to 19 months. When she had to leave, it was thought advisable to have them with two different nurses to avoid rivalry. Consequently Bill was assigned to nurse Hanni, with whom he remained from 19 months to his departure at 4 years 11 months. Bert unfortunately had two more changes, even returning to nurse Eva at one time.

Both boys proved that they were able to form object relationships. They formed them to these mother substitutes; they reacted to the nurses's day off by sometimes showing pleasure when they returned, at other times anger at having been left. Both were sensitive to disapproval, Bert far more so than Bill (Charts 23, 24).

At times when the twins were separated from each other owing to illness, the nurses were hopeful that they had gained an influence over them, but they were invariably disappointed when the twins were reunited, and when their former behavior was resumed and all improvement given up (Chart 24).

EVENTS BETWEEN HAMPSTEAD NURSERIES AND MR. BARRON'S HOSTEL FOR MALADJUSTED CHILDREN

There was no direct contact with the twins, from the time they left their mother, Bill four years one month (November 22, 1945), Bert one month later, until at the age of twelve years they turned up at Mr. Barron's Home for Maladjusted Children.

However, Mr. James Shields of the Institute of Psychiatry was able to collect information about them from the various agencies and institutions which had to deal with them during this period. The information comes from two sources—contemporary reports and retrospective ones—the first carry a note of bewilderment, almost of despair, the latter a note of amusement over the difficulties the twins created.

A summary of the salient facts pertaining to this period runs as follows:

When the mother realized she could not cope with the twins at home, she tried repeatedly to place them in an institution. They were first admitted to a residential nursery, which specialized for difficult children (November 22, 1945).

In April, 1946, when the twins were four and a half, a visiting welfare officer noted that they were "difficult," had violent outbursts against each other, but were improving rapidly. Need careful handling in quiet surroundings. Hopes their future will receive careful consideration and above all that they will not be separated. "They are so closely tied I think it would be psychologically dangerous to separate them."

In October, 1946, the twins, now five years old, were removed to a large children's home where they remained two and a half years (May, 1949).

In a contemporary report from the headmaster (March 24, 1949), twins aged seven and a half years, reference is made to previous requests to have the twins removed from the Homes. ". . . both very difficult on admission, little if any improvement."

Bill has made some progress in school under pressure and is beginning to read. Can add units and tens. A constant upsetting influence in the school, needs whole of teacher's attention, conduct often unbearable, disobedient, spiteful, antisocial. In the cottage a constant source of trouble.

Bert even worse than his brother. Very backward and lazy. Lefthanded, awkward, careless in writing. His numbers show fair progress. Conduct in school and in the cottage very unsatisfactory and most unreliable. Disobedient, spiteful, foulmouthed, constant source of quarrels and trouble.

Retrospective impression of some staff members:

Two teachers who remembered the twins reported to a welfare officer (May 14, 1954) that they were regarded as most difficult children, had to be separated early on, when Bill was moved into a higher class and later on the twins were put in separate cottages. They were always doing things to themselves, accidentally cutting knees, etc. Still just as troublesome separated, it was not a case of one influencing the other. In personality, no difference remembered, but it is claimed that they had no difficulty in knowing who was who.

The Matron of the Homes (May 14, 1954) said she remembered the twins well. "They were really handfuls but very lovable and friendly little people." When in mischief the teacher never knew which one to punish, with the result that they both got off with a caution rather too often. Neither regarded more difficult than the other, but it is easier for the staff to deal with them separately than together.

Early in 1948 (age six and a half) Bill moved into a different cottage, while Bert remained with the same housemother. But they continued to play together, either having their arms around one another or fighting violently. No nervous habits recollected, except occasional bed wetting, Bill more often than Bert. Neither regarded as dominating the other.

While in this home the twins had the minimum contact with their parents.

In May, 1949, at the age of seven years seven months, the twins went to a special boarding school. This is a small establishment for forty-five children, who are in three separate houses. The school is a separate unit and a fair proportion of the children attend outside schools in the area.

During their first term the twins were in the same "house." A retrospective report from the headmaster (November 25, 1953) says: "They were extremely aggressive toward each other and had outbursts of very violent behavior. Their general behavior was irresponsible, very noisy, and their language was appalling . . . this behavior persisted. It was noticed that Bill, although the larger of the two, was less sure of himself and usually had the worst of it in their fights."

The housemother in a contemporary report commented: "Bert: fights with his brother but is the quicker thinker and generally outwits Bill. An objectionable child.
"Bill: resents his twin and causes fights. Filthy mind and bad influence on other boys."

The schoolteacher who had them both in his class was not so distressed; he commented:
"Bert: a nuisance, but improving, a busybody, persistently monopolizing, aggressive, disobedient, daring, talkative. Making progress.
"Bill: a general nuisance, but improving, aggressive, disobedient, very daring, persistently talkative and mischievous. Could do much better work. Schoolwork generally a little ahead of Bert."

The psychotherapist notes (August 26, 1949) that there was much tension between them.
"Bert: more sure of himself, better adjusted and happier, stronger and better liked than his brother.
"Bill: probably higher IQ but feels crushed by his brother. To be moved up to next cottage to encourage him and so that he will no longer be constantly compared with his twin."

Christmas term 1949 (age eight years two months):

Bert: with the same housemother who comments that the relationship to her is unchanged. His behavior "naughty," spiteful toward other boys, very highly strung. The schoolteacher describes him as noisy, daring, no team spirit.
Bill: the new housemother comments that he was rather out of hand after a visit to his home. His relationship with other boys is "fair"; he needs constant supervision.

Christmas, 1949:

> Bill: the same teacher refers to him as "overdependent, aggressive, fools about."
> Both: Individual psychotherapy ceased. "Very fair" at games.

Easter term 1950:

> The housemothers report that the twins are generally unchanged; Bill was unruly and troublesome after visiting his home at Christmas. Anxious to get on at school, always talking about his lessons.
> Bert is described again as highly strung, always in trouble.

> The school teachers' report indicates considerable progress. Their conduct is described in the same terms, but their educational progress is marked thus:

Reading: Bert reading book 4.
                  Bill reading book 5.
Spelling: Bert very good.
                  Bill good.
Arithmetic: Bert worked half of second book of sums.
                  Bill worked three quarters of second book.
Art: Bert fertile imagination but color and execution crude.
                  Bill more decorative and fastidious than last term, has delightful and delicate color sense.
Writing: Bert fair.
                  Bill very fair.
Practical work: Bert on the whole an excellent worker. Steady progress.
                  Bill fair ability. Behavior during this lesson quite good.
Sport: Bert?
                  Bill good. Steady improvement, better cooperation. Has made progress, works better in absence of his brother.

Summer term 1950 (age eight years nine months):

> Again the housemothers record no change in the boys' conduct in the houses, but Bert's housemother adds to the usual

description: "but has sunny disposition, will invariably laugh his way out of his difficulties."

The schoolteachers' reports indicate that each boy is maintaining his improved level of working, but each tends to do rather badly in the other's better subjects. Thus:

Reading:	Bert inclined to be careless.
	Bill very good, tries hard.
Spelling:	Bert good.
	Bill below average but not too bad.
Art:	Bert not nearly so good as last term.
	Bill some extremely sensitive work, takes great pains.
Writing:	Bert very fair.
	Bill not bad.
Practical work:	Bert poor, interfering, and quarrelsome.
	Bill tries, has quick good tool sense.
Sport:	Bert very good indeed. Alert, active, noisy.
	Bill not too good, very noisy.
Conduct:	Bert fairly good, disobedient at times.
	Bill talkative, has quite a temper, tearful when not having his own way, yet works well, tries to be helpful.

During this term the boys were in different classes.

Reports for the period Christmas, 1951 until December, 1952 indicate that the twins maintained good but not outstanding progress in their lessons first at the special school and then in separate schools in the area from January, 1952.

In the houses their behavior showed no marked change, but their problems decreased in intensity. They both were able to get on "well" or sometimes "very well" with other boys. Their relationship with the housemothers shows the least improvement, such terms as "very little improved," "not greatly improved," "same" appearing in the housemothers' report to the end. The relationship between the twins is reported to be "more friendly," "not quite so violent," as well as the more usual "much ill feeling." They are sometimes described as "very lovable nature," Bert "lovable" boy, "quick-tempered" Bill.

The special schools' achievement can be summarized in the reports that they prepared when the twins were about to be discharged:

Psychiatrist's report (October 29, 1952): "On admission Bert dominated and overwhelmed Bill, but now Bert is less aggressive and Bill is quietly confident and making better progress than his brother. Both are still occasional enuretics. . . . Bill is quieter and more considerate than Bert.
"Bert seems to care very little about others . . . they are now friendly and seem to have lost their hostility for each other."

The headmaster (November 28, 1953): "both boys have been very good; both play in their school soccer team. Bill has made considerable, measurable improvement in vocabulary from 27 to 67 on Burt's tests in two years, but in numbers when he is very impetuous the figures are 26 to 54. His IQ on the latest testing was 95.
"Bert's improvement in vocabulary is from 22 to 77 and in numbers from 29 to 48. His IQ is 98."

The school authorities urged that the children should go home 1952 (eleven years): "It is thought that if the boys do not get back home now, they will never get back. It is realized that the situation at home may break down, particularly in the case of Bert, but it is a case of now or never." They were at home from December, 1952 to October, 1953.

The mother complained three months after the twins had returned home that she could not control the boys. They would not do anything she asked them. If she forced them or sent one up to bed as a punishment, they crashed and stamped around up there.

They refused to go to bed, fought over washing. They continually fought between themselves. If they were asked to sit to listen to the radio, one kept poking the other and there was no peace for the rest of the family. They swore a great deal, their language was filthy, other children ceased to play with them. "When they came home there was a constant uproar."

Things deteriorated further during the eight months it took to get the twins placed at the Hostel. They threw cups at one another; on one occasion one took up a knife to strike the other, but the mother intervened.

At the school they attended from their home no abnormality of behavior was noted, although the level of their work appeared to be below that which they produced previously and it was noted that they spent the best part of their time outside classwork in scragging one another. They were not allowed to sit next to one another in class.

Mr. Shields saw the twins at age twelve years five months at the Genetic Unit of the Institute of Psychiatry where their status of being identical twins was investigated. Mr. Shields's report runs as follows:

Establishment of Monozygosity, or Being Genetically Identical Twins

The twins turned out to be alike in eight different blood groups. Their fingerprints were taken, and they were given phenylthio-carbamide to taste, which neither of them tasted as bitter. If one knew nothing at all about them except their blood groups and fingerprints, one would predict that there was only a 1.3 percent chance of their *not* being genetically identical twins. Needless to say, I confirmed their striking likeness in build, eye and hair color, and appearance generally, down to a pimple on the nose. Indeed, the feature by which I found it easiest to distinguish them was the fact that Bert wore two badges in his lapel, while Bill wore none. Bill was still a trifle bigger. Taken along with this likeness in appearance monozygosity was regarded as firmly established. Incidentally, both boys showed me with pride the scars they had on their legs from various accidents. Bill had had two lots of stitches on his left leg and two years ago he broke both wrists.

Other Findings (age twelve and a half)

Besides collecting reports from people who knew them between the ages of four and twelve, I also took the opportunity of giving them some intelligence tests we had recently given to a group of normal twins of their age, and of having EEGs done. Their EEGs were closely similar. Dr. Pond thought both records showed poorly organized rhythmic activity and should be regarded as mildly abnormal for their age. On Thurstone's Primary Mental Abilities Test, Bert scored higher than Bill, but they scored just as well as twins attending the ordinary schools, and the difference between them was no greater than the average for identical twins. They both did relatively well on tests of spatial perception. Previous tests on the Binet Scale at ten and a half years and at eleven and a quarter years centered round IQ 100, sometimes one twin, sometimes the other, doing a little better on the day of the test.

These results brought out further similarities between the twins in maturational level. From the evidence of the EEG there is the possibility that constitutional factors play a role here in addition to psychodynamic ones. However, with identical twins it is the differences that are of particular interest. I shall comment briefly on the personality differences as they struck me at the time.

In the first place, there seemed to have been a change-over in some aspects of the relationship between the twins. In the Nurseries, Bill had been the more aggressive in their mutual relationship and was thought possibly to be retarding Bert's development. At the special boarding school, the psychiatrist referred to Bert as "overwhelming" Bill. Around the time I saw the twins, Bert was still reported as being the more aggressive, Bill the quieter. Bert was also the more anxious, for instance, over the intelligence test I gave them and over the Rorschach given in the Hampstead Clinic. Bert's nails were more badly bitten, and he had a more neurotic score on a questionnaire. Bill on the other hand was doing better at school; he could sometimes settle down to read a book. He was a little ahead in physical adolescent development (information from Mr. Barron). He could perhaps have been regarded at that time as being neater and more fastidious—witness his art reports; another psychologist had recently commented that Bill was fussy about neatness and straight lines; after the fingerprinting Bill wanted to wash his hands straightaway, while Bert did not mind so much having his hands covered with black ink. The difference is relative only and must be seen in the setting of essential similarity—on the one hand, aggressive, uncontrollable, accident-prone, anti-social, and with serious problems in relation to each other; on the other hand, friendly, enthusiastic, "lovable" (as they were so often described), good at sport, and now of adequate intelligence.

THE TWINS AT MR. BARRON'S HOME
FOR MALADJUSTED CHILDREN

The following material was taken from Mr. Barron's notes and reports concerning the twins during the first eighteen months of their stay in his Hostel, that is, before the start of their analytic treatment. The twins turned up at the Home for Maladjusted Children at the age of twelve years (1953) brought by their mother. Mr. Barron writes:

The mother made a poor impression on me; she said she and her husband had decided to get rid of the twins; and added, "I wish you joy with them, I don't wish to see them again." She could give no intelligible description of their behavior, and they themselves acted as if they did not hear what I said. I took them . . . to the gardener; when I later went to find them, the gardener came running toward me: "Come quickly, quickly, they are murdering each other." The boys had attacked each other with choppers and were still fighting, rolling on the ground, punching and kicking each other. . . . The boys took no notice of me. I had literally to pull one off the other and hold them apart. As I stood holding them apart, they continued the quarrel as if I were not there. . . . Each boy's eyes, his whole attention was completely absorbed in the other twin. In an effort to make some contact, I demanded to know which was which. Two voices replied simultaneously and identically: "I'm Bert, he's Bill." They were jeering at me in unison. Rather desperately, I demanded to know which was Charlie and which Sydney; Bert admitted to his second name of Charlie and I said they would be known accordingly, whereupon Bill said, "Eh, it's not fair, why should he be a Charlie and not me." I thought this was a joke, but Bill was serious.

I have recounted this opening scene because it is a keynote for much that follows. They had no object relationship except in attacking each other, or together, as a gang, attacking the group.

The twins were introduced to the group at teatime on their first day, a short time after their fight. From the moment of entering the room, they began to shout disparaging remarks to each other about the other children, to giggle together about a child's peculiarities, to push and misuse any child who was near them. . . . They disregarded the staff member conducting the meal and turned what was normally an orderly social occasion into complete disorder.

Unlike rebellious children they followed the routine, but reduced everyone about them to incoherence, and turned the Hostel mealtimes, playtimes, and bedtimes into chaos.

The twins were deliriously happy in the chaotic conditions to which they reduced every activity. Their excitement would mount as the whole group was drawn into their aggressive abuse. When the twins were finally frightened, they lost their confidence and would whine, accusing the other children and adults of being against them. They would leave the room and sulk separately in odd corners, later complaining that no one liked them.

The very existence of the Hostel as a social group was, after a few weeks of the twins, threatened. Separation seemed the only practical way out. Throughout this period it seemed to us that it was Bert who was the most unmanageable and aggressive, the mother and stepfather sharing this opinion. Therefore tentative plans were made to have Bill go home to his parents, Bert to remain in the Hostel. But since separating the twins had already often been tried with no success and physical separation could possibly hinder their psychological separation, the plan was given up.

Instead it was decided to isolate the twins to some extent, for their own protection as well as that of the Hostel life. In order to reduce the daytime hours spent with the group they were sent to a distant day school. I acted as their close keeper at all other times. I hoped in vain to develop a relationship to them. But it was impossible to make emotional contact with the boys, and their disruptive behavior continued whenever our police system failed. I could not for four months even tell them apart; if some distinction appeared, such as Bert's red nose or Bill's boil, the other boy speedily developed the same.

On the point of abandoning the twins, I tried an "Aichhorn technique": to show myself to each boy the sort of person he showed by his behavior that he admired. Their behavior shocked others into submission—so I shocked them. To give two examples: I challenged them to a swearing match (they retreated); and I drove them wildly and fast in my car, frightening them after their initial defiant jeerings. This worked like magic, in the sense of procuring a dependent relationship at last. They competed for my attention, they sought my company. I no longer had to be keeper to them: they were my keepers. I was literally followed about by one, or more usually both boys. No moment of my life was private. They walked into my bedroom, they would wait outside the toilet for me. I was not permitted to have conversation with my children, my wife, or even with emotionally unimportant people such as county officials. They would butt into every conversation. They would demand my attention. They would ignore everybody. The most intense emotion on the part of anyone else would be completely ignored; but toward me every nuance of feeling, every nuance of voice was noted, recorded, and responded to.

Eventually we managed to distinguish them, which helped toward separate relationships, but the boys themselves began to let distinguishing signs of dress, hair, etc., appear.

Although they had a relationship to me, it was only on the basis of including me in their gang. They expected me to gang up with them against the other Hostel children, who in turn became jealous of the attention I paid the twins and attacked them, and I had to try and protect them. However, Bert was attacked one time and he struck his assailant with a dinner plate cutting him in the ear severely. (It is interesting that in his other hand, the right one, he was holding a knife, which he did not use, thereby showing some control.) The boy fainted in a pool of blood and Bert thought that he was dead and showed anxiety. This show of fear enabled the group of boys to identify with him, comfort him, and accept him. Bill was furious that Bert was accepted into the group and accused his brother of being a murderer.

My relationship with Bill was now strong enough to make him stop attacking Bert, and he too was accepted into the group.

Both boys had made exceptional educational progress at this time.

The mother was pregnant during this period. But although the boys went home for weekends, they consistently refused to believe this fact. Instead they made excuses to avoid going home. When the baby was born, Bert was nauseated in the presence of his mother. He was excited by the baby, but unable to touch the little girl. Bill was affectionate toward her, kissed her, and was proud of her, pushing her out in the pram.

The dependent relationship that had been fostered in the boys had now to be given an aim. Analytic therapy became the aim. The preparation for treatment consisted in telling the boys that in their present state, in spite of their improvement, they would never be able to live outside an institution or be able to live independent lives. They themselves now began to wish for treatment and finally demanded it repeatedly and urgently.

DECISIONS FOR AND EVENTS DURING THERAPY

For the boys to have the head of the Hostel as their therapist, the person who had personally provoked and furthered their dependency to him, was inevitably adding a serious complication to their treatment. Besides, that the twins should have the same therapist was bound to cause still further difficulties.

The only reason for accepting such a situation was that there was no alternative. To remove the boys from the Hostel to London was an impossibility. There was no other therapist in the neighborhood—therefore this attempt of therapy within the Hostel and with Mr. Barron, the head of the Hostel, seemed the only possible way to help. Mr. Barron himself was fully aware of the difficulties inherent in the situation.

Both boys started their therapy on the same day, June 13, 1955, when they were thirteen years eight months old. Bert was willing to start, Bill reluctant and bargaining; when he saw that

Bert would be taken in any case, Bill said: "Well, if he is going to, I might as well." The boys then found it difficult to decide which should have the first session. Bert came first.

The material in the first weeks concerned Bert's acquisition of a bicycle (Bill already had one). Bert was proud of and pleased with his bike; determined to look after it as well as Bill did; he feared that it might not work properly and that he might not be able to control it, especially downhill.

Each boy feared to formulate or verbalize his thoughts and feelings because to do so seemed equivalent to revealing himself to his twin. Further, it appeared that each boy feared that the other would murder him. Each identified with the other and assumed that his thoughts were identical with those of the twin and thus feared an attack.

The competition between the boys proved to be the main spur to all their efforts. Bert was a fraction shorter than Bill and be- cause of this felt inferior to him. Bert had many fantasies and fears related to his twinship: was he only half a boy, was he defective, why did his mother have to have a baby twenty min- utes after him? He was extremely resentful of his mother for not leaving him his birthright of being the firstborn. He denied feeling aggressive toward Bill, and maintained that it was Bill who tormented him. He recounted an accident to his own leg and brought the memory of damaging Bill's leg with a red-hot poker; finally, with marked affect, he said, "I feel I would like to murder him sometimes."

Bert had a screen memory of a lady telling him he had not put his knife and fork correctly on his plate and that he must copy Bill and he tried all the ways he could to copy him; but however hard he tried, he was unable to get it right.

One recurrent dream of Bert's, of being chased and locked in a cupboard, led to the memory of an event important in both boys' material. Bill, in the Children's Home, had been naughty and was shut in a cupboard, screamed that he was hurt, but jeered when he came out. Bert was then naughty and, being mistaken for Bill, was put in the cupboard again, where his finger was jammed in the door, but his screams ignored. When he was let out, his finger was found to be broken.

It was clear that the twins had murderous intentions toward each other, and that Bert only by exercising rigid control over himself or by getting Bill to join with him in attacking others had in fact avoided murdering Bill. The twins also entertained a sadistic love play. Bert, after a ritual of chase provoked by Bill, would rhythmically punch the arm, leg, or trunk of his twin.

Bill in his turn was jealous of Bert's new bike. He, like Bert, thought his twin could read his thoughts. He was indignant when it was suggested that he might be frightened that Bert could hurt him, but then recalled incidents such as the poker throwing. It was clear that Bill's method of avoiding awareness of his impulse was to provoke behavior in others which he could then adopt in turn. He could masturbate only in a group; also, he incited a group to delinquent acts in which he then joined, such as stoning a passing car.

Bill also felt abused that he was a twin. He felt he had come late into the world, at the wrong time; he should have been the only one, he had no right to be there at all, since his mother had had her baby already when he arrived. He wondered whether, being a twin, he was not incomplete. He was overwhelmed by conflict in his feeling toward his twin. He had many accidents, connected with fears of identification with the twin. If Bert had an injury, Bill acted as if he were responsible, and damaged himself. When Bert cut his leg severely in a fall, Bill fell from a tree and broke his leg.

Bill's whole outlook depended on competition with his twin; if he seemed likely to succeed in a situation which unconsciously meant disposing of his twin, he failed. In a football match, where at his own request he was allowed to play goal over the head of a rival, he let sixteen goals through, even scored one against his own side; after this he had an accident to his leg; and then could not play because he was unable to get his football boots repaired.

CHOICE OF NEW SCHOOL

The boys had done remarkably well in the school they had been attending the last two years. They took second and third places and were recommended by the headmaster for a technical school when his school closed at the end of 1955. They therefore had the choice to go either to another secondary school or to the technical school. Neither boy was able to make a choice.

Bert wanted to go to the technical school, but was afraid of not doing well. Yet if he did not go, and Bill went, it would be unfair. He was the eldest, he ought not to be faced with an equal choice but with the first choice. (He asked if they could go to different schools, but this was impossible to arrange.) In his sessions he abused Bill and his mother, and told how he enjoyed tormenting boys he disliked. He showed how he wanted to avoid being excited by Bill, but also showed his fear of desiring a separate school: "I never want anything until I see Bill with it." When he saw Bill in a fight, he had to join in to fight the other boy and then fight Bill, "I was jealous of him hitting Bill, I wanted to do that myself." He showed his demand that Bill should have no life apart from him, in effect, that he should be part of his body.

He met interpretation of his homosexual trends with silent resistance. He acted out his fantasies with another boy; when the boy had a tonsillectomy Bert became silent, identifying with his suffering. He wanted to visit the boy in the hospital, but fear prevented him. These fears concerned his inability to achieve anything he desired; the mere act of wishing denied it to him. He told how he dressed and made up like a girl to make the other boys laugh. When it was interpreted that perhaps he wanted to be loved like a girl, he told of a girl who was obviously attracted to him without his being aware of it. The analysis showed that he had fantasies of being the girl in a pair of twins.

At this time he was flooded with material that he could not bring under control. Outside the sessions he acted the fool.

Bill, too, was overwhelmed by the choice of school. It was clear in the analysis that he wished desperately to go to the technical school, but he was inhibited from knowing this, because if he knew it, Bert would know, and would want to go too. He said, "I only get what I want by not wanting it."

Bill's main affect was anger against all the authorities, past and present, who had deprived and bamboozled him, and against the twin, competition with whom was all that mattered. He wallowed in bitterness, said he had never been allowed to take the educational opportunities, which, in contrast to Bert, he had deserved, and claimed that the present choice was really beneath him because he should have had a better one.

His wish to go to the technical school also was affected by the fear of losing influence over Bert and the stimulating comparison with him if the latter went elsewhere. And, in that event, he would be near fulfillment of the forbidden wish—to get rid of Bert.

He was very resistant to interpretations of this ambivalence, proclaiming loudly his negative feelings toward Bert. At this time he incited the outbreak of sadistic love play, but was infuriated by the suggestion that he provoked Bert to punch him; according to his feeling, it was Bert who tormented him.

In the end the authorities decided for them by sending both to the technical school.

BREAKDOWN OF SCHOOL AND HOSTEL

Although Bert had wanted to go to the technical school, he was afraid to meet aggressive boys there. This was a projection of his own aggression toward Bill.

The material in therapy showed that his removal from his former school to the technical school reactivated memories of past separations.

He felt it was Bill's fault that he had been thrown out of his home in his infancy. He claimed that he had to make more moves than Bill, that Bill was always allowed to remain. He brought a screen memory of the parting from his mother when the boys went from home to their first residential institution. He remembered that the mother left with them a joint parting gift, and that he had clung to this toy, refusing to part from it and not allowing Bill to have it. In telling this memory, it became confused with other partings, or reunions, and separations from Bill. A state of mourning set in for the old school, displaced from Bill. He blamed Bill for taking his mother from him and in the past causing him to be moved from one place to the other. In the Hostel he ill-treated especially the younger children (Bill was, of course, considered the younger by him); these children represented Bill as well as his younger siblings. He was blaming them as well as Bill for pushing him out of his home.

In an effort to solve the ambivalence toward Bill, he became a twin to himself. He was in reality gratified that Bill was sent to the same school, but angry that this was so. The disappointment was the unfulfilled wish to manage without him. He mourned the old school, but he believed that he suffered loneliness and loss because he was a twin. If he could be a twin to himself, he would not suffer this loss.

Bert told of a game he played with himself: he would pair off two words and see which he could retain longest in consciousness; this went on to material about hurting and being hurt, which leg was last hurt, and then to looking for something, but he did not know what.

At school he was failing miserably. He could not cope. He spoke with great admiration of Bill, envied the quantity and quality of work he could produce. It was useless for him to try and compete in learning or in sport. The only way he could compete was by being a nuisance.

In the Hostel he began to learn American social history. This connected with Hanni, the nurse they had formely had, Bill in particular, in the Hampstead Nursery. She had continued to write to them on their birthday and at Christmas over the years. It seems as if Bert was trying to win her back from Bill.

His damaging and disruptive behavior in school was intolerable, and complaints also poured in from railway, bus companies, and his own home. He was finally expelled from school.

Bert made a twin relationship with another boy (Peter) who replaced the real twin. Through this relationship, it was possible to learn of the erotic nature of the fights between the twins. He was unable to take part in boxing because it meant covering his hands with gloves, which upset the balance of his hands for him. He could fight only if he fought with his bare fists and feel the impact between his skin and the skin of his opponent. He and his friends resorted to delinquent acts, raiding the larder and roving around the countryside at night, reactivating in this way what he used to do together with Bill.

He had acute fantasies of being too small for his age. His failure everywhere only increased his acting out. It was decided to stop the sessions of which he did not make proper use. He was disturbed by Mrs. Barron's pregnancy. It seemed probable that Mr. Barron would be able to help him more by resuming the solely educational role than by also being his therapist in this crisis.

He was expelled from the technical school and found a place in a modern secondary school, where his ability placed him in the top of his class. In the Hostel his feelings of inadequacy and of being too small were allowed compensatory expression; he formed a gang, playing at rebels, and became leader of the younger boys and of the football team.

Bill in his turn in the technical school was surprised to find the new buildings familiar, not realizing that what was in reality familiar was Bert at the desk next to his. He did not mention Bert's failure in school, but instead was behaving badly himself.

Complaints from home and the bus company were reported
about him, too. He hoped to provoke his removal from a situation with which he was unable to cope.

At this time the twins had formed an antisocial gang in
school; that no one could distinguish them roused Bill's anxiety
and loss of identity. He began to panic at his learning difficulties, cheating and copying Bert's exercises. All that mattered was
that he should not fall behind Bert, although Bert was doing so
badly. The rivalry was expressed in an incident where Bill, with
his bare hands, took a hot iron bar from tongs which Bert was
holding. He said, "When I saw him with it, I just had to have it."

In reaction to the attention which Bert was getting by means
of his impossible behavior, Bill brought thoughts about his unknown father, with complaints that a boy is no good unless he
knows about his father. He hoped that each time he moved to a
new place he would meet his father. But he also feared intensely
what would happen when they met. He fantasied of having a
devoted father who faced death and torture to reach his own
son.

He had the fantasy that his position of being the younger but
larger twin could be tolerable only for a girl, not for a boy.

After a weekend at home, and at the time when Bert had
formed his football team, Bill collected a rival group and began
to make a cricket pitch next to and overlapping Bert's football
field. The two teams fought until the two leaders faced each
other. They were on the point of striking each other, when Bert
suddenly rushed screaming from the field, got Bill's bicycle and
smashed it. This reduced Bill to raging sobs. He acted as though
the attack on his bike had been an attack upon his body; he
did not repair the bike, but retained it as a reproach against Bert
and as proof that he ought to be separated from his murderous
twin.

There came a time when he retired to bed with a swollen
ankle, after keeping secret that he had infected his foot. The
injured place oozed and he compulsively sucked it. This revolted

him, but he was driven to do it by the fear of "losing something good from my body." He also fantasied that he was two persons, the good right half and the bad left half, the good half always getting damaged, and the bad half angry at being left out. As he was in the fantasy a twin to himself, he needed only to damage one half and preserve the other. He identified not only with Bert but at times with Mr. Barron's pregnant wife.

He was accident-prone; one accident clearly occurred because he was in danger of realizing an ambition. When success was in his grasp, the successful activity became linked with the desire to be the only one, to dispose of the twin. On such occasions he actively damaged himself; for example, he ran full force into a wall, severely damaging his knee.

One determinant of the need to hurt himself was the fear that if he did not do so, the twin would. Thus he cheated the twin of the pleasure of hurting him. Another determinant was that, when he saw his twin hurt, he felt he was responsible for the damage and therefore he damaged himself, to prevent the twin from taking revenge upon him. Once when he saw his twin in pain, his death wishes came so near to consciousness that he assumed the twin would become aware of them and damage him in revenge. At this point the therapist unfortunately fell ill. The Hostel had to close for two months, and the twins were sent home.

REACTION TO HOSTEL CLOSING AND RETURN HOME

Forced to return home abruptly and without preparation both boys acted out their feelings in a violent manner.

Bert stayed out at night, spent his time in pubs and with gangs of Teddy boys,[2] and had a fight with a soldier whose jaw he broke; finally he attacked his mother at the midday meal. His stepsister had dropped bread in his soup plate, to which he had

---

[2] Teddy boys are adolescents or postadolescent young men who affect an Edwardian style of dress and haircut and who often travel about in gangs provoking fights, much as zoot suiters used to do in America.

retorted by calling her a bastard. The mother intervened, saying it was he himself who was the bastard. He attacked the mother violently, was pulled off by Bill with whom he then fought, and ran finally from the house. When the police, called by the father, looked for him he came forward and gave himself up, saying he was the culprit. He found it difficult to convince them, as it was now Bill who had hid himself, afraid that he would be mistaken for Bert. It was clear that Bert did all he could after Bill had pulled him off the mother to avoid further provocation.

Bill had great difficulties at home as well, covering an intense conflict over his twin. He had, in fact, acted out the wish to be rid of Bert. Bill himself had hit the mother some weeks previously, but she had not charged him in court as she did with Bert. He was able to repeat the pattern according to which he did something first, with the effect that when Bert followed suit, the latter was considered to be the real offender. This is a reminder of the incident of the cupboard and the broken finger.

When the Hostel reopened, in September, 1956, Bert was in a Remand Home awaiting trial before a juvenile court because of his murderous attack on the mother, while the parents had requested that Bill be permanently discharged from the Hostel and live at home.

Bert, from the Remand Home, repeatedly asked for Mr. Barron. The latter had faith that he could get Bert back into his Hostel. With difficulty this was accomplished. On his return, Bert was withdrawn and inhibited and then began to attack other children, usually the smallest, with alarming violence. Treatment was resumed because of the real concern that he might harm someone. In his sessions it was put to him that he might end up by killing somebody. It became clear that he attacked the little ones in the Hostel because he blamed his stepsiblings for his banishment from home, not only now, but from his infancy onward. He also complained that they had a father while he had none.

With the re-establishment of the transference, Bert demanded to be sent back to the Remand Home. When surprise was shown at the nature of such a wish, Bert himself was astonished. It showed how terrified he was of the impulses which he could not control. He was jealous of Bill at home with his mother and feared what he might do to him. The specific event leading up to this material was that the mother had sent him birthday greetings via Bill with a promise that she would knit him a pullover, "like the one I made for Bill."

Regarding Bill it was agreed that he should be discharged from the Hostel and return home as the parents had requested, on condition that he should continue daily sessions. At this he was very disappointed. He denied that he had difficulties at home, concealed and lied about his twin's crime as though it was his own. He had a fantasy, contrasting his own unhappy lot, beset by family cares, having to do a morning round to get money for clothes, with Bert's happy lot in a group with all the company, food, and clothes he wanted. He thought Bert might escape and he be taken in his stead. The policemen became father figures, and Bert was imagined to be with the missing father. The guilt was reversed, to deny that it was he, Bill, who had deprived Bert of the mother.

Bill's sessions at this point had to be used to check his acting out, to prevent him from following Bert into the Remand Home. He came near to it, after an incident when he caused a bus to crash by inciting some "silly girls" to throw apple cores at the driver and then joining in. His difficulties at home were exemplified by an incident when his mother was ill and he attempted to give a helping hand like the others. He dug up the whole garden, destroying the plants and obliterating the paths. In reality, he secretly resented doing work for others and thought that such a situation did not occur in an institution.

THE END OF SCHOOL LIFE AND CHOICE OF JOBS

At this time the twins went to different schools. Bert seemed to have cut himself off from Bill after his release from the Remand

Home, when at a first meeting they had resumed their puppy play. At school, he spoiled the last few weeks of his attendance, provoking his headmaster by trying to belittle him, by smoking in class, etc. If the headmaster had not been very sympathetic, he would have been severely punished. As it was, he was removed from attendance some weeks before the end of term to avoid expulsion.

The problem that now arose was to find a job for him. He had two ideas about work, to do hostel work like the head of the Hostel, his therapist, or to join the army. As a first step toward learning a skill for community life, he chose gardening. This was determined by a wish to make his body stronger than Bill's; hence the need of a healthy outdoor life. Both of his choices were based on homosexual inclinations. He was set to work in the Hostel garden, but this proved a failure. He was unable to work because of the longing for his twin when alone, so that he left to seek companionship; but when he worked with somebody else, ruthless competitiveness was aroused.

The army for him was the abode of killers, but also the protective institution where men were permitted homosexual contacts in the form of "puppy play."

Material relating to the father now occupied the sessions. Bert demanded to know about his father. His therapist informed him that the father was a market porter, was married and had children, when the mother had the twins, she had expected to marry him but had refused to break up the father's marriage. His mother wrote answering Bert's request for his father's name, but he lost the letter, then spent days going through the telephone book hoping in this way to recall his father's name. He wished to find his father but was afraid of him as well. He told of a childhood fantasy that soldiers like his father get more money for every person they kill. His daddy had killed hundreds of people. One day he would come back to kill Bill, but he might mistake him for Bill, and kill him, Bert. In bringing this fantasy, Bert told how he had felt compelled to fight the young soldier.

He was so sure that the soldier would kill him that he fought with all his strength and with his second punch broke the soldier's jaw.

Surprisingly, regarding jobs, he acted on his own. With another boy he went to the Forestry Commission, inquired about the conditions for work and both signed up.

Bill's school life also was very stormy. His desire to be rid of his twin and his guilt at having succeeded in this were uppermost. An example of his acting out was a football match. He could not face the position of goal, as this was the position where Bert had played. When changed to another position, he could not play then, as it meant to mark another man. Everything associated with his twinship became intolerable, even the voice of one person talking to another on the bus. In the transference, the therapist was accused of being cruel; Bill felt helpless, so helpless that boys at school knocked off his cap and he did not know what to do about it. He showed clearly at this time how dependent he was on his twin for dissipating his aggression. He was so terrified that his own aggression would lead him to kill the other boys that he could not defend himself at all. He begged for boxing gloves (in contrast to Bert, who could only fight bare-fisted). His fear of his own aggression was reinforced by Bert's absence in two ways; the sight of Bert was a reassurance that he had not destroyed him, and their horseplay acted as a safety valve. He began to hang about the Hostel before and after his sessions, hoping unconsciously to find Bert. Consciously he was aware of his wish to be back at the Hostel. He started a course of acting out in which, unknown to his therapist, he brought something of Bert's possessions with him on each visit, until all trace of Bert was removed from the home; the stepfather as well forbade the mention of Bert in the house.

It became necessary in the sessions to concentrate on restraining his acting out. He fought his teacher, and gave his headmaster cause for frequent beatings. He would come to the sessions in suppressed excitement, very voluble but almost unintelligible.

One determinant of this was that all correction or misunderstanding of his speech was linked to the time when the twins could understand each other without words. In the treatment it appeared that his behavior turned on the lack of a father. How could he be expected to manage if nobody would put things right: neither the headmaster who beat him nor the analyst who failed to protect him and did not arrange for him (as he did for Bert). He half craved to get back to an institution. His provocation at school passed all bounds, and finally, before the end of term, he was withdrawn from school, as Bert had been. It was an achievement that he was not formally expelled or brought before the courts.

Choice of work came up in the last weeks of his school life. He said that he wished to become a teacher; this was in identification with the punishing headmaster and the disappointing therapist. The headmaster was cast in the role of the hated father, but was also the father whom he wished to follow.

He complained that his mother had decided that he would have to join the army immediately on leaving school. This was interpreted as his own wish in identification with his own father, a wish which he characteristically projected onto the mother. He made her force him to do what he really wanted, namely, to return to an institution and be under the control of authority.

On leaving school his stepfather found him an apprenticeship with a patternmaker, a job which could eventually lead him to work with his stepfather. With the beginning of his working life Bill failed to keep to his sessions and broke off treatment. Fifteen months later it was learned that he had changed jobs and was working on the railroad, while still living at home.

BERT AT WORK

As soon as Bert started work with the Forestry Commission, his behavior in the Hostel became much more mature, he got himself up early, made his own breakfast, and washed up before leaving.

He also came eagerly to his sessions and used them to gain insight into his disturbed working relationships.

He had chosen this job because it started out with a twin relationship, although the boy who signed up with him soon withdrew. Bert first worked with a very disturbed and unpopular man, but admired his skill and knowledge and tolerated his fault-finding and high-handed manner and competed with him. He also hoped to gain the great physical strength which some of the men displayed. He earned ten to fifteen shillings more than his wages because of good work. His next fellow worker was an older man, a slow and thorough worker, whose ways he found intolerable and with whom he coped in a kind of hare-and-tortoise race. He would let the man get ahead of him and then race to overtake him, thus introducing the element of competition which was necessary to his functioning. When he had to be absent at one time because of illness, another boy took his place. This created a three-cornered situation, which was beyond him. His therapist had to use all his skill to prevent him from giving vent to his aggression against this boy and from killing him. His work deteriorated, he earned considerably less. He spent much time sleeping and playing cards, an identification with his stepfather. When women were given the job that he had neglected, he was angered. He asked to be given another chance, was able to work again, and was soon being taught the most coveted job of felling trees. He was given a big axe which became his most treasured possession, but at the same time he was unable to use it properly, fearing he would cut himself down instead of the tree. His stance when wielding the axe was that of a sprinter, ready to run as if the axe were the aggressor. Turning his own aggression against himself was the only way in which he could keep control over his murderous impulses.

FOSTER FAMILY

Bert now had to leave the Hostel and a foster home had to be found for him. Some time was spent searching, and he had to visit various members of a Rotary Club who were trying to help him. Here he gained much pleasure from the fact that he was known by his own name now, not as Billybert or Bertbilly as had been his fate repeatedly.

The foster family that took him in were a young couple with two children, a boy and a girl, both under five. He became fond of the foster mother, appreciated her care, but kept away from the house except for eating and sleeping. He fantasied that his own mother would become jealous of this woman and would take him back into his own home. He could not decide whether to write to his mother giving her his address, or to leave it to her to search for him. His indecision was based on his longing for his twin and his fear that Bill might come and destroy his foster home. This fear sprang from an unconscious fantasy of making an exchange with Bill—Bill to have the foster home and Bert the mother. He coped well with the foster father, achieved the position of eldest son, became a hero for the little boy, and successfully managed the little girl through a feeding difficulty. Instead of bullying her as the parents did, he would take her on his lap and get her to eat in identification with himself. He perceived and understood that her difficulty arose from his entry into her home and her jealousy of her older brother.

LONGING FOR HIS TWIN

Bert had now an hour's journey to his sessions and was often late, losing his way. This made sense when it was discovered that he was traveling toward his own home. Then he began to arrive an hour early, in reaction to a fantasy that his therapist was seeing his twin and he would thus meet him. He obtained much infomation about his twin on these journeys, for he was often mistaken for him. On discovering that Bill earned more than he did, he began to earn more himself. One day, he "accidentally" saw Bill on a bicycle in his work clothes. He remarked that one could see that this was no ordinary kid for he "held himself like a king." On an impulse, he wrote to his mother that he would visit her. He took all his money from the savings bank and in new clothes started for home. Before going into the house he found Bill playing football and watched him, noting minute details of his appearance and behavior. Then he invited him and the boys into a pub and stood drinks lavishly. Bill responded by producing from his pocket a giant packet of expensive cigarettes.

On this occasion Bert's visit home went off well. His mother drew him aside and spoke tenderly to him. Yet on a subsequent visit she told him to get out. Bert reacted first by taking his stepfather's chair and reading his paper, then he said, "Well, goodbye Mum," and walked out.

On both occasions Bert had taken all his money to give his mother. He was wondering secretly whether his mother had been a prostitute (they were bastards), and in this way he acted out the wish to buy her from his stepfather.

BERT FIGHTING AND BEING BEATEN

During the last six months of Bert's treatment there was a mounting crescendo of fights. He severely injured a paper boy who was cheeky to him, so that he had to be in a hospital for many days. He blamed the therapist for his belonging nowhere, neither to the ordinary youths of the town because he was under the court and had been brought up in an institution, nor to the "club" of criminal youths who had graduated through the approved schools and Borstals.

He picked fights in the dark of a cinema with a gang of Teddy boys. They threatened to beat him up, he took up the challenge and withdrew to the lavatory. There he disclosed his powerful body and challenged the leader of the gang. On seeing his murderous intention and powerful physique, the leader of the Teddy boys refused to fight. This made him afraid that he must be mad if he could frighten a gang of Teddy boys; he also feared that they would waylay him and kill him.

After this incident he became involved in fights with gangs in which he was severely battered. He came to his sessions covered with blood, his suit ruined, and told how he complied with the rules of boxing and never defended himself as the others did. He further described how happy he felt when booted by the gang. "I was so happy, I was so happy," he reiterated. The fantasy underlying this was that if he suffered intensely enough, his twin would come to him and together they would fight and destroy the gang, then would fight each other. Another version was that they would compete to see which one could overcome the greatest number in the gang, the winner to be acknowledged by the unknown father.

Fights on a lesser scale continued until he joined in with the gang. He wished to break off treatment, fearing the dark on his journeys to the sessions. Finally, he did so.

COORDINATION AND COMPARISON OF MATERIAL

When Bill and Bert left the Hampstead Nurseries at the age of approximately four years, the predictions as to their future development were not optimistic ones. There were too many factors which they had against them. So far as environmental circumstances were concerned, there was illegitimacy, residential upbringing, insecurity in the relationship to the mother, a stepfather who did not welcome their appearance. Developmentally, they were found not to be up to age in intellect and almost totally lacking in educational response. Emotionally, their strongest tie was to each other, and this twinship was a factor of overriding importance in disturbing other contacts. Their aggression was out of control, and any adaptation to group life almost nonexistent.

It was not easy under these conditions to make provision for their future upbringing. So far, in the Hampstead Nurseries, separation from each other had proved the only method which brought favorable results. Although, in the face of their close and exclusive attachment, this was not an easy step to take, it was considered in their case. There seemed to be a chance that Bert, less aggressive and more lovable and intelligent than his brother, might win the mother's affection. He was her firstborn son whom she professed to love best. On the strength of this she might be able to cope with him, and it therefore was thought that he should go home. This, of course, would leave Bill in the worse position, separated from his twin, unloved and rejected by the mother, with a very slender chance of finding somewhere in an institution a fatherly authority figure able to control and guide him. What was also considered was the possible guilt aroused by such arrangements in the favored twin.

However that might be, this was the first solution tried, with full awareness that in the case of these boy twins only the formation of new object ties could prove to be a beneficial factor in their eventual socialization. It was also considered as a possibility that all efforts might be in vain and that it was too late to undo the consequences of their failure in educational response in their first four years of life.

When investigating, on the basis of the material collected, the factors which are responsible for the difficulties of development, it is natural to give first place to the twinship of the boys, since this seemed the cause of their withdrawal from other human contacts. In the comparison between past and present, accordingly, the material is arranged in the following order of importance: identity of appearance; mirror image; struggle for their own identity; excitability; antisocial development; differences in the personality of the twins.

IDENTITY OF APPEARANCE

As identical twins, Bert and Bill were the mirror image of each other, at first with no distinguishable marks. The complications in their lives caused by this fact hardly altered over the years, although in time the effect of it on their own feelings began to have increasing repercussions.

So far as the environment was concerned, their identical

appearance led to confusion and to consternation in those who had their care. As reported in the material, the mother herself was put out by her uncertainty in distinguishing between the twins, never knew for certain whether she was handling one or the other, made statements concerning one which, in reality, referred to the other child, and in her preference for Bert or Bill was guided by single traits such as activity, aggression, mischievousness rather than by an attraction emanating from the whole personality of the child. There was no doubt that under such circumstances her object cathexis of the children was uncertain, weak, shifting, and lacking efficiency and warmth.

The difficulties which arose with their nurses were not dissimilar. Here it was above all the doubt whether affection or dislike, praise or blame were attached to the right or wrong child, a difficulty which persisted far beyond the Nurseries into their latency periods and adolescence. At times it led to their being treated with unjust severity (see the incident of Bert being mistaken for Bill and shut in a cupboard); at other times it led to their being let off too lightly to avoid injustice (see the matron's report, 1954). In either case a correction applied with such uncertainty cannot but have had a negative effect. Even in adolescence, Mr. Barron paid tribute to the effect on him and the whole Hostel by their identity of appearance by reporting that he could make no contact with them until he knew "which was which," and that "no separate relationship" started until it was discovered that Bert's and Bill's "jaws were slightly different."

Insofar as their personal problems with identity of appearance were concerned, there was a definite difference between past and present. As infants or young children they were first oblivious and then enjoyed being like each other (see Mirror Image), and there is no doubt that in latency they made use of it in the service of delinquent behavior. It was only toward and in adolescence that this impinged on their problems of identity and aroused resentment and anxiety, as revealed in the treatment situation. It showed manifestly in Bill's fear that the police might mistake him for Bert when arresting the attacker of the mother, or catch him instead of Bert as a fugitive from the Remand Home. In both cases identity of appearance had become a symbol for identity of crime or guilt. It also showed, less overtly, in both boys in their inability to tolerate the physical presence or nearness of the twin (see Choice of New School).

But even in adolescence, after the twins had parted company, their identical appearance was still used in the service of their positive attachment, for example, on the occasion when Bert used the confusion between their looks to glean information about Bill.

MIRROR IMAGE

The relationship of infants to their own mirror image has been studied at length,[3] and descriptions have been given how children not only enjoy meeting their own reflection but pet and stroke the image, etc. Confusion between their own mirror image and sight of the twin was noted with Bert and Bill at seventeen months and again at two and a quarter years. There is little doubt that living in the presence of the twin was for them synonymous with living in the presence of their own reflection. There also were indications (see Chart 20) that the intensity of their reaction to being separated from each other contained narcissistic elements, loss of the twin representing in this sense the loss of a portion of their own person.

In infancy, the twins' relationship to each other was compounded, therefore, of a mixture in which it was impossible to assess the relative importance of narcissistic trends on the one hand and of object-directed strivings on the other. Teaming up together in mischief, doing exactly the same thing at the same moment without giving a visible signal to each other, moving about the room in the same position and with identical gestures (p. 38) point to narcissistic unity and identification rather than

[3] See Lacan (1949), and also *Twins* (1952), Chart 24.

any known form of close early object relationship. So does the understanding without words, the deliberate copying games, calling each other by the same name, displaying the same needs and wishes at the same moment (p. 20). Doubtless, this identification based on narcissism was broken up only gradually by the dawning realization that the twin was not merely a duplication of the self, whose identical reactions heightened the wishes, needs, impulses of their own person, but also a rival to the self, capable of monopolizing wanted objects and means of satisfaction. This realization reached a climax in the later feelings of rivalry and the conviction that pleasure gained by one twin automatically implied the failure of the other twin to attain a coveted object or desire.

On the other hand, the unconscious material elicited in the treatment of the boys in adolescence emphasized the elements of object cathexis even in their earliest relationship. It is well known (see A. Katan, 1937; Anna Freud, 1958) that in adolescence, the individual institutes a struggle against his early object ties partly to remove these persons from being drawn into his regressive incestuous fantasies, partly to prepare himself for forming new ties to strangers outside the circle of the family. This struggle against the early objects, normally the parents, can take various forms from bodily removal and avoidance of their presence to emotional indifference toward them, or of passionate hate and denigration.

That Bert and Bill reacted toward each other in adolescence in all these manners, overtly and unconsciously (i.e., removed themselves from each other, avoided each other, abused and hated each other, etc.), seems to prove that they were, indeed, each other's earliest love objects, not only each other's narcissistically cathected mirror images. In this case, it is the later analytic explanation which makes a decisive pronouncement on an instance of uncertainty in direct observation.

On the other hand, narcissistic elements did not cease to play their part even at this late stage. When at sixteen, Bert saw Bill from the distance on his bicycle and reported in his session that he "held himself like a king," there was no doubt about his narcissistic enjoyment of this "mirror image," in the middle of all the negative, derogative, hostile feelings toward the twin which belonged to the rejection and reversal of the object relation.

STRUGGLE FOR THEIR OWN IDENTITY

All adolescents have to go through a phase when they struggle to establish themselves as a person in their own right vis-à-vis themselves, their families, their contemporaries, and the wider community. What they come up against during this process are the preoedipal and oedipal identifications which have become part of their own superego. To grow truly into himself, the adolescent finds himself therefore at war not only with the objects but also with the moral and aesthetic demands, aims, and ideals of his past.

In Bert and Bill, with their abortive relationships to adults and the defects in their superego formation, little or nothing of these normal conflicts became visible in the adolescent material. For them, to "be a person in their own right" had one meaning only: to be without the twin. If, in their case, adolescent treatment had not been preceded by a detailed observation of their infancy, the therapist might have gained the impression that here were children in whom hostility for an ever-present rival and competition had played a decisive role from earliest beginnings. This would have been an error. It is true that the twins were in rivalry from infancy: in the relationship to their mother when both cried for her, wanted to be picked up by her first, fed first (Charts 17, 21); in the Nursery when both wanted to be loved and cared for exclusively (p. 21ff.); when they wanted to grasp and possess the same toy at the same moment. But this rivalry, although present, was not the element which shaped their childhood. The factor responsible for this was the opposite one of extreme closeness and possessive intimacy with the twin, the copying games, the understanding without words, the constant companionship, the increase in personal power and efficiency through ganging up with the twin (Chart 20), the complete absence of loneliness. The intensity in their rejection of the twin in adolescence has to be understood therefore, not as commensurate with infantile rivalry, but as being in reverse ration to the earlier closeness.

To get rid not only of the external presence but also of the internal image of the twin was the aim for which both boys struggled in adolescence and for the accomplishment of which they were willing to accept the therapist's help. Their efforts were given expression in treatment in various ways. There were manifest complaints about the twin birth, memories and cover memories which confirmed the harmfulness of the twinship; direct threats expressed against the twin. Less directly expressed, there were also the hostilities against other children as displacements from the twin as well as displacements onto inanimate objects such as the bicycle. Finally, there was the full impact of the murderous wishes which both boys harbored against each other and which determined much of their behavior. It is significant in this respect that both were fully aware of the other's enmity against themselves and were afraid of it; but that both, before treatment, were equally unconscious of their own wish to kill, and of its projection onto their partner.

In spite of this, the advantages of twinship were not given up easily, and made themselves felt by means of regressive pulls back to the infantile enjoyment of them. This becomes very evident in Bert's treatment, at the time when he tried in fantasy to become "a twin to himself," substituting for the rejected brother a play either with words, or with the right and left part of his own body.

"Togetherness" in infancy also persisted in another form, namely, in the constant thought preoccupation with the absent twin, the ongoing comparison of earnings and possessions, the fear (and underlying wish) for his reappearance and its consequences, etc.

EXCITABILITY

In normal development a child's involvement in autoerotic activities limits the influence which the objects in the environment can exert on him. His ability to provide pleasurable sensations and excitement for himself renders him independent to some degree of the objects, of their approval and disapproval, and of their pleasure- and comfort-providing actions.

With Bert and Bill, to excite the twin and to be excited by him took the place of autoerotic stimulation, as shown in the first four years by their touching and biting games, their puppy play (pp. 21-26). Since the twin and the games with him were ever present, the effect of this on withdrawal from environmental influences was considerable.

There was also the added factor that "autoerotism in partnership" produced a higher degree of stimulation than is seen usually when similar activities are carried out in isolation, the excitement of each partner acting as a further seduction and incitement for increased abandonment on the other. With Bert and Bill this came under observation from their crawling days onward and destroyed completely any atmosphere of internal or external peacefulness in their lives. Whatever was initially merely interesting to them was turned by such interaction into intense agitation which intensified and increased until they were both overwhelmed by it (especially Bill, see p. 25). Nothing else mattered at such times (p. 24f.). Touching each other's bodies often started in a gentle way, but turned invariably into rough handling (pp. 24-25, 34; Charts 15 and 16); what started with rubbing ended with biting, etc. It was also notable that this tension was heightened, not diminished, when both their attentions were directed toward an ulterior aim (such as the mother's attention) and when they were in rivalry. In these instances they were deaf to any interference and completely unaware of any approach to them (p. 34; Chart 19). Tension was accompanied by screaming (especially shrill and intense in Bill).

Excitement of this kind was generated not only in partnership, as shown by Bert's banging his head against a table leg on his own, and developing head banging as an "autoaggressive" activity (Chart 16) which was taken over only subsequently by Bill (Charts 21, 25, 26). But even this became a common activity since at two years five months the twins, reunited after a separation, greeted each other by banging their heads against each other. To such exciting pleasures, pain was no barrier. They inflicted it on themselves, on each other (as well as on other people), for example, by biting (especially Bill).

There is the possibility that the twins' mother fostered rather than discouraged these attitudes by enjoying activity, aggressiveness, and mischievousness, first in Bill and later in Bert. But this was not really the impression recorded in the observations. It was rather that the twins, through constant interaction, had a highly developed erotic response to every kind of tension and influx of stimulation and used every opportunity offered to extract the highest pleasure yield from the events.

Comparing the shared infantile autoerotism of Bert and Bill with the equivalent features as they appeared in their later treatment, the outstanding impression is one of sameness, of an intact survival of the infantile trends without adaptation, modification, and certainly without sublimation. There was the same uncontrollable excitement which they engendered in each other, and which did not allow them to have a moment's peace. There was the same heightening of tension in rivalry, as expressed by Bert: "I never want anything until I see Bill with it," or by Bill when he seized a red-hot poker because Bert was holding it: "When I saw him with it, I had to have it," an excitement which did not allow for any consideration of consequences and urged them as blindly toward wish fulfillment as it had done at the toddler stage.

What had not changed either, in spite of adolescence, was that the mother (probably by virtue of her absence and imaginary, rather than real, role) was continually in the center of their thoughts as the coveted prize to be won away from the other, especially so in states of tension and excitement. When Bill was claimed by the parents in adolescence, and Bert rejected, the former could not do enough to erase every trace of the brother from the home surroundings. This, very effectively, revived and reversed the infantile situation, when Bert was home and Bill relegated to the Nursery.

It was not only the bodily presence of the brother which influenced the other twin, any reminder of a relationship between two people was enough to cause tension. In Bill's words: "Even the voice of one person talking to another is unbearable." At the same time the competitive element which had meant companionship in their past was too precious to be missed (see Bert and his "hare-and-tortoise race" in the Forestry job.)

Unchanged continuance of the past was most noticeable in the openly homosexual elements in the adolescent twins' relationship. Here, bodily nearness to each other was sufficient to cause touching, whether this was of friendly or of hostile kind. The early "puppy play" was still there, even if developed into a sadistic rolling on the ground, punching rhythmically the arm or body of the twin. As in the past, such games served skin erotism. If Bert was unable to fight with boxing gloves (because he needed to feel the bare flesh), and Bill could fight only when gloved, this showed both boys' fixation to skin erotism, even if in this case Bill had gone further than his brother in rejecting it.

Homosexual possessiveness of the other's body also showed when Bert, after seeing Bill fighting with a stranger, reported to his therapist: "I was jealous of the other boy hitting Bill. I wanted to do it myself."

Secondarily, their own body fights were also displaced onto the world at large, with distorting consequences for their conception of reality. The army, for example, was seen by both boys as an assortment of people who fight—as in their puppy play— and fighting as an exciting fantasy could be increased to murdering, turn into an orgy of killing, as in the imaginary picture of their soldier father who was thought to have killed hundreds of people, and would finally destroy the twin.

Another feature which remained unchanged from infancy to adolescence was their masochism. Just as painful head bangings had been pleasurable in the Nursery, beatings provoked by Bill in school, by Bert from the gangs, were welcome. When Bert came to his session in a pitiable state, kicked and maltreated by the gang members, all he could describe was an overwhelming feeling of excitement and pleasure: "I was so happy, I was so happy."

The same feelings could also be aroused in them by self-inflicted damage, i.e., by their accident proneness (Bill more than Bert). Significant in this respect for both of them was engineering situations which subsequently they could not control; Bill taking off his bicycle brakes, or running in front of an oncoming car; or, as shown in the follow-up, Bill possessing a motor cycle which Bert envied as a "death machine," and on which he already had had six accidents.

This is not too unlike the accidents which the twins inflicted on themselves in the Nursery, such as Bert falling out of his cot at fifteen months, hurting his finger on a tin at eighteen months, falling, cutting eyelid, having to be stitched at two years four months; or Bill "being insensitive against pain, whether he has hurt himself or is hurt by other children" at two years five months (Chart 24). Mr. Shields also reports from the examination of the boys: "Both twins showed me, with some pride, the scars they had on their legs from various accidents. Bill has had to have two lots of stitches on his left leg and two years ago he broke both wrists," at twelve years five months.

There is only one difference emerging here between past and present. Perhaps already as a result of treatment, Bert especially became aware of the dangers in which he placed himself, to the degree that he pleaded even to be returned to the Remand Home where he would be controlled by external authority.

ANTISOCIAL DEVELOPMENT

It is obviously out of order to apply the term dissocial or anti-social to infants and toddlers since no understanding for social necessities and little compliance with them can be expected of them. In spite of this, many of the observers who saw Bert and Bill in the Hampstead Nurseries were tempted to regard them as belonging to this category. They stood out among the other population of the Nurseries as being wild, passionate, over-excited, aggressive, out of control. They were the despair of their nurses and they created pandemonium (p. 25f.). As they grew from infants into toddlers and from toddlers into nursery school children, they did not quiet down in their behavior, and they did not become more constructive in their actions.

There were several features in their early development which gave rise to grave concern regarding the possibility of future social adaptation.

There were, for one, those inherent in the fact of twinship, namely, the absence of a symbiotic relationship with mother or mother substitute which could lead to useful identifications; and instead the symbiotic relationship with the twin which served merely to intensify existing behavior patterns by reciprocal in-fection and cross-stimulation.

There was an overdevelopment of narcissism (owing to the narcissistic tie to the twin) and an underdevelopment of object libido, caused by the insecurity of the mother relationship and institutional life with consequent withdrawal from the adults and disregard for their wishes.

There was imperfect differentiation between self and twin, their own identity at the toddler stage tending to become lost and identification with the twin exaggerated. There are many observed examples of this with Bert and Bill, especially in rivalry when a rapid change of identity took place. In wishing for what the rival had at the moment, the child experienced his own self as frustrated, but identification with the twin served to give him a share of the latter's enjoyment—a process tending to interfere with the development of a clear concept of the self.

Their age-adequate advances in speech and muscular control were placed at the service of pleasurable interaction with each other and used for the expression of passion and excitement in shouting, screaming, joking, "puppy play." There was no constructive use of toys and no beginning neutralization of drive energies.

There was little use of mother or nurse as comfort giver. On the contrary, due to the existing rivalry, turning to a shared adult (mother or nurse) merely served to heighten tension and increase excitement.

There were few advances toward other children who were treated in the main as disturbers, or as if they were the furniture. Only occasionally a child was used as substitute for the twin, usually in the twin's absence.

Lastly, and perhaps most ominously, adult objects, even if cathected, were not used for the purpose of imitation, identification, and ideal formation. Bert and Bill were not unattached in the Nursery, in the sense in which autistic children are withdrawn. They had a special relationship to nurse Eva, for example, who took care of both of them from the age of four to nineteen months. As toddlers, they expressed their positive feelings about being in her presence by increasing excitement, flinging themselves about, throwing toys and plates, laughing and screaming alternatively. When she left the room, they would scream with despair; when she reappeared, scream with pleasure. They expressed their competition for her attention by biting and hitting her and each other. But the relationship went no further than this. The nurse had no influence over them and no power to control them, which distressed her greatly.

By the time Bert and Bill arrived at their treatment in Mr. Barron's Hostel (age twelve), there was no doubt that they could be classified legitimately as antisocial. They were unruly, boisterous, intolerant of authority exercised over them, in constant difficulties with housemothers, matrons, teachers, headmasters, always on the verge of being excluded or expelled from school. They were in conflict with the police, and Bert was brought before the Court. They either fought gangs or themselves became members of a gang of Teddy boys with whom they shared the characteristics of indifference for the feelings of other people, enjoyment of terrorizing, of harmful and cruel acts, and a continuous dissatisfaction that went with the desire to oppose law and order.

Every analytically trained therapist who treats an antisocial boy is faced in the patient's material on the one hand by the delinquent's mood of bitterness and rage against parents, family, community, and on the other hand by the "delinquent character," i.e., by the patient's inability to control himself or be controlled; the urgency of his desires; the impulsiveness of his actions; his irritability and, at the same time, the repetitiveness of his behavior. All of these were present in the case of Bert and Bill. The questions which every therapist invariably poses to himself are whether and how far the patient's resentments are justified, i.e., whether he had been rejected and discriminated against in reality or merely in his imagination; which was the point at which his antisocial development deviated first from the norm; and, above all, is the patient's irresponsive, infantile way of pleasure-seeking equivalent to a breakdown, a regression from a more advanced level of socially adapted functioning, or is it representative of an arrest at the normal todler stage, i.e., at the level of irresponsibility and primary process functioning?

In the case of Bert and Bill, we were in the advantageous position of being able to check the answers suggested by the treatment material against the childhood records of the boys. Both boys filled their sessions with bitter accusations against the mother who, according to them, had "cheated them of their birthright" (Bert), against the unknown father who had deserted them (Bill), against the siblings who had displaced them in the home (both), and against the stepfather who had thrown them out. A fantasy image of the unknown father appeared (Bill) in which the latter was a cruel and victorious killer of men, but also a hero who braved every danger to find his son. In these family romances of both boys, realistic and imaginary elements were blended in the usual manner: it was real that the mother had ceased her regular visits to the Nursery shortly before the birth of the next baby; also that they were unwelcome in the family (above all due to their being unmanageable) and that they had never had a proper chance of home life. What the material at this stage did not reveal was the fact that there were chances given in the Nursery to form attachments to mother substitutes (nurses Eva, Hanni), of which they were unable to make appropriate use. The image of the nurses did not appear until after adolescence and after the relationship to the twin had ceased to be an active force. There was no reality behind the father fantasy, except the detail of the soldier's uniform worn in the war, seen at seventeen months. The actual father was a kindly, inoffensive, modest married man onto whom the heroic killer attitudes were projected from the twins' own wishes.

The other question, whether Bert's and Bill's delinquency represented an arrest in development or a regression, was answered fully by the comparison of the boys' behavior in and outside treatment with the Nursery records and the follow-up of behavior during latency. Treatment material showed that they were at the mercy of their instincts with regard to rivalry, competition, the expression of hate displaced from the twin onto other children: all this an exact repetition of their inner state of mind described in the Nursery records (p. 25f.); that they were impervious to influence by adult authority as they had been as infants (Chart 24); that they expressed their possessiveness of adults by hurting and attacking (compare Bert's attacks on the mother with the boys' behavior to nurse Eva; Charts 23, 24); that they used other persons to reproduce the twin relationship; that they had pleasure in creating chaos in their surroundings (compare Mr. Barron's report on their influence on the Hostel with the "pandemonium" created in the Nursery; p. 25); that there was fear of each other, of aggressive boys at school (Bert), of the army (Bill), but no evidence of guilt for any of their actions (compare the lack of the precursors of guilt in infancy such as the rarity of the occasions when they felt sorry for having hurt a nurse; Chart 24). Above all, the quality of their relationships remained the same: they formed attachments narcissistically, on the basis of feeling that the other person resembled themselves, or possessed qualities admired by them, rather than relationships based on cathexis with true object libido (compare here the infantile relationship to the twin with their fascination with Mr. Barron after he had impressed them by being "reckless," their friendship with Teddy boys, etc.).

On the basis of these items it may be justified to draw the conclusion that the twins' delinquency did not represent a regressive process, similar in structure to a neurosis, but an arrest and defect in personality development, i.e., in defense organization, ego control over the impulses, and in superego and ideal formation. It may also be justified to conclude that these defects are due to imperfectly developed early object relationships and undue autoerotism and narcissism developed in the twinship.

DIFFERENCES IN THE PERSONALITY OF THE TWINS

So far, for the purposes of this study, Bert and Bill were treated as if they were indeed "identical," not only in looks but in personalities as well. Actually, this was not the case; although they had many important characteristics in common, there were at the same time differences in their personalities significant for their fate, their treatment, and their future development. So far as could be ascertained, none of these personal differences was the direct result of being either first- or second-born since Bert was, in his treatment, seen to be as resentful of having a brother born in immediate succession to himself as Bill resented having been immediately preceded by one.

As shown by the Nursery records and further by the result of

Mr. Shields's inquiries, there was a gradual changeover (from Bill to Bert) in regard to physical strength and aggression toward the twin. An opposite changeover was felt to happen in Nursery times in regard to cleverness, since first Bert, then Bill were observed to have the best ideas and to initiate games. In one of the residential homes (at seven years nine months) Bert was regarded to be the "quicker thinker"; at the same time another opinion considered "Bill's schoolwork generally a little ahead of Bert." Actually, it was the psychologist's opinion that the twins were both of average intelligence, sometimes one, sometimes the other doing a little better on a formal test.[4]

There is no doubt that, so far as the use of intelligence was concerned, rivalry, competition, and the general wish to outdo the twin acted as a source of stimulation for them and proved beneficial for their school successes.

What proved to be the most portentous difference between them was Bert's greater sensitiveness and responsiveness in infancy. Initially, this was probably no more than his reaction to Bill's greater size and strength which threatened him. However this may have been, it was Bert who cuddled into the arms of nurse or mother while Bill appeared indifferent to attention (Charts 16, 18), and it was this greater gentleness which prompted the mother to take him home at four and a half years while Bill was left in the Nursery. This meant that Bert experienced, for a few months at least, the sensation of being the unrivaled eldest son in the home, preferred to his twin, and that he had a chance to develop the rudiments of normal family relations. That he had a possessive oedipal relationship to his mother at this time is suggested by two later reactions, both turned into the negative, it is true: by his murderous attacks on the mother when

[4] Age	Bert	Bill	Test
10½ yrs.	98	95	Binet (IQ)
11¾ yrs.	99	106	Binet (IQ)
12 5/12 yrs.	104	88	Thurstone's Primary Mental Abilities (Total weighted score)

she taunted him with his illegitimate birth; and by his reaction of avoidance and disgust to her pregnancy. More important still: it may have been this boost to his object libido which came to the help of his treatment by cementing the treatment alliance with Mr. Barron and lessening the narcissistic versus the object-related elements in the transference to him.

In contrast to this, Bill, as the rejected twin, showed through his later childhood more of the characteristics of the unloved "institutional" child ready to revenge himself on others, more eager to inflict pain on people or animals, found to push a boy in front of an oncoming car, inciting other children to unlawful acts, causing a bus to crash, etc. He turned the tables on his twin when he finally succeeded in inducing the parents to allow him home and keep him there for good, but at the age of almost fifteen, this was too late to make up for the missed oedipal relationship.

In contrast to Bert, Bill did not resent the mother's renewed pregnancy. Also in contrast to Bert, he could not maintain the treatment alliance with Mr. Barron and broke off his therapy abruptly, as many children or young people with institutional backgrounds are apt to do.

FOLLOW-UP

Contrary to the more pessimistic predictions which were expressed several times during the boys' treatment, their antisocial outbursts ceased after adolescence. Since the material concerning this consists exclusively of external data (in conversations, letters, etc.), it does not allow for valid conclusions as to the reasons for the change. We can only speculate what played a part in it and what significance should be allocated to the various factors.

There are external and internal circumstances to be considered in this respect. Among the former we list, with regard to Bill, his reacceptance by the family at the age of fourteen years eleven months; with regard to both boys, their bodily separation from each other which marked at the same time the breaking up of the antisocial twin gang. To the internal factors belong, above all, the effect of treatment in which the interpretation of the unconscious hostility to each other played the leading part. Since both boys were inexorably tied to each other by this unconscious hostility, the analysis of this element may have been decisive in enabling them to grow apart and to form new and positive relationships.

INFORMATION ON BILL

There is only meager information about Bill after he left his treatment at the age of fifteen years. As reported before, he had two jobs until he settled down as a bus conductor. He continued to live at home and no further complaints from the parents reached the authorities. One source of information were letters written by Bert containing the following facts about Bill: At age thirteen years four months he (like Bert) was collecting books as a hobby. At fifteen years two months "he has grown much stronger and heavier than Bert." At sixteen years nine months he "has just bought a death machine with the help of his dad— a 350 B.S.A. motor bike." At seventeen years eight months he had an accident on his motor bike; and he "has had five accidents since last November, but this one is the worst . . . he has had some stitches" in his face.

At nineteen years, Bill "is quite happy in his work. Bill is courting still and is still saving like mad to get married."

At nineteen years two months, he is reported to be engaged to his girlfriend Julia.

At twenty years nine months, Bert writes, "Bill got married to a girl called Julia. I don't know her well except that she was at school with me."[5]

---

[5] According to Mr. Barron's impression, Julia was in love with Bert at that time, a fact of which he was oblivious.

At twenty-one years, "Bill seems to like being married; he does not talk of anything else."

A second source of information was Mr. Barron himself who wrote to Bill after hearing of his engagement and received the following answer:

> I have just recently got married and was very lucky to get a house, it was offered to us so we took it, it's much better than living with in-laws.
>
> Bert has been in the Air Force for three years now and he is enjoying himself. He has been abroad quite a lot, and is in Singapore now.
>
> My mother has been a different woman this last year or two, we have got on quite well together. She is very pleased that I have got married and a house of my own, and gets on well with Julia (my wife). They have got on well together from the first time I took Julia home.
>
> My mother is very pleased to have heard from you. Give my regard to Mrs. Barron and the little ones who have grown up now.

Bill also visited Mr. Barron with his wife to introduce her, which Mr. Barron describes as follows:

> Bill makes a very good impression. He has a quiet manner and was well dressed in very good taste. He is obviously extremely pleased to have a home of his own, and his conversation was mainly about the things he had grown in his garden and the plans he has for cultivating it next. He spoke of the difficulty he had at home after his stepfather's death, and was able to give a vivid description of his mother's depression and said that although he sometimes found himself arguing with her, by and large he was able to "coax her along."
>
> He showed considerable enterprise to find a house before he married. His wife impressed me as a very nice person.

INFORMATION ON BERT

In marked contrast to his brother, Bert was not offered new opportunities to establish a real family relationship after his treatment. On the other hand, he showed the same ability to make new contacts. He selected for this partly the actual foster family where he was placed after leaving the Hostel and for the other part began to form an elaborate and constant tie to a figure in the distance whom he treated as an imaginary mother substitute.

As mentioned before, in their early years in the Hampstead Nurseries a young nurse in training, Hanni Koehler, had been assigned as mother substitute to the twins when they were twenty-one months old. She took care of both for a short time and then was chosen for Bill exclusively at the age of two years eight months to three years ten months. After the closing of the Hampstead Nurseries she had tried to keep in contact with them by sending them cards or presents for Christmas and their birthdays. She received no replies until the twins were thirteen years and three months when Bill thanked her for a Christmas present. Her correspondence with Bill ended with this. But Bert, surprisingly enough, took over from here and from then onward communicated with her with increasing frequency and intimacy, treating her quite clearly as an important person in his life. His letters, which began at thirteen years four months, i.e., when he was still in the Hostel, were written in the beginning mostly at times of stress and loneliness, for example, when Mr. Barron fell ill, later when Mr. Barron left the Hostel, when he himself started work and had not found a place to live, etc. The letters ranged over many topics such as work, foster family, his own family, and included a real concern about Hanni's doings and family members. The following are some quotations:

> [At age fifteen years two months:] When I leave school and live in digs I may never see Bill or the family again because I am in the care of the County Council.
> [At sixteen years five months, he writes about a new job as mate on a delivery van.] I have changed my job of working on the Forestry Commission . . . because I wanted to have my thoughts to myself looking at the scenery of the Surrey downs

and the countrysides of Kent, and also because I wanted to travel a bit. . . .

I would not say I was handsome, if you are judging me by that photo, I would say it was the summer air because I was on holiday.

I do get very lonely even when I am around with the other boys, I feel as if I am not one of them. I sort of doze off and when someone speaks to me, I just don't know what he is talking about, I try to keep myself to myself, sometimes I go for long walks by myself in the eve until about 10 o'clock. Sometimes I go into the café and get a drink and sit in a corner table by myself and think about all sorts of things and I don't speak to anybody. I don't really want to bother you with my loneliness. . . . P.S. I enjoy every minute of reading your letters and writing to you, but when I write I am in a sort of dream so you must excuse the spelling and writing and the mistakes.

[At sixteen years nine months, when he reports on Bill's motor bike, he says:] All the boys and girls I know asked me how long and where I got my bike, but I had to tell them it was not mine but my brother's, they said they could swear it was mine. I hope to get a motor bike soon, a much bigger one than Bill's.

At eighteen years he wrote to Hanni as well as to Mr. Barron that by the time he heard from them, he would be in the R.A.F. and had joined up for five years; that he had been thinking a long time about it before deciding to enlist. He did not yet know what trade he would want to take up, but would try for a physical training instructor. "When I come home on leave my mother and father say I can come home to stay." He had been visiting them regularly and was getting on well with them.

At seventeen years, "I went home to see my mother and family, they seemed very glad to see me."

Further letters to both reported from his R.A.F. address that he had finished his training and was off to Malta, that his stepfather had died of lung cancer but that his family had not been able to reach him as he had not given them his address, "My mother did not like that much."

There was an interruption in letters since Bert omitted to send his Malta address to Hanni; but they were taken up again at twenty when he was back in England on the point of leaving for "another 2½-years tour of duty in Malaya or Singapore."

At twenty years two months, "I spent Christmas at home and really enjoyed myself. Mum was very pleased because we all could come home and Teddy got a few weeks from R.A.F. training camp. Bill has got engaged to a girl from N."

Quotations from the letters that follow contain a surprising amount of interest in his family without any reference to the fact that he had been the one rejected by them, nor do they show any hate or rivalry for his siblings. Apart from the flow of information about Bill quoted above, he reports the following about his younger brother:

> Teddy, my younger brother, has just left school and will be entering the R.A.F. as a boy entrant. [About his little sister:] I took my small sister out for a walk. She is very sensible when crossing the road, and in her talk is very grown up. [About his mother:] Mum is not the same as she was when Dad was alive, she seems to be drawn into herself and won't get out anywhere anymore, she gets very moody at times, it is very difficult to know what to do for her.
>
> [At twenty-one years:] I always visioned my birthday at home, but it looks like I was robbed of it. . . . [He goes on to say that] everyone at home is just fine. . . . Mum has decided that she may get married again now that her children are gradually leaving her to go out and fend for themselves, Mary[6] has got herself engaged to a London policeman.
>
> [About Hanni's child, Judy, and her home he writes at sixteen years four months:] Has she any playmates of her own age to play with?
>
> [At sixteen years five months:] It is rather a funny thing you should have mentioned the way Judy pronounced my name the way she does because my landlady's little boy calls me "Bertrey." . . . It is a very kind thought of Judy's to be thinking of me that way, it had me quite taken back.

6 His younger stepsister.

[At sixteen years nine months:] . . . so glad that Judy can talk and recite nursery rhymes, it is surprising what kids of two or three come out with. My landlord's little girl of three says the most awkward things at times that you don't know how to answer them.

[At seventeen years:] Judging by the photos of your new home it looks very comfortable and warm, as you say it looks very English. . . . I hope Judy will get used to living in her new home.

The best way to get the tree down is to get some experienced men, who will chop the top branches down and work it downwards until there is nothing left.

[At eighteen years:] Is Judy at school yet and does she like it? My landlady's daughter has started school this summer and she is thrilled with it . . . give Judy a big kiss for me.

[At twenty years three months:] I hope you enjoyed your Christmas as much as I enjoyed mine, and Judy, too, all my best, give Judy a big kiss from me.

[At twenty years four months, on receiving a photo of Hanni's daughter:] Judy does look very well, doesn't she? I never expected her to be so big. I have always imagined her as a very small girl.

You never told me you were going to have another baby. You must be very happy to have a little boy and Judy will have someone to look after and spoil.

Bert also describes some events which give some clue to his reactions to his surroundings and his attitude to life in general.

[At twenty years three months:] Singapore is not quite what I expected it to be; in fact, it is totally different except for the people. For a start it is very smelly and full of diseases of every description . . . for some places are notorious for fleas, flies and violent Chinamen.

[And in another letter:] Now I find it very nice, it [Singapore] compares with London any time, the people here are very different from what I expected, they are very polite and ready to help us, but they are also ready to rob us whenever they can, it does not seem possible that these things go together, it is very educating to see them. . . . I have tried some of the Chinese foods and like them. My favorite is Masi

Gorang; if you go out to a Chinese restaurant, you will have to try some, it's delicious.

[In this same letter he also refers to] Jane, my girlfriend. [In another letter:] I have been on a two-month detachment at Gan. Gan is an island 600 miles South West of Ceylon among the Maldive Islands, it is 1½ long by ¾ wide and is used by the R.A.F. as a stepping stone for transport Command; it is spaced evenly between Singapore and Aden exactly 200 miles from each, we had a fabulous time there. The sea is nice and clear like the Med. and lots of fishing, boating, swimming and sunbathing. But there is one snag and that is, that there are no Females, to see or talk to, except one Nurse and a W.V.S. woman. I expect I will be there for Christmas as well, apart from the Female situation, it is about the best posting that the R.A.F. offer.

[And in another letter:] I have decided that I should take up a hobby, out here you have to do something or you go nuts, the hobby I have taken up is aeroplane modeling. I have alreadymade a good start on a stunt model, have flown it twice and wrecked it twice, I flew it today and it went straight into a post and broke the left wing into bits, it's great fun making them and mending them when they crash.

It looks like everyone has decided on some fighting, what with the Cuba situation and India with China. It's about time we were put on active service again like at Cyprus, it would relieve the monotony of training for it like we are always doing. I know it sounds a bit macabre and gruesome but that is how I feel, even to spend a few weeks on Jungle patrol in Malaya or Borneo would help a bit.

[Then the allusions to marrying become more frequent.] Bill writes to me ever so often, he likes married life and has managed to get a house which is very lucky for him, it is next door to his in-laws. I went to school with his wife, she is a nice person, although I do not think she has forgiven me for pulling her pigtails. I wrote a lot to Jane my girlfriend and I have no trouble in that direction. We have an understanding together that restricts neither of us while we are split up, it works, because for 4 years we have been courting and for 2½ years of that time I have been overseas. She is a wonderful girl and I hope to marry her when I get home in 1964.

[And the last letter:] I have only another 9 months to do in

Singapore and Jane is very pleased. She says that I am not going overseas again without her, so it looks like I have been given direct order. You asked me what I am going to do when I leave the Forces. Well, I really don't know, I first have not given it enough thought. I may even decide to stay in the RAF. I like the life and the travelling but I do not like the moving every two years or so, especially if I marry, it just is not fair on the woman and she won't like it when we go away for months at a time, which we do too often for the married men in the SQD. Their whole attention is not on the job half the time and that can cost someone his life. Jane would have to put up with quite a lot. So I will have to make my mind up as to whether I want to get married and settle down in civy street or stay in the forces and enjoy myself while I can, it's a difficult thing to decide as I don't think I am responsible enough yet for married life, even though Jane thinks I am.

CONCLUDING REMARKS

Quotations from Bert's letters have been given at length because of the striking contrast which emerges between the unruly, inconsiderate, antisocial boy in the Hostel and the thoughtful, sensitive, and attached postadolescent who he turned out to be. What is stressed in the letters repeatedly is on the one hand his sympathy with mother figures and their concerns (his own mother, Hanni) and on the other hand his understanding of small children and their needs, i.e., feelings which were manifestly lacking in his past (compare his attack on his mother, his hate for his younger siblings).

Another new feature in his personality is the withdrawal into himself and the enjoyment of solitude, both feelings probably possible only after separation from the twin.

It is a further interesting point to view the intense hostility of the twins to each other, as revealed in their treatment, in the light of a remark made by Bill to Mr. Barron during the follow-up visit with his wife at age twenty-one. When asked if it had been wise to separate him and Bert when it happened, he answered that he did not think so as he missed him so very much.

It is also interesting to note that, after all, the fates of Bert and Bill remained intertwined: Bill chose for his wife a girl formerly in love with Bert, while Bert chose as his "pen-mother" a woman who had been Bill's nurse much longer than his own.

Part II
Development of the Blind

Chapter 12

PSYCHOANALYTIC OBSERVATIONS OF BLIND CHILDREN

Analytic observations of the psychic development of the blind open up the possibility of examining certain issues that deserve our theoretical interest. We know that vision plays an important role in normal development. Processes connected with vision have, in the form of scoptophilia and exhibitionism, a place among the component instincts in the sexual life of men. The mechanism of identification is dependent on vision; most iden-

This paper was first published as "Psychoanalytische Beobachtungen an blinden Kindern." *Internationale Zeitschrift für Psychoanalyse und Imago,* 25:297-335, 1940. An English version, entitled "Psychic Problems of the Blind," appeared in *American Imago,* 2:43-85, 1941. The paper published here is a new translation based on the German version.

This study would not have been possible without the interest, help, and cooperation of Siegfried Altmann, Director of the Isrealitisches Blinden-institut, Hohe Warte, Vienna. Mr. Altmann not only shared with me his extensive knowledge of the blind but also gave me access to the Institute.

I also wish to thank Dr. Gabriel Farrell for granting me permission to visit the Perkins Institute in Watertown, Conn. The attitude of the teaching staff of this Institute—their untiring efforts, enthusiastic cooperation, and devotion to their work—creates an inspiring atmosphere and holds out the promise that the improvements of methods in the education of the blind which I suggest in this paper are entirely feasible.

227

tifications occur on the basis of visual perceptions. Reality testing, one of the most important functions of the ego, makes extensive use of sight.

When this sense is lacking, the child lacks elements which seem indispensable to us to normal development. It is therefore worthwhile to follow the consequences which the lack of sight has, on the one hand, on sexual development and, on the other, on character formation. Lay opinion generally holds that the blind are very cheerful, most friendly, and unaggressive, but that their love of truth is unreliable; whereas the deaf are said to be disagreeable, unfriendly, suspicious, and tending to paranoid ideas. Analytic investigation of character formation should enable us to determine whether these general statements are correct or not.

The lay opinion generally held about the blind, deriving for the most part from novels and fiction, is that although the blind have one sense less than the normal person, they compensate for this lack by having their other senses of touching, hearing, and smelling more highly developed. It would therefore only be natural to take for granted that in the education of the blind every effort has been made to stimulate these other senses.

Astonishingly, however, this conclusion does not at all coincide with the facts. In reality, the blind child is brought up precisely like the sighted child. The teaching of reading by means of Braille, of writing on specially constructed boards, and of arithmetic with special counters is obviously an unavoidable exception. For the rest, the education of the blind has not been geared to their lack of sight; on the contrary, the blind are expected to adapt themselves to normal education as far as is possible.

In order to introduce the problems with which this paper is concerned, it seems to me necessary first to present a picture of the world in which the blind child lives, especially with regard to the differences in the behavior of the environment toward the blind child, in the blind child's contact with people, in his conception formation and language development. The blind child's unconscious life is accessible to us only via the detour of his conscious one. This part of my considerations is a necessary preparation for the analytic conclusions which I subsequently intend to draw.

DIRECT OBSERVATIONS OF BLIND CHILDREN

The conscious psychic life of the blind child is built up mostly on misconceptions and misinterpretations of what he has experienced, as the following examples show.

I observed a group of children in an institution for the blind in Vienna[1] for a prolonged period of time. These children surprised me by talking of the city, the streets, the city life in the same way as seeing children. Knowing that these descriptions could not be based on their own observations, I began to listen to the children more attentively. It became clear that these blind children talked to each other about things that were completely foreign and inaccessible to them. They talked of the color of their clothes; after a day in the country, of the beauty of the mountains; but they did not mention the texture of the clothes they wore, or the sensation of the air and sun on their skins when they were on the excursion.

One day I took some of these children for a drive in the car. They asked continual questions: "Where are we going? What are we passing on the road? Are there any trees? What color is the sky? Are there any animals in the fields?" The more I told them, the more they seemed to enjoy themselves. After a while I let them get out of the car and we walked a short way along the edge of a wood. The children were of course awkward; they tripped and fell in this unfamiliar region and did not show any signs of enjoyment. I encouraged them to feel the flowers, the

[1] Israelitisches Blindeninstitut, Hohe Warte.

trunks of the trees, and the meadow, but I found it difficult to direct their attention away from my descriptions to what they were exploring themselves.

On the whole, however, this excursion made a deep impression on the children, who continued to talk about it for many days. They told the other children about what they had seen, described the animals, the woods, the fields, and the sky; that is, they repeated word for word what I had told them on the way, but they did not bring in their own observations. I could conclude only that what they had heard was evidently more important to them than what they had themselves experienced.

At another time one of these children told me about a visit to the zoo. I asked him what he had liked best. "The monkeys," was his prompt reply. "One monkey chased another one and bit it until it bled." After further questioning he admitted that he had of course not seen it himself, but that "Someone told me." I then asked him what he had heard while he was there, and received a description of sounds made by a camel and a duck. He said one could not hear an elephant, but one elephant looking for sugar had blown at the sugar and that was audible. This description was apparently based on a real sense impression which he evidently had asked to have explained afterward.

It is important to note that his first account dealt not with his own experience but with the monkey scene about which he had been informed by others. We may assume that the dramatic scene in the monkey house attracted and excited the other, sighted children who were standing around and watching, and that the blind child heard their exclamations and laughter and sensed the various other indications of their excitement. The exclusion from this excitement on the one hand aroused his envy of the sighted; on the other, he reacted to the emotional contagion by getting excited himself. We could say he behaved like a person who hears a joke he does not understand but who nevertheless laughs with the others.

Impressed by these and similar observations, I realized that these blind children were living a double psychic life. It is true that they led a life of their own that in many respects was enjoyable; and, further, that they lived in a group where all the children had the same defect, though to varying degrees. Their everyday life was adapted to their needs: they had special books, occupations, entertainment, and friendships. They competed with each other and envied each other, as normal children do. Above all, they enjoyed the security given them by the Institute, which represented school and home for them.

But in spite of all this everyone of these children realized at a very early age that the world around them was a seeing one, that he was blind, defective, and therefore an exception. It seemed clear that from that moment on the blind child's attention was focused entirely on the seeing world. They tried to imitate the sighted in every possible way, thereby adjusting to this world as far as they could. They do not for a moment forget that they are blind, but their main goal in life is to make others forget it, i.e., to cover up their blindness. In some respects this attitude can be compared to the relationship of every normal child to the adult: he, too, attempts to imitate that which at the present time is still unobtainable for him. The wish to be grown up thus corresponds, in intensity and significance, to the blind child's wish to see.

In his contact with the outer world the blind child cannot avoid being continually awkward and therefore constantly having his own incapacities brought home to him. Since blind children are often not aware of the mistakes they have made, they cannot always immediately hide them in the same way as the seeing children; they must find their own methods to cover up their inferiorities. For example, a blind child lets something drop and, though he gropes about, he still is unable to find it. The next time he will simply let the object lie instead of hunting for it unsuccessfully. If a sighted adult is nearby, he will automatically bend down to retrieve the object, thus making it unnecessary for the blind child to try to do so. The blind child learns through such experiences that his clumsiness will be less conspicuous if he makes no such attempts and that in this respect his dependence on the seeing person is less humiliating than the disclosure of his incapacity. In this way the blind child learns to make himself appear even more awkward than he really is. He makes believe that he is helpless when he really is not.

The reaction of seeing people to the blind is one which the blind meet at a very early age, and one which is apt to make them very much aware of their blindness and of being different from those who can see. The blind child's feeling of being an exception on the basis of his defect is from early childhood on constantly confirmed and reinforced by the emotional attitude that the sighted have to him. Every sighted person who is not familiar with the blind through daily contact with them meets them with shyness and embarrassment, sometimes even with dislike and repulsion. It seems to me that these very sensitive blind children react from their earliest childhood on to this unnatural behavior on the part of the adults and in the course of their development become increasingly aware of it. They realize that they are being avoided, that they are pitied because of their blindness, that people who see are revolted by it and are even afraid of them. We know that this fear—as dread of a defect in oneself—comes into play not only in regard to the blind but in regard to all cripples.

The awkwardness of a blind child and his inferior position in comparison with a seeing child are especially marked when the blind child finds himself in new surroundings or comes across new objects. It naturally takes him much longer to get acquainted with his surroundings; he has to feel the furniture, to walk the distance from one object to the other, before he can have some idea of its dimensions. Objects also have to be picked up and handled and compared with others before they are recognized and correctly identified; and the more complicated the object, the longer is the process of recognition. Many objects are never known clearly as a whole, for instance, buildings, trees or large animals, for without sight only a part can be grasped and even this often remains vague.

On such occasions the blind must become keenly aware of the enormous superiority of the sighted. Those who see can orient themselves with a single glance; without the slightest hesitation they can immediately describe their surroundings; they need not laboriously investigate each object in order to use it correctly; and they can move about in unfamiliar places without bumping into them and without giving offense. Experiences of this kind indelibly impress on the blind child's mind the conviction that the seeing are omnipotent.

This relationship between the blind child and his seeing environment gives rise to his double life, which consumes the greater part of his psychic energies. Their constantly being in contact with the world of the sighted, which differs considerably from their own, continually interferes with their capacity to adapt to life on the basis of their own limitations and abilities. The sighted persons who live in this other world move about and behave differently: they can do things that are impossible for the blind; they can talk and laugh about things of which the blind are completely unaware; they seem to criticize and ridicule the blind who try to imitate them; and they seem to shun the blind for being incapable of understanding their world.

It is only natural that the blind are curious about and full of envy of this foreign world and that they develop intense wishes to possess this sense which they lack and which obviously opens up inconceivably marvellous feelings and sensations. They try to adapt to this world as far as is possible, and make every effort to imitate as best they can the object of their envy. They attempt to attain the impossible by unsuitable means and in this process neglect their own sensory world in favor of seemingly participating in the sighted world. They speak the language of the sighted, although many words have no meaning whatsoever for them, and behave as if they recognized and understood what in reality must forever remain a mystery to them.

ANALYTIC OBSERVATIONS OF BLIND CHILDREN

I have chosen certain parts from the analysis of two blind children to illustrate specific points in the development of this double psychic life of the blind.

CASE 1

Jacob was an eight-year-old boy who had been completely blind from the first month of his life. He was small for his age and had a sickly appearance. He was sent to me for analysis because the director of the Institute was worried by his neurotic behavior. He was inhibited in his schoolwork and had difficulty in keeping up with the other children, although he often made very intelligent remarks which showed his marked powers of observation. He was often very depressed and oversensitive, feared being laughed at and criticized, and immediately withdrew from group activities when he felt he could not do them as well as the other children.

Jacob understood very quickly that analysis could help him, and before a resistance set in he was eager to come to his hours and ready to talk about himself. The course of his analysis did not differ substantially from the analysis of sighted children, but for my presentation I have selected only material that is relevant to the focus of this study.

Concept and Fantasy Formation

I shall first examine Jacob's concept formation which in many respects seems to me to be characteristic of blind children. We can distinguish three types of concepts which are grouped according to their correctness: the correct and honest ones; the misunderstood and dishonest and fantastical ones; and those that contain elements of both. I also want to bring out how his fantasy life then developed further on the basis of these conceptions.

I shall first illustrate some correct concepts.

Jacob tried to describe his idea of snow to me. "It is hard. I can tell whether it snowed when I walk on it; I can kick it with my feet. Of course, I have felt it. I have touched it on the windowsill. When it snows into your face it feels like rain, only warmer." This is a description built entirely on his own observations.

On another occasion a child was given a paint box as a present and Jacob tried to describe this object and how it is used to me: "The paint box contains little cakes; to paint you must put water on a pencil and then write with it." This description, too, is a correct rendition of his own observations.

Jacob had had a visitor. He first told me that the lady was beautifully dressed and then that she had brought him a present, a train. He added, "The engine had no string. I know it because I felt that there was none. There were hooks to hold the cars together; they were stronger than those you have on your train and the cars did not constantly come apart." He told me that the train had made a noise, which he demonstrated by banging two of the cars together. He then described how he had led his visitor into the gym so that he could be alone with her. "I took her by the hand and led her. She took the train out of something. I do not know what it was, and she put the train on the table. I know that because the train rattled as she put it down." In this description we find a combination of honesty and pretense. Jacob can of course not know whether his visitor was beautifully dressed; but the rest of his description corresponds to his own observations.

But his own observations did not suffice to give him a correct picture of what was going on. For instance, when Jacob was running his locomotive on the floor of my room, it would hit something and fall over, but the wheels would continue to turn with a buzzing sound until the spring was unwound. For Jacob this was a wonderful experience; he would beam all over and clap his hands. Misinterpreting the sound, he thought that the locomotive was racing across the floor. He would call to me:

"Look how fast it is running." In this instance, Jacob behaves like a seeing child who builds up a wishful fantasy based on a single sensory impression. The noise by itself is enough to arouse in him the wished-for image of the locomotive racing across the floor. The concept he has therefore corresponds to reality in only one point; the rest is based entirely on his wishes. But this kind of wish fulfillment is made easier for the blind child because his reality testing is impaired due to the lack of sight.

Let us compare these descriptions with the following remarks. Jacob mentioned a shopwindow: "The toys are placed behind transparent windows, you cannot touch the toys, I would so like to see them." One can feel Jacob's tremendous wish to know what a window is like, but the words he uses do not mean anything to him; they are simply taken over from the seeing world. His utterance thus gives the impression of dishonesty.

At another time Jacob told me a fantasy: "We are driving a car and meet a horse. The horse is frightened of us and in his fright he kicks the steering wheel with his hoofs." Here we are not sure whether his idea of a horse is entirely false or whether he is possibly using the horse as a symbol to express a sexual fantasy, or whether it is a combination of both. A second fantasy aids our understanding. Jacob spoke of having lived with his aunt, who had a stable. "Once I led the horse into the stable and fed it; then the horse lay down and covered himself up. He covered himself with straw all the way over his head so that he would be warm and comfortable." He related this event as though it was a memory, which to him sounded neither improbable nor in the least fantastic. Now we know that he simply has a mistaken idea of a horse; he imagines the body of the horse in accordance with the image of his own body.

Jacob met the same difficulties when he tried to understand complicated technical matters. After a drive in a car he wanted to know how the motor worked. I attempted to explain that a motor needed energy to make it run. As an example of air pressure I used the force of breath and let him blow on strips of paper, showing him how his breath blew the paper away from his mouth. For the same purpose we made paper bags; I let him blow into them and explode them, showing him the hole where the air was forced through. He got very excited and kept shouting: "I see, I see." I asked him what he meant. He repeated: "I see the hole where the air comes out." Then he continued: "With a gun you see the bullet only after it has left the gun." Another time he said: "You can see the motor in the car when it is running." Exploding another paper bag, he commented: "Now I am the motor." And still another time he said he would blow out bags until he had blown out a window. "If I am near enough to a window, it is bound to blow out." He added: "Air bites." Here one gains the impression that he really had formed some concept of compressed air and what it could do, but a few days later he tried to explode some paper bags in which he himself had punctured some holes.

Apparently, he had formed his concepts in the following way: "I see, I see" simply meant: I understand that the air comes out of the hole because I can feel this hole. His next remark about the bullet leaving the gun showed that he was capable of appropriately applying this piece of knowledge in another context. That one can see the motor when it is running evidently means only: if I can hear the motor running, surely you can see it. He can only hear action and has every reason to assume that the same is true for vision. His exclamation "I am the motor" corresponds to an omnipotent fantasy that accompanies the explosion of the paper bags. His expectation of the window blowing out is a logical sequence to his ideas of compressed air: if the air is strong enough to burst paper bags, it surely must be powerful enough to blow out the glass of a window. From this point on his thoughts take an aggressive turn: "Aid bites" seems to be based on an experience of air being bitingly cold, but he complements this notion with that of a vicious, biting animal. His subsequent attempt to explode paper bags that are full of holes makes one realize that his newly acquired knowledge is still on

very shaky ground: it can at any moment still be replaced by
his previous misconceptions. This whole chain of Jacob's thoughts
is an excellent example of the typical way in which the blind
child combines correct and incorrect conceptions; misunder-
standings; imitations of what the seeing world understands; and
the superimposition of fantasies which deal with sexual symbols
and conscious and unconscious wishful images.

Reality and wish-fulfillment elements could be distinguished
even more clearly in another remark of Jacob's which he made
on the same day that he received the train from his visitor. After
having described his impressions of how he was given the train,
he continued with the following fantasy: "The train ran into
the dining room and back again. The doors of the dining room
were open and the train went very far, through the open doors,
into the other room. It went everywhere, going faster and
faster; it bumped into the piano and took it along with it. It
went all the way to your room; you were lying in bed and snoring. I crawled into the room and screamed; at first you kept on
snoring, then you woke up." In this case Jacob acted in a way
that is characteristic of children's fantasies; he made a sudden
transition from reality to the fulfillment of a conscious wish, that
his train would run faster and faster and be more and more
powerful; and, secondly, to that of an unconscious wish, to come
to my bedroom while I am sleeping. The excitement that accompanies this unconscious wish finds its symbolic expression
in the increasing speed of the locomotive.

It is only natural that the wishful fantasies of blind children
turn again and again to the wish to see. Jacob provided the
following example of this type of fantasy. He asked me for a
photograph which I had taken of him to send to his parents. He
asked me to show him where his face was on the picture, insisted that he too could see the face, and pointed to it with his
finger. I turned the picture over and he continued to point to
the place where his face would have been if I had not turned it
over. When I expressed surprise at his persistence, he told me

that he had been to the oculist, that he had been tested, and that he could see a ray of light. The oculist had held up his hand and he had been able to see it and to count his fingers. With increasingly mounting excitement Jacob flatly insisted that he could see. He sounded so very convincing that I asked the director of the Institute to give me detailed information.

Indeed, Jacob had come to the director, too, assuring him that he could suddenly see; whereupon the director had permitted Jacob to go to the occulist and be tested. Jacob had guessed several times correctly and just as often incorrectly what was shown to him. The occulist had made no statements about Jacob's capacity to see, but since that time Jacob was convinced that he could see. Upon returning to the Institute, Jacob forced the director to test him again. The director held a flashlight up to his eyes, and Jacob said he could see it. Then the director went to another part of the room and again Jacob said that he could see it. Jacob himself had asked the director not to lean against the door, because otherwise he could tell from the noise where the light was. Finally, the director held up his hand, without the flashlight, and Jacob again maintained that he could see the light. After this examination, Jacob suddenly pulled himself up very straight and proudly declared: "Now, I can see; please, tell all the children that I can see." It was this scene that Jacob wanted to repeat once more with me. Instead of examining him, however, I explained to him how much he wished he could see and that often one believed that something one wishes for had really happened. In this way I told him why he believed he could see, but that in reality this was not so. Jacob thereupon dropped this theme and instead started playing.

This example provided by Jacob lends itself particularly well to trace in detail the elaboration and collapse of such wishful fantasies. The fantasy that he could see is in the service of warding off the intolerable reality of his blindness. The intensity with which he acts out this fantasy succeeds in convincing not only himself but even his environment. It is not clear how far he himself can still distinguish between fantasy and reality. At any rate, it would be incorrect to say that he consciously tried to deceive the doctor and the director; he even warned them not to use measures that would help him to tell where the light was. The strongest motive of his fantasy becomes clear at the end of the scene when he asks the director to tell the teachers and children that he can see. He wishes to see, and this means to him that he wants all the pupils and teachers of the Institute to stand in awe of him as a sighted person and to envy and admire him for the miracle that has happened to him.

The occurrence of such wishful fantasies as that acted out by Jacob becomes even more understandable when we consider the fact that occasionally such miracles do indeed happen in groups of blind children. Shortly after the incident described, a girl in Jacob's immediate group did in fact gain vision. She underwent an operation, remained uncertain for a while, but when the bandage was removed from her eyes, she could for the first time in her life perceive light. From then on her visual capacities improved very slowly with the help of intensive exercises. Throughout the weeks of this development the entire Institute was in a state of high-pitched excitement. The children and teachers became intensely involved in each phase of the preparation, operation, the period of uncertainty, the fears and hopes, living through them as though their own fate were at stake. The girl was everyone's heroine and everyone identified with her. The envy of the miracle that had happened to her was counterbalanced by the feeling that the same thing could happen to each one of them.

It is easy to understand that each child must feel very tempted to create such a dramatic scene, with himself as the center of attention, if reality circumstances do not succeed in bringing this about. It would nevertheless be incorrect to suspect Jacob of merely trying, consciously and forcibly, to alter reality. The analytic observations made it quite clear that the acting out of his fantasy had little or nothing to do with conscious intentions.

His acting out was driven by an unconscious motive that was sufficiently powerful to override his capacity for reality testing for the time being.

Anxieties

I now take up Jacob's anxieties which, like his fantasies, can be divided into three groups. In the first are real anxieties, i.e., above all, fear of dangers that are especially threatening to him because of his helpless situation and fears that, to a large extent, were conveyed to him directly by his parents. A second group of his anxieties is based on faulty conceptions of reality. Finally, like all children, he has anxious expectations that derive from either faulty or correct reality evaluations but then take on fantastic elaborations.

Jacob told me one day that he was very angry, so angry that he wanted to take a stone and smash a window. He then remembered: "When I was still at home, I loved to listen to stones falling down. I threw stones up onto the roof and listened to them rolling down. In this way I once broke a window and was spanked. Our house was very near the railroad." Here he is describing the enjoyment he experienced when he listened to the noise made by rolling stones, and simultaneously tells us that his pleasures had unfortunate consequences. It surely is not surprising that a blind boy throwing a stone can accidentally create damage. He does not complain about his parents for spanking him; on the contrary, he justifies their behavior by explaining that, living so close to the railroad, they had to be very careful with him. He understands that being blind, he might do many harmful and dangerous things. He can inadvertently break a window by throwing a stone; in the same way, without intending to, he might wind up on the rails where the train would run over him. His parents are therefore quite right to fear for his safety and to be very strict with him to make him cautious.

The parents' strictness and precautions evidently combined

with and extended into a whole series of real anxieties that Jacob had. He was afraid of getting, all alone, into surroundings with which he was not fully familiar, e.g., to remain in the garden without being accompanied by someone. He was afraid of electricity and gas. He avoided electric switches and warned me not to touch the gramophone; one could be killed by touching an electric wire. He told me that there was a huge gas switch in a closet in the Institute, but that he never went there. He might turn the switch on and might not be able to turn it off again as quickly as a seeing child. These are fears based on realistic concepts. He also told me that one might easily be killed by gas bombs. Only policemen would be safe because they wore gas masks. He had the idea that the gas enters the body through the open mouth. The sighted could see the gas and run away in time. Here, too, his concepts are on the whole correct, except for the admixture of a slight misunderstanding. Jacob understands that sight affords the possibility of recognizing and avoiding dangers, and of somehow protecting oneself in time.

Superimposed on these realistic anxieties were other anxious expectations that clearly bore the stamp of neurotic anxieties. When he went down the stairs, he was afraid that someone would come up behind him and push him down. When he was walking on the sidewalk, he was afraid that something or someone would come up from the street and push him down.

His fears of animals were restricted to two types: horses and moles. He was afraid of horses because he had heard that they could bite. With regard to his fear of moles, however, I would assume that the choice of this animal as an object of anxiety was a symbolic one and was probably based on the fact of its blindness.

Jacob also described a fear with which we are familiar in neurotic children who see, but which is evidently magnified by the lack of vision. He feared that, without his knowing about it, someone might be in the room and overhear what he was saying: "It might happen that Mary is in the room. I know she is not here, but she could be here and I would not know it. I just now have the feeling that she is here." In this way he is attempting to express his feeling that he could sense whether or not someone was present, but that, having no means of verifying his impressions, he found it very difficult to disbelieve his feeling that someone was watching him. In this instance one can see very clearly how the inability to test reality by means of sight facilitates and intensifies the fear of being observed.

This fear of being observed is closely related to another anxiety, the fear of the toilet, which manifested itself especially during Jacob's visits to my apartment. He became very reluctant to use my toilet, which was locked with a key, unlike the Institute's toilet, which was shut with a bolt. He thought a bolt worked much better in shutting out the external world. He feared that someone was watching him while he was on the toilet. Here there was a link to reality: he had heard of bathrooms with windows through which the teachers could look in to see when the children were finished. At the same time he was afraid that someone in the waiting room might hear him when he was passing wind or a stool in the toilet. Here he clearly shows how his conceptions of the omnipotence and omnipresence of the sighted have been extended to include hearing and smelling. His anxiety, however, is in no way different from the imaginary anxieties of sighted children who fear that God can see everything they are doing under their bedclothes at night.

It is more surprising to find the well-known fear of darkness in a blind child; yet Jacob very convincingly described his fear of the nightly darkness. I responded by telling him that, being unable to distinguish between light and darkness, he was obviously repeating something he had heard from seeing children. But he persisted in describing in great detail the anxious feelings that settled over him when the lights were turned off at night, when everyone was quiet, and there were no sounds. In the middle of the night there were no noises, but one could hear them again in the early morning. He was afraid of going to the bathroom as long as everything was quiet. He waited until the first street car went by, and the waiting was dreadful. Thus, what Jacob calls his fear of darkness is in reality a fear of stillness, but in every other respect it is identical with the nightly fear of sighted children.

Jacob was afraid of going into the dining room at night because a ghost might jump at him and frighten him. When he was in bed at night and heard a horse coming up the steep road, he feared it might climb up the side of the house, come through the window, and run over him. At night he was also afraid of volcanoes and tornadoes. He imagined that a witch outside his window could magically make volcanoes explode and thus destroy everything.

While this type of symbolic and neurotic fears can scarcely be distinguished from the anxieties of sighted children, there exists a fear that is specific to the blind and that, unlike in the case of sighted children, can dominate the blind's entire lives: that is the fear of being left alone. Jacob was continually afraid of being left alone, that something dreadful would happen to him if he were left without a seeing person to protect him. On several occasions I had the opportunity to observe him in such a panic-like state. This usually happened when the person who brought Jacob to his analytic hour decided to do some shopping on the way to the office. Before entering a store, he would place Jacob on the street, with his back to a wall, and tell him to stay right there. And Jacob would stay, pressed against the wall, completely immobile, full of fear that his escort would forget about him and not return, or fearing that something would come up from the street and knock him over.

Such situations show the extent to which the blind feel dependent on those who are taking care of them; the blind feel they are completely at the mercy of the seeing and fall into a state of utter helplessness and despair when they are forsaken and abandoned to meet the real and fantasied dangers alone.

Jacob developed a whole series of ideas and fantasies concerned exclusively with overcoming this fear of being left alone. He wanted a dog which would see for him. In fantasy he had such a dog; it would always stay with him, lead him wherever he wanted to go so that he would never again need a human being and would never again be lonely. If anyone wished to do him any harm, his dog would protect him, bite the assailant, and chase him away.

While this fantasy contains many realistic elements—we know there really are such dogs trained to lead and protect the blind—we are forced to admit that all children have fantasies of this type. In them a large and feared animal, a father symbol, is changed from an object of anxiety to a protector who will henceforth shield the child from all dangers and ward off all attacks on him.

Jacob found other ways of coping with his fear of loneliness and these decisively influenced his attitude to the outer world. He became an avid collector of postcards, stamps, and all kinds of pictures, continually begging for new contributions to these collections. This seemed to me a very extraordinary thing for a blind child to do. At first I could not understand what pleasure he could be deriving from such a collection. He learned to recognize the pictures from descriptions he remembered and could distinguish between them in terms of some minute peculiarity, a tiny scratch, a bent corner, or a small tear; but at best they could be of value only in competition with other collections. As far as the stamps were concerned, he had no way of telling them apart and I was baffled by his interest in them.

But gradually I realized that Jacob's passion for collecting did not serve the functions usually connected with this activity. He collected not for himself but for his teachers and the seeing children in the Institute. He was giving all the things he had so carefully and enthusiastically collected to others, though not to his closest friends and not always to the same persons. Thus, his presents were not a sign of friendship but rather a way of wooing and bribing people. He understood that he needed the seeing adults and children and that they would be more inclined to do something for him if he could do something for them. By giving presents he strengthened his sense of security; he bribed people in the hope that they would lead him, take care of him, and protect him from dangers. He thus used the sighted in the same way as his imaginary dog: they are his eyes, and in order to share their capacity to see he is ready to do everything to gain their favor.

In this context it is of interest that Jacob was unable to refuse anything that was asked of him by a seeing child, and, without any protest, would give away his most treasured possessions. He could not afford to incur anyone's displeasure and anger and thus possibly lose their help. This danger loomed larger than any other consideration.

This is a character trait which I have found in all the blind children I have had the opportunity to observe. It is natural that the blind, despite all their efforts to make themselves independent, always remain dependent on the help of others. There is a multitude of things that they cannot ever do alone. True, they learn to read, but only Braille; they will never be able to read street signs, public notices, danger signs, etc. They do hear all sort of noises, but have to rely on others to explain unaccustomed noises to them. Many events that happen around them remain completely unintelligible to them; for example, they realize that an accident has occurred in the street, but only because people are excitedly talking about it; to understand what took place they require explanations from the sighted.

In the Institute where Jacob lived the blind children valued children according to the amount of sight each possessed. For example, Jacob told me that in the garden he preferred to play with children who could see, even if they could see only a little, because they could help him and lead him around. But if one just wanted to talk to somebody, it did not matter whether he could see or not. Not only for Jacob but for all totally blind children, it was very important to keep on friendly terms even with those other children who were a little more fortunate than they were. This was made easier by the children who could see a little. Being very proud of their superiority and even boasting of it, they were very ready to help the completely blind child in any way they could. The fact that they could give aid represented a welcome proof of their superior abilities.

This description of the blind child's character development, toward dependence on and submission to those who can see, points to a possible explanation of their apparently contented, cheerful, and unaggressive disposition, which seems so little suited to their unfortunate fate. It is possible that in their constant attempts to win the favors of the external world, the blind succeed in repressing all those tendencies and traits which would be likely to alienate those they need. The fear of losing the object's love is one of the reasons for the repression of aggression, but in the blind it is further reinforced by a very pronounced fear of the consequences of their own aggression, as the following observation illustrates.

While playing ninepins, Jacob once hit me with the ball. Until I mentioned it, he had been quite unaware of it, but then he became very frightened and upset. He behaved like someone who is overwhelmed by the breakthrough of unconscious aggressive impulses. Evidently, not knowing about the consequences of his action here takes the place of not knowing about the existence of aggressive impulses.

On another occasion, Jacob's teacher gave the children a few canaries. Jacob was delighted, but on reflection he decided he would not feed the canaries when the teacher was away. "I might squeeze them to death. When the teacher is away the children will all crowd around the birds and they will surely be killed." It is not too far-fetched an assumption that this was the expression of an unconscious death wish against the birds. But he had more reason to fear its realization than normal children

do. Since he had less control over his actions than they, it was
entirely possible for him to kill the birds without noticing it.
The fear of his own uncontrolled aggression governed all his
relations to other people. Like all blind children, he was extraordinarily cautious in his actions and precisely because of his
anxiety extremely inhibited in all spontaneous expressions of
aggression.

His manner of playing ninepins illuminates his attitude to
aggression with particular clarity. I placed the ninepins at the
end of a long table, and put wooden blocks along each side to
make an alley for the balls. Walking from one end of the table
to the other, Jacob would feel the balls, roll them, and be very
pleased when the ninepins fell down. He himself introduced
a number of inventions to make the game more complicated. He
called a large ninepin the king, the next smaller one the queen,
and the little ones the children. He was especially delighted
when he hit the king. He even succeeded in rearranging the pins,
but he had to be very careful not to knock down the other pins
in the process. Sometimes he would say to me: "I cannot see
and therefore it takes me so much time to do it; please, you
arrange them." Occasionally he told me what to do: "Throw the
ball in the direction where you can see the pins." At other times
he even asked me not to roll the ball back to him but to put it
in his hand, "because I cannot see where it is when it falls
down." Suddenly he began to do the same thing with me, hand-
ing the ball back to me and putting it in my hand. In other
words, he treated me as though I also were blind, but, noticing
it, he said: "Shut your eyes and throw the ball with your eyes
shut." But then I never succeeded in hitting the ninepins—to the
great delight of Jacob, who was very pleased that he was better
at this than I was. He then wanted me to feel his toys, took my
hand and put it on several objects, or simply demanded: "Feel
it." Apparently, he has suddenly succeeded in turning his aggression to me: if I am blind as he is, he can finally feel superior
to me.

CASE 2

Sylvia was almost four years old when I saw her for the first time. She was well developed for her age, had a charming manner, and a very expressive animated face. She had beautiful dark brown eyes which did not give the impression of being sightless.

Her parents were Polish Jews. Her father was a leatherworker who made and sold leather straps; her mother worked as a charwoman several times a week.

Sylvia had been blind since her birth, or since a few days after her birth. Her condition was diagnosed as blennorrhea, an inflammation of the conjunctiva caused by a gonorrheal infection at birth. A country doctor had urged the mother to take the child to Vienna where something could be done for her eyes. The mother accepted this advice. The oculist recommended surgery in the hope of making it possible for the child to differentiate light from dark. But soon after she was taken to the hospital, Sylvia came down with scarlet fever and had to be transferred to another hospital. At the end of six weeks she was returned to her mother. By that time the idea of eye treatments had been dropped, despite the mother's urgings. Instead, Sylvia was admitted to the Jewish Institute for the Blind, where I had been working. Sylvia was far younger than any other child there, but her charming, winning personality and her unusual intelligence induced the director to accept her. He knew very well that sending her back to the little Polish village would deprive her of all hope for further mental and physical development.

As the youngest child in the Institute, she was given a great deal of attention and was much indulged in, to which she reacted, surprisingly, with natural good manners and great friendliness. She proved her intelligence by rapidly learning all the languages she came in contact with. At home she had spoken only Yiddish; during the six weeks she had been hospitalized, she became fluent in German; and shortly after her entrance into the Institute, she also picked up Polish from the Polish-speaking children. After the first week she knew the names of all the children in the Institute. Almost every day she learned new songs; her hearing was excellent and she had a very sweet voice and thus found many willing teachers. She had a large vocabulary and conversed with ease on many topics. The listeners were constantly amazed by her great familiarity with many cities and many different countries.

Sylvia did not come to me, as Jacob did, because of neurotic difficulties. She appeared to be quite normal and in no need of analysis. Her visits to me initially served only the purpose of analytic observations. I had intended to refrain almost completely from making any interpretations and to restrict myself entirely to comparing her development with that of seeing children of the same age. Nevertheless, my contact with her developed very much like that we know to be characteristic of the situation in all child analysis, in which the material proceeds from the surface of consciousness to the deeper unconscious layers.

Real Anxiety and the Need for Security

Sylvia's mother was devoted to her child and tried in every way to protect her. She always carried her about and taught her the necessity of staying where she was placed so that she would not come to any harm. When her mother left the house, Sylvia was forced to sit for hours on a chair and wait until her mother returned, which she did without protest. Her mother did not give her anything to play with because she was afraid Sylvia might hurt herself; she was especially afraid Sylvia might stick something into her eyes. She did not allow her to crawl on the floor, probably because she feared that Sylvia might get dirty.

The result of this training was that Sylvia could walk only when somebody held her hand. She cried out with fear the moment her hand was let go. When she first came to me, she sat on a low chair in front of a table that had toys on it. At first she would not even lean forward to touch the toys. With great anxiety she resisted all attempts to put her on the floor. She felt secure only on a high chair, far away from the floor. She explained to me that the floor was dirty, that she could fall down and hurt herself—even that the floor might kick her. These notions obviously were remnants of her mother's warnings not to leave the chair.

Whenever it was necessary to leave Sylvia alone for a while, she made absolutely sure not to be left standing without support. She insisted on either sitting on a chair or leaning against a wall. Such places chosen by the adults apparently gave the child some semblance of security. The voluntary confinement contributed to her sense of protection; chair and wall were safety zones, whereas the unknown and unfamiliar surrroundings were full of threatening dangers. A seeing child will gain a comparable sense of security by looking at the familiar objects around him.

Sylvia invented other ways of strengthening her sense of security and easing her mind: left standing or sitting, she would put her arm around her neck and hold herself. If no one was there to hold her, she held herself. That is to say, she took over the role of the protector and, with the help of this identification, she alleviated her own anxiety.

Similar measures enabled her gradually to learn to walk in the course of half a year. One day the other children suddenly discovered that Sylvia was walking alone in the garden; they formed a ring around her and expressed their admiration. In a state of intense excitement, Sylvia had taken one hand to grasp the wrist of her other hand, thus leading herself around in a circle. She repeatedly mentioned that a fox terrier was leading her around. This first attempt to walk took place in the afternoon and she insisted on walking incessantly until her bedtime. In her bedroom upstairs she continued to walk and to feel every object she encountered. The next morning she woke very early and immediately tried to walk, but cried bitterly in the belief that she had forgotten how to do so. She calmed down only when she again managed to lead herself by her hand. She continued to walk about in this manner for several days. In this, we can clearly discern the mechanism by which she wards off anxiety. She identifies herself with the person who led her about; feeling the pressure on her wrist, she no longer feels alone and now feels protected as before.

Sylvia used the same mechanism not only to master anxiety but also to repeat pleasurable experiences originally involving others. For example, she played a game with her hands, in which one hand was her uncle and the other hand herself. With the Sylvia hand leading the uncle hand, she said: "I am leading my uncle." Or she would take something from the uncle hand and put it into the hand representing herself, announcing: "My uncle gave me a present."

Relations to Inanimate Objects

With the decrease in Sylvia's fears and anxieties, her attitude to inanimate objects began to improve. I had initially picked out several toys for her to play with: a table, a chair, a dog and a cow, doll dishes, and a doll which was always dressed in the same clothes. She recognized the table, chair, and dishes; and she knew the two animals as such, but could not distinguish the cow from the dog. The most treasured toy was the doll, which she immediately called "mummie" and with which she played a great deal. She learned to undress the doll, but that was all. She continued to mistake the doll's arms for its legs, and vice versa; she was unable to find its face and frequently searched for its mouth on other parts of the doll's body. The only thing she could identify instantly was the doll's hair, perhaps because it was real hair. On the whole, however, she did not really play with the doll or any other toy. She enjoyed picking it up and swinging it back and forth, or rhythmically knocking it against the table. Such rhythmic movements are frequently found in the blind, who either sway their own bodies or swing an object to and fro.

Acoustic Perceptions

As far as the sense of hearing was concerned, Sylvia was extraordinarily attentive to noises. Often she suddenly stopped her play, sat quite motionless, listened. Usually it was not difficult to determine what had attracted her attention: a bird call, people talking in the street, a newsboy calling out the papers. On these occasions I did not have the impression that she was listening more intently than she usually did. On the contrary, I frequently called her attention to noises which she apparently had not heard. At other times her acute sensitiveness to noises was astonishing.

She would often surprise me by asking: "What did you brush off your dress?" when I had done no more than touch the material; "Are you tired?" when I had leaned back in my chair. Or: "You wiped your mouth, didn't you?" "What are you writing?" Faint inconsequential noises and very slight movements had far more significance for her than they do for sighted children. Once she held the stem of a flower in her hand and said she was making "sash." It took me a while before I realized that the noise she was making by squeezing the juicy stem between her fingers was very aptly described as "sash." Children who see do, of course, frequently make similar observations, especially where pleasurable activities are involved. Nevertheless, one could say that Sylvia grasped, by means of hearing, a whole series of events that normal children would have understood simply by looking.

Sense of Smell

With regard to the sense of smell, there is no question that Sylvia attempted to use it as a substitute for seeing to the extent that her environment did not interfere with this. The blind, and sighted children too, are again and again taught to refrain from smelling things and admonished not to mention odors and smells. For example, when Sylvia's mother was asked whether Sylvia liked to smell things, she avoided an answer with obvious embarrassment. We can be sure that in the past she had frequently scolded Sylvia for showing an interest in smells. The very nice woman who brought her to me every day was shocked when Sylvia took her hand, smelled it, and said it smelled nice.

Sylvia spontaneously divided people into those who smelled good and those who smelled bad. When she liked someone, she took his hand, smelled it, and with great affection remarked: "Oh, you smell so good." Once I heard her say to a specially favored person: "You smell as good today as you did the last time I saw you." When she felt that someone was angry with her, she maintained that that person smelled bad.

When Sylvia was first placed in the Institute, her mother was not allowed to visit her because it was thought that this would make it harder for her to get used to the Institute. One day, however, the mother accompanied Sylvia's uncle, who paid a visit to Sylvia. The mother planned to remain perfectly quiet in order not to give her presence away. As soon as Sylvia entered the room, she became quite agitated and immediately asked: "Where is my mother? I know she is here; I can smell her."

Sylvia also applied this classification to objects whose smell we do not notice. The wall smelled bad; pillows had no odor at all; tulips had an awful smell. Apparently, she was repelled by the clammy-wet feeling of the tulip's stem and displaced her disgust to the odor. She did not recognize a rose by its fragrance but immediately knew what it was when I put it in her hand. Similarly, she recognized a lily by the shape of its leaves. A little later I tried to teach her to recognize several flowers by their distinctive odors, but she found it easier to recognize things by touching them.

Tactile Perceptions

Her sense of touch was remarkably little developed. One reason for this was the lack of early training. In her overanxious cautiousness the mother had prevented Sylvia from all play with objects. Another important reason was a habit she had developed: she used one of her hands almost exclusively for rubbing her eyes. This behavior had assumed almost ticlike and compulsive proportions. All other activities such as holding and feeling objects could be carried out only with the other, unoccupied hand. The touching of objects seemed to give her little pleasure; she had constantly to be invited and encouraged to do so. Yet she was capable of stringing beads, undressing her doll, and, with much help, putting its cap and shoes on again. Very slowly she learned to take off her own shoes, attempting to pull the laces through the eyelets. After she had been visiting my room for several months, she began to touch the things in my room. She recognized the objects which she used every day— furniture, dishes, books, a pocketbook. All other objects remained strange. She called a statue of a man a tree; a radiator, a carriage; a lock on the door, a hook.

If one closely follows the clues she uses for naming objects, they turn out to be correct. We are astonished by her behavior only because our visual associations are so very different from the associations she makes to what she touches. For Sylvia this period of misnaming objects is a transitional stage during which she learns that most objects are not what they appear to be at the very first moment. With the decrease of her inhibiting anxieties, the sense of touch became increasingly more useful. For instance, a year later she noticed that my hands were rough and advised me to use some cold cream. She also mentioned the veins on my hands. By that time she had become quite adept at feeling objects with the tips of her fingers, using an almost imperceptibly light touch.

In addition to the usual sense perceptions, Sylvia began to show an awareness of the nearness of objects. For example, sitting on a chair, Sylvia let me push her around, a game she called "playing train." Sitting with her hands in her lap, she would suddenly stretch out her hands when we came near a piece of furniture and say: "Something is there, what is it?" While we are familiar with this ability in the blind, we do not know how they achieve it. Several authors attribute these and similar perceptions to skin sensations, especially in the forehead, which is supposed to be very sensitive to changes in the pressure of air; other authors speculate that acoustic impressions are involved.

Orientation

The blind child's difficulties of orientation in new surroundings were especially clearly shown by Sylvia when early in the summer I moved to a house in the suburbs. During her first visit Sylvia was very excited, repeatedly asked for confirmation that she was in a strange place, kept on saying the name of the place as if to impress it on her memory, and over and over again told herself about all the new things she had encountered on the new route to my place. Apparently, by clinging to words and names, she found it easier to orient herself. But her coming upon a blanket which we had used in the city suddenly plunged her again into deep doubts about whether we were not at the old place after all. As if under a compulsion, she had to repeat all questions and replies over and over again in order to explain the change of place to herself.

On the other hand, she had no difficulty in quickly finding her way again when I moved back to my city apartment at the end of the summer. On the very first day she walked straight to the chair, which she found in its customary place, and exclaimed: "Here is our express train."

We generally assume that blind adults have a good sense of spatial orientation. Observations of blind children permit us to follow the development of this ability through the many efforts and difficulties. For example, while I was in the country house I took Sylvia up a flight of stairs to my room every day. She never learned where the steps began or where they ended, although she was very interested in them, especially because they were circular, which she called "funny steps." After she had learned to walk by herself and could get about the room alone, she often lost her way. She could not find her way from a table to the sofa which was only two yards away. She usually started on a rug in the middle of the room; but the moment she stepped off this rug, she knew that she had lost her way and would try with her feet to find the rug again.

In the case of Sylvia, it is of course possible that her entire attention was taken up by the problem of walking alone, so that she had little left to give to the task of orienting herself. It is also possible that her wish to be led and protected stood in the way of her acquiring a better sense of orientation. I observed other blind children who completely lost their previously acquired sense of orientation when they were under the pressure of anxiety or excitement. Evidently, spatial orientation without the help of vision requires great concentration, which can be achieved only in a state of psychic equilibrium that is undisturbed by emotional pressures. On the other hand, the sense of spatial orientation can also be interfered with by the child concentrating his affects on an adult, as was the case with Sylvia.

Attitude to the Outer World

Sylvia's relationship to adults was in many ways similar to that of Jacob. The most striking character trait in Sylvia was her great friendliness toward everyone, of which the following is a good example:

I was playing a game in which I threw blocks a certain distance away and invited Sylvia to listen where they fell down so that she could retrieve them. I soon noticed that she perceived the noise of the falling object only when it landed very close to me. Her concentrated attention was so exclusively directed to my person and everything connected with me, that the rest of the room and the various noises in it seemed hardly to exist for her. This exclusive focusing of attention on me resembles the normal infant's attitude to his mother in his first intimate relation to her (see Chapter 4).

I had arranged for Sylvia to see a special teacher several times a week, who was primarily concerned with developing her sensory awareness in order to counterbalance the almost purely intellectual stimulation which she was getting at the Institute. I arranged for their first meeting to take place at my house. When I told Sylvia that this teacher was coming, she became cross and upset. She did not want to know anything about this teacher and did not want her to come. When this lady actually arrived, Sylvia gripped my hand very tightly, and did not let it go throughout the course of our joint conversation. At the same time, however, she was most friendly, talked continuously to her, asking her what she would teach her and acting as if she were delighted at the prospect of going with her. The teacher could only feel convinced that Sylvia was very much looking forward to being with her, and I should have thought the same if the pressure of Sylvia's hand had not informed me differently. The same process was repeated before the first lesson for which the teacher came to fetch Sylvia from my house. Sylvia became agitated and apprehensive, but said: "Please, don't tell her that I do not want to go with her; she might be unhappy about it." With the teacher's actual appearance Sylvia's behavior changed completely: she hugged the teacher, wanted to touch her entire body, and asked to go with her at once.

This excessive friendliness is obviously a reaction formation and serves to ward off her anxious and hostile feelings. Instead, she identifies with the object of her hostile thoughts and, on the basis of this identification, then becomes unhappy herself when someone refuses to go with her. Like Jacob, Sylvia has already grasped the importance of keeping people well disposed toward her.

This sudden turning toward a person who until then had been rejected is instructive in still another respect: the moment Sylvia let go of my hand and turned to the new teacher, it was as if I had ceased to exist for her. She was fully absorbed by this new relationship, and whatever had preceded it was for the moment blotted out.

Such observations can be made with almost all blind children. Similar to the deaf or hard-of-hearing person, the blind need a great deal of psychic attention to maintain their contact with another person. The effective tie to the object cannot dispense with the perception of the other person's reactions. Whenever one sense is lacking, more attention has to be concentrated on those that are left. For this reason relationships of the blind seem in many cases to be one-sided since in a given situation they can focus only on a single person or a single occupation. It is difficult to determine whether this process occurs only on the level of sensory perception or whether it also includes their affective life. I shall return to Sylvia's emotional object relations when I discuss Sylvia's instinctual and affective life.

Concept Formation

Sylvia's excellent intellectual development showed up primarily in her rich thought processes and her large vocabulary. The latter was so far in advance of her age that in many instances one must suspect that she used words without understanding their meaning. One day, after she had used the word "jealousy," I asked her what it meant. At first she thought she didn't know, but then immediately talked about not liking it that Jacob too came to see me; she would prefer to be the only one who came to me. A moment later she stated that a teacher told her that Jacob had died.

She talked of the darkness. "It is dark; a room is dark, here [she meant at my place] it is light. I can see." This would seem to indicate that the concept of "darkness" had a special emotional connotation for her. What "dark" really meant to her could of course not be determined.

At another time she told me: "My mother sees; my father sees; Sylvia, too, can see." I explained that she was blind, to which she replied: "I can see." Here she was using denial, the same mechanism we found in Jacob, but she nevertheless had some awareness that her mother and father had a sense more than she did.

She wanted to read. I told her that later on she would learn to read like the other children in the Institute, but that did not satisfy her. She wanted to read my books and then asked me: "Am I blind, what is blind?" She had understood that she was blind, i.e., that she could not do a number of things that others could do. Here her understanding stopped.

Once when she was at her special teacher, a sighted girl of the same age came in and sat down at the table with her. Sylvia picked up a toy from the table and held it out to her. "Look at this, is it not beautiful?" This indicated that she was already able to appreciate the sighted child's capabilities.

At another time she told me that her uncle had taken a photograph of her to send to her father. When I asked her what a photograph was, she answered truthfully: "a piece of paper." A little later she begged me for this photograph, asking: "Isn't she beautiful?" Then she added "It is made of paper; no, of cardboard. What is on it? Her photograph?" She then took it and rubbed it against her eyes. "Now I have taken a photograph." She knows that a photograph has something to do with eyes and believes that eyes and picture must touch to produce a photograph: This sequence of behavior affords us some insight into her real conceptions. The question "Isn't she beautiful?" simply indicates the tremendous effort she is making to adapt herself to the thinking of the seeing.

A few additional examples:

She mentioned a store window. "It is a room with many things in it." She asked whether she could tear up a pencil and when I said no, she wanted to know what could be torn. When I gave her a piece of paper she tore it into shreds, showing that she knew the meaning of tearing. She called a green wooden rabbit silvery and shiny, showing that these words had no meaning for her except by association, i.e., she had heard these words used in connection with other objects.

Several times during the summer when Sylvia was with me I had the opportunity to observe her during a thunderstorm. At first she acted as though she did not notice it, asked for a book and pretended to read it to me, but she read a story about a thunderstorm. She then asked me whether it was a big bird, whether it had a mouth, whether the rain came out of its mouth, and whether the storm could walk. When there was a very loud clap of thunder she became frightened and buried her head in my lap. She begged me not to look out of the window, but immediately noticed it when I turned my head slightly to look out. Full of fear, she said: "You shouldn't look out." I asked her what she meant. "You shouldn't look with your eyes," she replied. She then took her doll and placed it on her lap facing her, and bent her head as if she were looking at it. She then turned toward me as if she were looking at me. "Now I am looking at you." She put her doll on a little toy piano and announced: "My doll is looking at the piano." She leaned over the doll as if she herself were looking, then asked for a picture book and read poems (she had memorized) to the doll. These examples show that she could guess from their position that people were looking at something and that she could use the most minute clues as an indication of their having changed positions. She also understood that people used their eyes to write, and demonstrated her understanding by asking for a pencil and paper and beginning to scribble like normal children; however, she changed over to Braille after a while.

One day Sylvia was very much afraid when she heard a dog barking outside the house. Half crying she said: "The dog will beat me, he is angry with me because my hair is untidy." She showed me with her hand how the dog would beat her. At another time she heard a cock crowing and asked whether it was tied up. In her mind, a horse consisted of a head, a tail, eyes, hands and fingers. Her concepts of animals are reminiscent of Jacob's idea of a horse, which he imagined in terms of his idea of the human body. Sylvia's idea of the tied-up cock is

based on a confusion with dogs, but then she also thought of
dogs as human beings like herself. So far she has had little
opportunity to learn about the differences between the various
animals or between animals and men, and for this reason simply
builds up her conceptions on the basis of what she is familiar
with and knows about the human body.

It is quite striking that she did much the same with inanimate
objects. She wanted to know whether a lamp could speak and
whether the lamp wore a hat (she meant of course the lamp-
shade). Although she used a streetcar every day, she asked
whether a streetcar had hands. One day she complained about
the wind having blown off her hat, and demanded a piece of
string to tie up the wind; someone probably suggested that she
tie up her hat, but imagining the wind as a person, she thought
it would be better to tie up the wind so that it would leave her
alone. Even such abstract concepts as winter, summer, noise
were persons whom she could take to bed with her. In the
course of her frequent explorations of my room, she once found
a pair of tweezers on a table. She became terribly excited, repeatedly opened and shut them, and was convinced that she was
holding a bird in her hand. The open points reminded her of
a bird's beak, and this one detail was enough to fire this child's
fantasy and to conjure up the image of a whole bird.

This behavior is characteristic of all blind children. The
recognition of objects is a very difficult task for them; therefore
they begin to make things easier for themselves: having recognized a single characteristic of an object, they stop all further
exploration and instead let their fantasy activities take over to
fill the gap. On the one hand, this results in a continuous stimulation of fantasy activities—and it is this factor that accounts
for the richness of their fantasy life. On the other hand, it also
leads to the incorrectness of their realistic thought processes,
which in turn is the true reason for what so frequently is called
the blind person's lack of truthfulness.

The blurring of differences between the world of humans

and the world of animals, on the one hand, and between animate and inanimate objects, on the other, reminds one of the fables, which play such an important role in children's literature. The normal child uses personified animals and objects as a transparent disguise for playing out his conflicts, which in an undisguised form would induce too much anxiety. But his use of displacement differs from that of blind children. The normal child displaces his problems with the most important persons in his environment to animals and things, thus placing them in a realm a little removed from his own. The blind child, on the other hand, by virtue of his reduced sense perceptions and his more tenuous contact with the outer world, faces different developmental conditions: as a consequence his thinking remains egocentric for a far longer period than the sighted child's. His concepts of objects are therefore determined less by perceptions of the external world than by his own bodily sensations and images.

In this context I should like to refer to an interesting study on the plastic works of the blind by Ludwig Münz and Viktor Löwenfeld (1934). On the basis of experiments carried out at the Jewish Institute for the Blind in Vienna, the authors demonstrate that in their Gestalt concepts the blind rely far more on the inner perceptions of their own muscular movements than on the impressions derived from touching external objects.

Sylvia furnished further proofs for this assumption in her ability to imitate, with the professional skills of an actor, the posture and the facial expressions of other people. She changed her voice, depending on whether she spoke of her father or her mother. Talking about her grandmother, she would go about the room bent over and trembling, giving a perfect portrayal of a very old woman. The first achievement was of course derived from acoustic impressions, while the latter can probably be explained by the fact that in touching her grandmother's body Sylvia felt the trembling. But then she even imitated my facial expression, began to smile like me, and to adopt some of my other expressions. Here there evidently must have been a certain connection between moods and the accompanying bodily sensations which she experienced on her own body, then transferred to the other person, and subsequently reproduced again in her own body.

Sylvia's Instinctual and Emotional Life: Her Relationship with Her Mother

When Sylvia first came to the Institute she did not appear to miss her mother very much. She was almost continually entertained by the teachers and children and was hardly ever left alone. Yet there were times when she asked to be put on a windowsill, and she was content only when her wish had been fulfilled. At first this behavior appears to be unintelligible, but it is not very difficult to explain: she must have been recalling the time when she had scarlet fever and was hospitalized in the ward for contagious diseases and her mother was only allowed to look at her through a window. By sitting on the windowsill she attempted to re-create the feeling of her mother's nearness. And when she spoke of going back home to visit her parents, she said: "They are certainly sitting at the window and looking out to see whether I am coming."

In her sessions with me thoughts of her mother certainly predominated. When I gave her a doll, she at once named it "Mummie," and from then on used the doll to represent either herself or her mother in her play. She told me that the doll was calling her, but she would not come and get her—surely an admonition which her mother had given her. Or she suddenly banged the doll against the table, saying: "Look, how she is carrying on." She played that she was going out with her mother, that they were taking a trip together. She asked the doll whether her eyes hurt, in a tone of voice full of the love and concern that her mother had expressed to her. She informed me that Mummie would soon be able to walk alone, and that Mummie was going to make every effort to be able to walk alone. When I praised her for having accomplished something, she suddenly became very excited and said: "Now I can go to my real mother." In all these instances, the doll clearly represented herself, but at other times the "mummic" doll was her mother.

With the help of this doll Sylvia acted out scenes from her past or wishes that pertained to the future. For example, she said: "Mother is going to bring me something beautiful." And then she took the doll up on her lap, kissed and hugged it, calling it "my beautiful mummie."

One day she complained that she did not like being at the Institute: "I only like to be here because my mummie is here." At that time the mother doll had become something very real for her. She then made up a game in which the doll walked over the table: "I am coming to you; I walk with my feet very slowly; I am already with you. How are you?" Then she and the doll lay down on the sofa and together they went to sleep.

At a much later time she invented a game with a ball, which she called her child. She would throw the ball away and become very upset and unhappy if she could not immediately find it. When she finally retrieved it again, she kissed and hugged it, but could not resume the game: she was too afraid of losing her dear child. Instead, she took the ball and lay down on the sofa, tightly clutching the ball in her arms. It is clear that this game depicts separation and reunion between Sylvia and her mother. She throws the ball away as she felt she was thrown away by her mother.[2] It was not difficult to guess what function this game served at that particular time. She had very recently been ordered out of the kitchen in the Institute and had complained bitterly that nobody liked her and that everybody wanted to get rid of her.

At a later time she created new variations of this game. When she could not find the ball, I had to hand it to her, and she would

[2] In this context see Freud's description of a game played by a child who had been left alone by his mother (1920, p. 15).

welcome it as her child. She then asked for the mother doll and gave the ball to the doll, saying: "The doll has a child." She put the doll on the sofa, the ball next to her. "She goes to bed with her child." Then she would get up on the sofa next to the doll. "Father mustn't disturb her, he disturbs me. It is so nice to be with my child." She held the doll close to her. "She will never leave me." She then admonished her child to be quiet, not to disturb her, and with a deep sigh of satisfaction added: "Now it's lovely." With the help of the doll and the ball and her own person she thus portrayed her entire family situation and, above all, her wish to be alone with her mother and to exclude the disturbing father.

After this play representation she also talked directly about her parents, asking when they would come to see her and when she could go home to them. She also told me why she thought she had been sent to the Institute. "My mother sent me away because she did not love me, because she wanted to get rid of me." At another time she added: "So that I can die here."

This material concerning Sylvia's relationship to her mother differs neither in content nor in the form of presentation from the analytic material of a sighted child. In a sighted child's longing for his mother, the visual memory of what she looked like, her facial expression, the clothes she wore probably would have dominated the picture. But the lack of vision in no way influences the significant affects—Sylvia's love for her mother, the wish to have her all to herself, the jealousy of the father, and her sense of being unwanted and rejected.

Traumatic Experiences

In much the same way Sylvia brought a lot of material about her eyes and her experiences in the hospital. For instance, she stuck a pencil under her arm, demonstrating how her temperature had been taken in the hospital. She related that she was given a bath in the hospital and then carried to her mother, who "kissed me on the cheek and arm." At another time a book she had been playing with suddenly became a hot water bottle which she got ready for a teacher in the Institute who was suffering from a stomachache. She explained: "He is sick and I must take care of him. A doctor came and put drops in his eyes and pinched his eyes." Then she played with a handkerchief, saying: "You are in my handkerchief, I am in a handkerchief." At the same time she put the handkerchief over her nose and mouth. I suspected that she was portraying the induction of anesthesia and subsequently learned that Sylvia had in fact had her eyes examined under anesthesia.

Among the toys she once found a football, but did not want to play with it. "It is wearing a dress," she explained. She called the slit where it was laced together an eye and stuck her finger into the opening. She played at putting drops into this opening and then pinching the two sides together. After this play she told me quite directly, and for the first time, that she had come to Vienna because of her eyes. A doctor had sat her on a piano and asked whether she could see or hear. "I answered that I cannot see, but I can hear." She then rubbed her eyes, as she often did, but at the same time she played out the following scene: she picked up something, evidently a medical instrument, and poked it into her eyes. She asked for Mary (an old, broken doll which had only one leg and whose eyes had fallen out). Addressing Mary she explained that she had to stay with the doctor until her second leg had grown back again. Thereupon she immediately grasped one leg and one arm of the doll and assured her that she already had two legs now. Again she picked up the instrument from the table and made as if she were poking it into the doll's eyes. "Now you can go back to your mother, your eyes do not hurt anymore." She suggested that Mary be taken to the doctor. "He pinches her eyes and she is quite well; she can see now." I said that I did not notice any change in Mary, but Sylvia insisted that Mary was now quite well.

Another time she rubbed some ointment into Mary's eyes—

to make them healthy. Sylvia, assuming the role of the doctor, now repeated a remark which I had made to her: "You cannot always make things well again," but she added: "The eyes will move and then they will be cured." A little later she said: "The doctor cannot help her; she should go back to her mother." At times she even stopped rubbing her eyes and instead rubbed the doll's eyes.

This material leaves no doubt that the eye treatments had made a very strong impression on Sylvia, far stronger than any of her other illnesses. The scarlet fever, for example, is referred to only indirectly by two details: the thermometer and the hot water bottle. Her urgent wish to have her eyes cured seems to be connected less with the desire to see than with the idea that she was sent away from her mother because of her eyes, and could go back to her mother once they were cured. But even if she cannot be cured, she should still be with her mother. She blames her mother for the separation and is angry with her and, like all children, assumes that mother sent her away because she did not love her. The following material will show us that Sylvia also experienced the separation as a punishment for her misdeeds.

Masturbation and Castration Anxiety

As was already described, Sylvia rubbed her eyes compulsively, a behavior which the people in her environment considered a very bad habit and for which they had frequently scolded and threatened her in the hope of breaking this habit. After receiving such a scolding in the Institute, Sylvia told me: "If I do it again, I will be put in the cellar. Stella beat me and then sent me to the cellar where the rats and mice are." She was told that if she continued rubbing her eyes, she would become sick and ugly, and no one would love her. Her aunt, whom Sylvia liked very much and who occasionally paid her a visit, threatened Sylvia that if she did not stop rubbing her eyes, she would not come to visit her anymore. After this threat Sylvia was able to stop for a while, but instead she immediately developed a tic of her eye.

The way in which the hand Sylvia uses to rub her eyes is almost completely excluded from performing any other activity and the way in which the environment reacts to the rubbing of the eyes arouse the suspicion that in this case, as in so many blind children, we are dealing with a displacement upwards; that is to say, the rubbing of the eyes is a substitute for masturbation. I advised her to refrain from rubbing her eyes in the Institute because it annoyed everyone there so much, but told her she could rub as much as she wanted to when she was with me. Taking advantage of my permission, she quickly said to herself: "It won't do me any harm." I reassured her again that both her hands were good, even the one that rubbed her eyes, but that was not easy for her to accept. "My hands are good, but only this one is bad." One day when she was playing with the Mary doll, she pretended that she was going to bed with her, but suddenly pushed the doll away. "Mary is not allowed to come to me because she rubs her eyes. I will send her away, she can go to someone else." She could scarcely have found a clearer way of expressing her idea that her mother sent her away in order to punish her for this sin or bad habit.

Penis Envy

As Sylvia increasingly trusted me, she began to present me with material dealing with her unconscious wishes and desires. For example, she told me a story: a woman had a little boy who was very bad and trampled on all the flowers. While she related this, she put a flower she had been holding in her hand on the floor, stepped on it, and announced: "I am a boy."

She told me that a doctor cut a piece out of her arm. "But it grew back again. My father also had a piece cut away from him. My father has something that many fathers have." While she was talking she masturbated by putting the doll between her legs. It is clear that the blindness has not prevented her from obtaining a great deal of sexual knowledge. She is aware of the differences between the sexes, knows that a boy has a penis and that she, as a girl, does not; that all fathers have a penis, not only hers.

Observation of Intercourse

Sylvia mentioned that her mother went away in a carriage. "My father took a piece of flesh away from her." She was masturbating with a pencil, took up the mother doll, and said: "I stick it [the pencil] into Mummie." She tried to stick the pencil into the doll's hand and then into the leg, saying at the same time: "She likes it. It doesn't hurt." On the one hand, she seems to imagine that her father has castrated her mother; on the other, she already understands that intercourse is not an act of violence but is something pleasurable—a discovery that most normal children usually make only at a much later stage.

While masturbating she told me that she had a dream: "Someone took away my little point." I asked her which one. "The point of the cushion. My head is still here, but my hair is messed up. Hair isn't a little end, is it?" Her castration anxiety is quite apparent here, but like her masturbatory activity and eye rubbing, it has been displaced upwards. Evidently, her messed-up hair is a betrayal of her masturbation. We now recall the first fear she told me about: she spoke of a dog who wanted to hit her because her hair was messed up.

She played at lying in bed with a young married couple, both teachers in the Institute, who had occasionally permitted her to come to their room while they were resting. She said: "I want to stick it in." And she continued to play in such a way that everything got stuck somewhere: evidently, she was preoccupied with the fantasy that during intercourse the penis can get stuck in the vagina and cannot be withdrawn again.

While walking about in my room she suddenly came upon a tassel hanging from a key on a closet door. She screamed with terror when she touched it and for several days thereafter had a series of anxiety attacks. Suddenly, she was afraid of noise, of a bird's cry breaking the stillness, of a gramophone, of the merry laughter of children playing outside, of an airplane. As she heard each of these noises, she stopped whatever she was doing and then was too afraid to start again; or she tried to continue but stopped again, fearing that the noise would recur. When I asked her what she was afraid of, she replied that she might be taken away. In such a state of anxiety she had only one single wish: to lie down and go to sleep. When she was frightened by the children's laughter she explained: "The children could take me away. They could tear me to pieces. They could tear off my little point. Could you manage to have a little point grow on my head?" The noises evidently aroused a tremendous fear of castration in her. And her last remark indicated what she hoped for when she expressed the wish that I would make her "whole" again.

In the same connection Sylvia told me of her friend Raphael, a little boy who was very nice to her. He was one of the children in the Institute who could see a little. "I write to Raphael. I am Raphael." Later, when she was in a state of anxiety: "I am Raphael, he could be taken away and torn to pieces." I assured her that she was not Raphael but Sylvia; she was not a boy. "But I would like to be a boy." I asked her then what she thought was the difference between a boy and a girl. "A boy is called Raphael." She refused to talk about it anymore, but instead wanted to listen to my watch. "Raphael cannot hear it, his hearing is bad."

At another time she was pretending to read, babbling nothing but nonsense. I asked her what kind of language she was speaking. She answered: "The language of the blind," and was delighted that I could not understand her. Apparently she had succeeded, all of a sudden, to put us all into the same category of defective beings: Raphael's hearing was bad, she could not see, and I could not understand. In this way she was able to deny both her exceptional position as a blind person and her penis envy. I

would assume, further, that her pride in hearing the ticking of
the watch was related to clitoral sensations produced during masturbation. To the extent that no guilt was attached to them, she
experienced these sensations as pleasurable; but her fear of
noises, which forced her suddenly to stop all play activity,
pointed to noises (ticking, beating) having become a danger
signal in her struggle against masturbation.

She heard a boy speaking loudly in the waiting room. "He
will come in here and tear me to pieces." She then played a
game she called day and night: "I hear screaming in the night.
I scream sometimes in the night." Another time when she heard
a boy speaking angrily in the hall: "He will pull and tear me to
pieces. He will pull off my legs, my nose, and my little point."
But then she played lying in bed with the boy. This material is
very clear: she wants a penis; but when her identification with
a boy succeeds, she becomes afraid of losing her penis: it will
get stuck or be pulled off. The screaming she hears at night must
be connected with coitus observations. She identifies herself
with the woman who has a penis, and then fantasies that her
penis will be taken from her during intercourse.

Aggressive Tendencies

In her play Sylvia turned back again to the married couple,
the teachers. She fantasied that the wife took her into bed with
her and squeezed her. "The way I am doing it on my leg." She
squeezed her leg to show me what she meant. "She could take
away my little point. It stays stuck in the hole." Then she immediately continued: "Do Mary's eyes hurt her? He could hit
me in the eyes, he could tear out my eyes. Mother was angry
with me when I scratched my eyes." She rubbed her forehead
and told me she had scratched herself there. "I scratched my
eyes. My aunt told me that my eyes would get sick if I rubbed
them. The doctor scratched my eyes. I rubbed my eyes." Here
the connection between her genitals and her eyes is quite clear,
a connection that in her earlier material could be seen in the

form of a displacement upwards. She fears that her eyes will be torn out when she rubs or scratches them, just as her little point will be torn out when she plays with it. Her feeling of guilt relates equally to both activities.

In connection with these castration anxieties, Sylvia brought up angry and revengeful thoughts against her mother. "My mother has bitten my leg. I hit my mother because I fell off a chair. She pinched my ear. I won't do it again. I want to be with my mother." She took up the mother doll and kissed her, then hit her and made the mother doll hit her back. She explained. "She did not want to sit on a chair." She then made the mother doll pinch her, and the doll pinched her back. Next, the mother doll bit her in the foot, and Sylvia reciprocated by pulling out the doll's hair. "Now she will never do it again. She wants to stay with her mother." Sylvia holds her mother responsible for her misfortunes and tries to revenge herself by hitting and pinching. At the same time, however, she is terrified that as a consequence of her own aggression she might lose her mother. She promises never to be naughty again, if only her mother will remain with her.

She repeated the same behavior in the transference. She became very frightened and I asked her why. "I am afraid of you; no, of a thunderstorm." She then climbed onto my lap and clutched me tightly. "I love you so much. I am afraid of you. I don't know why." At another time she explained her anxiety in the following way: "You could take away my doll, you could take everything away from me." With this she indicates, as clearly as is possible, the whole development of her relationship with her mother as we have come to know it from the analysis of the feminine castration complex: she blames the mother for the defectiveness of her own body; at first, she imagined the mother as possessing a penis; then her castration is in some obscure way connected with the observations of parental intercourse. The love for her mother is now disturbed in two ways: on the one hand, by the aggressive feelings with which the girl reacts to the supposed defectiveness of her body; and, on the other, by the somewhat later idea that the mother herself is incomplete and not "whole." To overcome these disturbances the girl develops in reaction an overcompensatory positive mother relationship. She becomes overaffectionate, tied to the mother in an obsessional manner, reacts to every separation with longing and homesickness, and clings in every way to the love object whose existence is threatened by her own hostile wishes.

SUMMARY

I shall now attempt to summarize how the material obtained in the analyses of these two children may serve to answer some of our questions concerning the psychic development of blind children. There is no doubt that the ego development and character formation of both children were decisively influenced by the fact of their blindness. The lack of one group of sensory perceptions—the visual ones—disturbs and diminishes one of the most important functions of the ego, i.e., the testing of reality. Instead of compensating for this lack by greater reliance on their other senses, these children turn to fantasy to make up for what is missing. This leads to denial of reality and to wishful thinking, which in combination easily create the impression of insincerity. Since their physical defect is the most important factor in the life of the blind, this denial frequently extends to blindness itself.

Very early in their lives the blind become aware of the superiority of seeing people in all matters of practical daily life. Conscious of their own helplessness, they develop a relationship to the seeing people that is compounded of fear, envy, dependency, submission, and admiration. We are familiar with this attitude from the analysis of feminine boys and young men who assume a similar emotional position in relation to a powerful, admired, older man. This attitude invariably results in passivity, i.e., wooing, inhibition of aggression, and emotional surrender. Both passive men and the blind develop fantasies in which they identify themselves with their admired object, share in the envied qualities, and maintain a sense of indissoluble union with them. Jacob's analysis disclosed his fixation on passivity, which left him inhibited in almost all his activities; Sylvia, on the other hand, was able to find a way out and achieve some independence by means of her capacity to identify with the protector (mother, uncle, fox terrier).

The analysis of these two children did not yield much new material concerning their early sexual development, but it is astonishing how little Sylvia's observations of intercourse differ from those of sighted children. One reason for this may be the fact that almost all children make their coitus observations in the darkness of night so that visual impressions probably play a far smaller role than we generally assume. The child sees less than he hears and, above all, senses the exciting events that occur so close to him. We can assume that Sylvia used to sleep in her parents' bed and that this physical closeness made up for the lack of visual impressions.

There is nothing astonishing in the fact that the anxieties of Jacob and Sylvia are identical with those of normal children. The instinctual processes and the attempts at repression—the conflict that causes anxiety—are in no way related to vision. This is most evident in Jacob's fear of silence, which is the equivalent of the normal child's fear of darkness. Silence and darkness have the same meaning to the child: they mean being left alone without the prohibiting and protecting adults, and thus being helplessly exposed to his own temptations.

Where the displacement of castration anxiety and guilt from the genitals to the eyes is concerned (Sylvia), it is an open question whether this is primarily determined by the significance of the eyes and the damage to them, or by the attitude of the environment which condemns the rubbing of the eyes in the same way as masturbation. It should be stressed that all people who work with blind children know very well that such self-stimulating rhythmic, ticlike, and compulsive activities (eye rubbing, rocking, head shaking) occur wtih great frequency in blind children. Teachers of the blind generally regard these so-called "blindisms" as bad habits and make every effort to suppress them (Cutsforth, 1933).

The fragments of these two analyses unfortunately yielded very little material that would illuminate the vicissitudes of exhibitionism and scoptophilia. All we can say is that Sylvia's sexual curiosity found ample satisfaction without the help of sight. In Jacob's case, the link between ambition and exhibitionism is most apparent in his wishful fantasy to stand, as a seeing child, in front of all the children of the Institute and be admired by them.

The analyses of these two children did not go far enough to bring oral and anal material to the surface. As a result of their education, blind children usually take a very special pride in their cleanliness; that is to say, since all anal strivings have been rigorously repressed, it takes a longer than usual time to lift these repressions and make the underlying material available for analysis. In the case of Sylvia, who had such an especially strong tie to her mother, we can only guess at the state of her oral strivings, but the analysis itself did not really disclose them. We came closest to them in her fantasies of biting, which played an important role in her castration anxiety.

PRACTICAL APPLICATIONS

These theoretical considerations have many practical implications for the education of the blind. In what follows, however, I shall focus only on a few issues that seem to me to be of overriding importance.

The education of the blind has at all times had the same goal: to prepare him as far as possible to share the life of the seeing world. With his education successfully completed, he should somehow be able to find his place among the sighted, earn his own living, and take his share in their means of enjoyment. Yet we are only too familiar with the difficulties the blind encounters in his struggle for existence and his attempts to gratify his sexual desires.

The educators of the blind never lose sight of this goal: to adjust the blind to the normal world from the very beginning. To prevent his appearing different from the sighted, they encourage each attempt to adapt as a welcome advance in the individual's development. Their endeavors in this direction are made easier and facilitated by two special characteristics of blind children: the rapidity of their speech development and the richness of their fantasy life. These two traits are heavily relied on and exploited in order to compensate for the lack of important sensory perceptions.

The results, however, as the analytic observations show, are serious defects in the blind child's sense of reality which further complicate his social adaptation. The correct evaluation of the significant role that reality testing plays in the individual's entire ego development would induce the educator to put the greatest emphasis on the utilization and careful cultivation of those sensory functions that are at the blind child's disposal. The risk, by comparison, is a minor one: the period during which the psychic life of the blind differs from that of the sighted would be more prolonged.

The opportunity to familiarize himself with the external world and to build up a fund of real knowledge about it is especially important for the language development of the blind. The child acquires speech via his contact with the external world, i.e., he imitates the adults. In this way the normal sighted child learns the names of concrete objects and simultaneously acquires knowledge of their properties by means of his sensory perceptions. Gradually, he also acquires a vocabulary for more abstract conceptions, in imitation and emulation of the adults whose psychic makeup and language are based on the same sensory perceptions.

The blind child, on the other hand, learns the language of a world to which his access is largely barred by his inability to perceive it. There is no doubt that the blind child is quite capable of learning speech, but there is considerable doubt that what he acquires is an expression of his own inner life. A teacher of the blind, wishing to avoid this error, would have to find ways and means of excluding all those words and verbal concepts that have no meaning for the blind infant. And this would have to be done during the child's earliest years. Only as the blind child's reality testing and realistic thinking become more firmly established—only then can the blind child be gradually introduced to the entire vocabulary of the seeing, and even then this process must always be in step with actual advances made by the child.

Just as the blind child is offered a language that is ill-suited to his needs, so he can make next to nothing of many opportunities for enjoyment and sublimation that for the sighted are a primary source of gratification. We probably underestimate the amount of unbroken satisfaction that the seeing person derives from the various forms of sublimated scoptophilia in its widest sense, whether it is enjoyment of the beauties of nature, art, the human body, clothes. Very little has so far been done to provide the blind with comparable opportunities for pleasurable activities within the framework of their own perceptual world. A step in this direction was made by Münz and Löwenfeld (1934), who attempted to develop talents of the blind for modeling and sculpting. Comparable attempts in other directions might well lead to a variety of suitable interests and activities. And it is entirely possible that such endeavors might create the beginnings of a separate art of the blind, independent of the seeing world and different from its art.

These considerations have a direct bearing on the methods and techniques used in the education of the blind. Within the framework of this paper, however, I can only give an outline in the most general terms. Their education should begin in a kindergarten especially adapted to their needs, so far as the training of the senses is concerned; it should continue in a special primary school where manual work is given at least equal weight to purely intellectual stimulation, and writing (expression of thought) outweighs reading (the intake of new conceptions); the first half of high school, still taught in special classes, would introduce sciences in a practical and concrete manner. Only after these steps have been accomplished should the blind child be admitted to an ordinary school and be introduced to the normal intellectual life of the community. There is no doubt that in these circumstances the blind child's progress in adaptation will be slow, but his adjustment will not be made at the expense of developing such character traits as vagueness, submissiveness, and insincerity, which are the unavoidable by-products of our present-day education of the blind.

Chapter 13

SOME NOTES ON THE DEVELOPMENT OF THE BLIND

The aim of this study is to follow the development of the personality of the blind child, to contrast this with the familiar development of the sighted, to show up deviations, and wherever possible to explain them.

The material that we have at our disposal for this purpose is of various types: there are the observations made in our nursery group for the blind children, ages between three to seven years; there is the experience gained from the work with the mothers of these children; further, there is a group of babies now under observation and their mothers who are given help in raising them; and finally, there is the analytic material from five cases, ages between four to eleven years.

The blind are a minority in a world which is focused on the characteristics, needs, accomplishments, and behavior of the seeing. This means that although the blind themselves lack the stimuli provided by the visual sense, all the stimulation which

Reprinted from *The Psychoanalytic Study of the Child*, 16:121-145. New York: International Universities Press, 1961.

they receive via the object world comes from people who see and bears the imprint of the sighted world. It is therefore hardly possible to study the mental processes of the blind undistorted by the influences which are brought to bear on them from their sighted environment.

EARLY OBJECT RELATIONSHIP

Based on her work with the mothers of blind infants and children, Mrs. E. M. Mason has described repeatedly the difficulties and obstacles which mother and child meet in making their first contact. In contrast to the pride and pleasure which a mother feels in her normal baby, Mrs. Mason has shown how the mothers of the blind are affected by the first discovery of the child's visual defect whenever the discovery is made by them and confirmed medically. She has described their feelings of injury, of hurt pride, of guilt, and of the depression which make them withdraw emotionally from the child and sometimes unconsciously or rationally wish for his death. It is only natural that the baby in this most vulnerable period reacts to the mother's withdrawal and in his turn responds with passivity and withdrawal far beyond the degree caused by the visual defect itself. According to our observations, therefore, blind babies who need an excess of stimulation to counteract the lack of visual stimuli receive less than the normal child. This has far-reaching effects on the further development of their emotional life. It also has side effects on the development of all the ego functions of the child, which the present paper is trying to describe.

THE DEVELOPMENT OF MOTILITY

CONSEQUENCES OF RESTRICTION

From our observation of normal mothers of sighted babies we know how much pleasure they gain from each new activity of the child. The first turning toward the mother, the stretching out of the arms to be picked up, the reaching for a toy, the energetic kicking, the crawling, and the first steps, all cause the mother great enjoyment. The physical beauty of the baby as he develops his musculature causes the mother to give him unstinted admiration. This in turn stimulates the baby and he responds with a pleasurable forward movement in development. Joyce Robertson (1962) has described this interplay between mother and child as observed in our Well-Baby Clinic.

We know from the observation of children who have had their hands tied in infancy and were kept in cots and prams overlong as toddlers, that there are serious consequences to such motor restrictions. Under such conditions, some develop excessive autoerotic activities, such as head banging, rocking, sucking, or masturbation. Others become passive; others again react with a retardation of speech or a general delay in development.

According to our observation on blind babies on which Mrs. E. M. Mason has reported recently, retardation and restriction of muscular achievement are the order of the day. We see two reasons for this in the blind baby. Although the muscular impetus is the same, in the absence of vision the blind baby is not stimulated in the same manner to reach out toward people or inanimate objects. Hearing does not seem to give the same impetus to turn toward the source of sound as sight does. Secondly, the baby is not guided by the mother's look or her expression of pleasure in his activity and therefore lacks some of the incentive to repeat achievements. Lack of muscular response on the part of the baby again diminishes the mother's wish to stimulate the child by her own actions, so that a vicious circle is set up. The blind baby, although not intentionally restricted, behaves in many respects like a restricted sighted child.

It is essential to encourage the mothers to take the initiative in muscular action with their blind babies. This may include to take the babies' hands or pull their arms before the baby stretches them out in invitation, to put objects into the babies' hands and manipulate their fingers around them. The object of such activity is to prevent the child from remaining in or falling back to a passive attitude, which seems as natural to the blind child as it is his greatest danger. Mothers report that their infants do not seem to have spontaneous pleasure in feeling objects with their hands except those that make a sound.

There is another intriguing observation concerning the blind infant's use of arms or legs. Miss Isabel Harris reported on a blind baby boy (from eleven to seventeen and a half months) that he showed a decided retardation in reaching out for objects and feeling them. At the same time he showed great pleasure in the activity of his feet and legs, stretching them out and kicking. As he reached the toddler stage and could propel himself about, he used his lower extremities in all ways to make noises, banging his feet on the rug, on the floor, against the bars of his cot, experimenting in this manner with movement and sound simultaneously. Another infant under our observation showed the same tendency to find pleasure in his legs rather than his arms, the latter remaining quite inactive.

Similar attitudes can be observed in older children in our nursery group of the blind. The teacher who gives them physical exercises tries to induce the children to be freer in their movements. It is interesting that she remarked that the children tended to express all ideas with their feet; she had great difficulty to get the children to move their arms at all.

On another occasion Mrs. E. M. Mason has reported on observations of the toddler's stage in blind children, how they enjoy their newly acquired skills, how awkward they are, and how they fall about indiscriminately as do the sighted children. Also, just as the sighted child, the blind toddler soon grows confident, becoming indifferent to bumps and injuries. But only in the sighted child does this early confidence lead soon to the next stage of agility, competence, security, rhythm, and grace of movement. With the blind this early confidence is lost gradually. Although at a later stage the blind child may also become more agile and secure again, what counts next is that the difficulties he has to meet in the first instance increase rather than decrease. There is no diminution of the obstacles that the blind child may bump into, nor of the difficult unknown situations which he encounters. Experience makes him more aware of dangers rather than the opposite. Alongside his own fears run the justified worries of his mother and the constant outcry of "be careful," which accompanies all his activities and leads to the future dependence on the mother and other sighted people to be described later.

With sighted children it has been ascertained that emotional disturbances can betray themselves in awkwardness of posture. There is the suspicion that the same is true for the blind over and beyond the awkwardness which is caused by blindness.

Matthew (3 years) runs like a scared rabbit, starting in one direction and then turning to another; beyond expressing the understandable difficulties with orientation, this is also an expression of his fears.

Judy (4; 10) walks and runs stiffly, giving the impression of a puppet, this being well in accord with the stiffness and artificiality of her personality.

Gillian (5; 3) is slow and awkward, this being the result of her being handled and treated by her family like a doll with little chance for original expression.

All the children when running have the habit of running in the same spot, i.e., not advancing. In their case this is an understandable reaction, the outcome of a compromise between the desire for motility and a self-imposed restriction on motion in order to avoid unpleasant experiences and shock. But such reactions which start rationally lead easily into fixed mannerisms.

BLINDISM

All the children under our observation show the so-called blindisms, i.e., rhythmic movements of the body, rubbing the eyes, knocking of the head with the hands, swaying and rocking.

There is little or no thumb sucking in our nursery, although the normal amount of masturbation can be seen. It is difficult to say how far these rhythmic activities merely substitute for the more normal muscular activities and discharge of aggression which the children lack, and how far they have the full value of auto-erotic manifestations. They certainly share with the autoerotic manifestations a persistence which wins over all the parents' efforts at restraint.

With one child, Helen (7; 3), it became unmistakably clear in analysis that her swaying movements were substitutions for re-stricted and repressed aggression.

ORIENTATION

In normal child development, the infant learns without much difficulty to orient himself in increasingly larger space and, ex-cept for cases of very serious illness, we will not often find orientation disturbed. This is different with the blind. It is only natural that with the absence of vision to guide the child, orien-tation is slow to come, perhaps much slower than is ordinarily imagined. We find that even with the children in our nursery, in the well-known room, there is often difficulty to find the door, the toy shelves, or the snack table.

Winnie, a child of 4, who has for months been taken across the street by her therapist and is repeatedly asked to find the door of the Clinic, is, for example, still unable to do so and will also invariably walk into a mailbox on her way.

But orientation once learned and mastered is also open to secondary disturbance in every kind of emotional upset. Chil-dren who usually find their way in the nursery easily will not do so when there has been trouble in the home or difficulty with the teacher. They will get "lost" so far as direction is concerned, and getting lost will put them in a panic which resembles the panic of the seeing child who suddenly cannot find the mother. Thus, in the young child so far as our own observation goes, the amount of orientation to be expected at a given moment is absolutely unpredictable.

We have so far only made one assumption why this should be the case. In emotional equilibrium the blind child seems to help his processes of orientation in various subtle ways, such as concentration on listening for some accustomed noise, asking questions to be guided by the answering voice, increased listening, etc. It is possible that these activities, which make high demands on the child's concentration and ego functioning in general, cannot be kept up when emotions intervene.

It goes without saying that the ease with which orientation is disturbed, acts as a retarding factor with regard to all other activities.

DEPENDENCY

There is in every child's life a phase where needs cannot be fulfilled except with the help of another person who on the basis of this function becomes the child's first object, i.e., the anaclitic object. Normally this phase is outgrown with the increasing independence of the child's functions such as purposeful movement, knowledge of the environment, ability to grasp, to fetch, and to make contact with the source of satisfaction. As the child becomes more self-reliant so far as gratification is concerned, the quality of his object relationship changes and the latter is based on other factors besides need satisfaction.

It is this particular earlier stage which we see enlarged and prolonged in the case of blind children. Since vision is one of the important factors contributing to orientation and mastery of the surroundings, the blind child finds himself longer in the state in which need satisfaction is dependent on the objects, which substitute in this respect for the function of his eyes.

The mother on her part adds to this dependency. She is realistically aware of the dangers for her child; that without sight he will pull objects onto himself, bump into obstacles, and fall down into spaces he does not see, and she tries to guard him from such accidents. But, above all, because of her sorrow, and her guilt over her death wishes, she will protect and keep the child near her, thus encouraging dependency.

WISH FOR INDEPENDENCE

Although dependency can never be given up altogether by the blind child, he has at the same time the normal urge for independence. This shows in our nursery school children; the cry, "I want to do it myself," is the order of the day. They attempt persistently to become independent. The following is an example of a successful achievement.

The teacher starts to open the door for Winnie (4) who says: "Do it myself." She goes to the door, fumbles with the handle, opens it, shuts it, opens it again, and passes through with a radiant expression.

ATTEMPTED ACHIEVEMENT

Matthew (5; 6) wants to pour the orange juice into his glass. He tips the small pitcher toward the glass, but hardly any juice goes into the glass; the teacher then holds his hand to help him. He does not look very satisfied.

After many such efforts lasting over months, Matthew is able to fill his glass skillfully without help.

Matthew (6) fills a self-made clay bowl with water. He holds it under the tap and it fills up, but as he holds it tilted, the water keeps running out. The teacher comes and helps him to hold it straight. Matthew says: "I want to do it myself." This is only partly true; although there is the wish to do it himself, his insufficient ability to complete the activity depresses him and he is in reality complaining: "If only I could do it myself."

The wish to complete a task seems to contain the awareness that, if interrupted or helped, part of the pleasure is lost.

When the teacher tells Winnie (5; 4) she will show her how to put a screw into her puppet, Winnie asks: "Then will you let go?"

There are many activities which a blind child cannot learn to do even with persistence and skill. It may be too dangerous such as crossing a busy street, or it may be an impossibility such as picking up all the small objects that have fallen and scattered all over the the floor.

In all these instances the children realize there are other people, who can be successful where they themselves fail. They find it preferable on these occasions to accept the help of the sighted, i.e., to use the sighted as their eyes. This is another reason for the blind children to forego independence.

Matthew (6; 3) is trying to find the climbing frame; he calls out to Alan, a partially sighted child, "Show me where the climbing frame is."

Using the seeing in this manner became especially noticeable with Matthew (6) when his younger sister reached the toddler stage and became able to run about on her own. This younger sister, Dorothy, looks up to Matthew in admiration and thinks that he is marvellous in every way. At the same time Matthew can appeal to her for help and use her vision as his own. For example, she fetches whatever Matthew wants, picks up toys that have fallen on the floor, and hands him things even before he asks for them.

REACTIONS TO DIFFICULT TASKS

We have often observed how a child drops a toy or a spoon from a table, makes no effort to pick it up, and behaves as if nothing had happened, as the following example shows.

Judy (6; 6) is trying to match buttons; they fall with a clatter on the floor; she sits quite still, her face immovable, her hands motionless on the table. Since no one pays any attention, she soon moves away to another part of the room.

There are several possible reasons for this behavior. She may avoid in this way the difficult task of trying to pick up the scattered buttons. But the most likely reason is that she does not want to call someone to help her. Experience has told her that she will be asked to do it herself, which would take her a long time. Besides, at home, she has experienced the impatience and irritation caused by her slowness and therefore much prefers the task to be accomplished by someone who can see.

THE CHILD'S ROLE IN INITIATING DEPENDENCE

The children do not find their dependence equally restricting if they can initiate it themselves.

Gillian (6; 2) wanted to be as independent as Helen in going to the lavatory, so she asks the teacher to wait in the hall next to her. But at the same time she is very concerned that the teacher should be sure to wait and tells her to "knock on the wall and keep on knocking."

Judy (6; 2) is jumping off a chair and asks the teacher not to hold her. Then successively, as she jumps, she asks the teacher first to stand by the door, next to go as far as the next room, and finally to sit down in the next room. As Judy gains confidence she gradually removes the teacher from her vicinity until she can be certain that no help can be given.

Often children are observed to say, "I want to do it myself," and simultaneously to hold on to the person to whom they have directed this remark. To give expression to the double feeling: "Don't hold me, but let me take hold of you, let me be the active one," seems to be an intermediary step toward independence. In this way the children feel in control and have taken the initiative in spite of the dependence expressed by their behavior.

The stubbornness observed in our blind children is often no more than the expression of the wish to be left alone to try out experiences for themselves.

Winnie (5; 2) is in the far corner of the washroom and refuses to emerge. She asks the teacher to leave her alone so that she can "go by myself."

FEAR OF ABANDONMENT LEADING TO COMPLIANCE

Blind children are often treated like inanimate objects, picked up and dumped where convenient.

First, when our nursery opened, the children were brought by car service and often by different drivers. The drivers, good-natured men, would pick the children out of the car and deposit them in the hall. You could observe how the child resented being handled in this manner but at the same time would cling to the driver fearing to be abandoned. They know that if deserted, they cannot cope; therefore they prefer to be at the mercy of these strangers.

This remarkable degree of compliance is observed in all our children. They have learned from experience how dependent they have to be on those with sight, into how many dangers they run, and how many of their wishes are unobtainable when they are on their own. But this manifest compliance is no more than a thin disguise which hides the revolt against dependency. The latter shows in a tense posture, a clenched fist, etc. It shows also when helpful but ununderstanding adults push and lead children about without bothering to explain their actions. This is very different from the occasions mentioned before when a child takes hold of a receptive hand and demands to be taken where he wants to go, to be shown where a particular object is placed or where a noise invites investigation.

There are also incidents where pride in achievement and fear of independence are blended into a compromise attitude which is meant to please the adult through compliance.

Gillian (5; 10) puts the plug into the basin herself to wash her hands. She then pulls the plug out, and says: "Gillian cannot do it, you do it for me."

ANGER

In the nursery our teachers are familiar with a form of anger characteristic of all children who feel under the impact of continual frustration.

Alan (6; 11) tries to snap his belt shut which he has never been able to do alone. While doing this he repeats to himself in a whisper: "Do it myself, do it myself," although he is still unable to do it.

The whispered words seem to express anger over the frustration turned against himself, as well as his anger toward the teacher who finally comes to his help.

Matthew (6; 2) at times also whispers his wish to do something alone, the whisper expressing control of anger and fear of upsetting the teacher.

It is true that some of these examples could be taken as well from seeing children, but they would then occur at an earlier age, between two to three years. The phase of conflict between dependence and independence, which is comparatively short with seeing children, has to be immeasurably longer with the blind. With them it is less a stage of development than a continued testing of their own powers of accomplishment as well as of adult reaction to what they are doing. In reality, compliance with the desires of the sighted adult conflicts with their own desire for achievement. Still, there is no attempt at competition with the seeing, rather a wish to submit to the seeing person's impulsive need to assist the blind. It is only acquaintance with these compliant children which shows up the superficiality of this reaction and the negative attitude hidden behind the positive one. They suffer greatly when they compare themselves with the seeing; they are resentful and angry, and merely control their anger because they realize how much they need the seeing.

AGGRESSION

When we compare our observations of blind children with those of normal children of the same age, we are struck by the comparative scarcity of free aggressive expression, at least so far as our nursery group of the blind are concerned. The reason for this may lie in the two characteristics which have been mentioned before: the greater inhibition of muscular expression and the increased dependence on their objects.

We know from the development of normal children that the child's first aggression is directed toward the first cathected object, i.e., the mother; that it finds violent outlets in the toddler stage where the mother is not only possessed by the child but often maltreated; and that it reaches its height in the death wishes belonging to the oedipus complex. So far as the blind toddler is concerned, he seems to be prevented from treating the mother aggressively by the general curb on his muscular activity; so far as the blind child in the phallic stage is concerned, it seems to us that his death wishes are inhibited by his greater fear of losing the object, i.e., as mentioned before, by his dependency. What we find in our blind children actually is much less aggressive expression and much more fear of aggression.

THE CHILDREN'S FEAR OF THEIR OWN AGGRESSION

Most of our children, with perhaps one or two exceptions, are excessively sorry for every aggressive act. They show fear when they have hurt or hit another child accidentally. They are unusually concerned when they have dropped almost any utensil and believe it broken. As all young children do, they throw things frequently, but they do so in a curious way; they throw backwards over their shoulders rather than forward. As mentioned before, they do not dare to express open anger with adults when thwarted or interfered with against their wishes. They seldom express anger with their teachers and certainly much less with their mothers.

Although it seems to us that inhibition of muscular action and of death wishes are the major reasons for this behavior of the children, there is no doubt that absence of vision itself as well as the mother's attitude play their part. So far as the first reason is concerned, we can often notice that the children are made uneasy by their inability to check on the consequences of an aggressive action, that imagination at times leads them to believe that what they have done has had catastrophic results, a belief which may be strengthened either by the exclamation or by the silence of the attacked child. This fear of aggression is naturally strengthened by their mothers' excessive concern about any damage that they might cause inadvertently. The mothers' protective attitude toward their blind children is matched almost in all instances by an anxiousness to prevent any damage which their child could do to others.

THE CHILDREN'S FEAR OF BEING ATTACKED

We find that the children are as frightened of being attacked as they are of attacking. While we think that this is due in the main to the fear of their own aggression, it is certainly heightened by their being less equipped for holding their own in any fight with playmates. They are not able to see the angry expression on another child's face or take notice of a threatening posture; lack of free movement makes it impossible for them to run away or to take evasive action. Where adults are concerned, an angry expression on the mother's or teacher's face does not warn them beforehand of a reprimand. Any such attack whether coming from a child or adult therefore has a surprise quality to which many of our children react with outbursts of despair.

At least in the beginning of our observation, almost all the signs of aggression noticed by the teachers were abortive or merely verbal ones which neither reached nor harmed the object for which they were intended.

Judy (6; 11) is having difficulty in hammering one of the pegs through the hammer-peg toy. She changes to another peg and says: "It's hearing a lot of hammering on its head." The teacher asks her if she thinks the peg can feel. Judy says, "No," but rather doubtfully, and appears to give this peg a rest from time to time.

Matthew (4; 11) learns that his teacher is not coming that day and he begins to cry and then becomes quite angry, saying to the substitute teacher: "I don't want you. I hate you."

Judy (5; 11), while washing up, says for no apparent reason:
"I want to splash and splash and splash your eyes right out."

The nearest to an exception to this general picture is Winnie,
now at the age of five in analysis, who can hit out especially
when she is jealous. But even she expresses her violent self-
assertive or hostile feelings more often in profuse swearing than
in muscular action, Occasionally, Matthew can do both.

Matthew (4; 11) bumps his head on the door, he kicks out at
the door and says: "It nearly pushed my blasted eye out."

VERBALIZATION WITH BLIND CHILDREN

The role of verbalization in early childhood has been described
in an instructive paper by Anny Katan (1961). When describing
verbalization as an important ego achievement of the normal
child she views it from three important aspects: (1) as verbalization of "perception of the outer world in order to obtain fulfillment of wishes and needs"; (2) as verbalization of feeling which
"leads to an increase of the controlling function of the ego over
affects and drives"; (3) as verbalization of thought and feeling
which "increases for the ego the possibility of distinguishing
between wishes and fantasies on the one hand and reality on the
other," i.e., of reality testing.

The blind child verbalizes in a manner similar to a sighted one
in many ways, but there are differences. In one way lack of sight
stimulates verbalization in the blind child, who tries to make up
with words for what he does not see. He finds uses for speech
that the seeing do not require, that is, for orientation, to collect
characteristics for differentiating between persons, to discover
some mark by which an object can be recognized. He asks questions, the main object of which is to provide clues.

On the other hand, lack of sight makes many words meaningless or gives them a different meaning. Therefore, concepts may
be completely misunderstood or only partially understood; or
words may be used merely to imitate or to parrot the sighted.

With none of the blind children under our observation did we find any attempt to build up a language which is based strictly on their own perceptions and sensations. On the contrary, the use of words and expressions which are different from the sighted causes embarrassment to the children as well as to their mothers. The children evidently fear to display the inadequacy of their functioning of which they are dimly aware and therefore make every effort to conform. The mothers' wishes certainly go in the same direction.

FIRST WORDS

Naturally, this difference does not show in the first stage before verbalization proper, when the production of sounds and sylla-bles is based above all on mouth pleasure and only gradually serves the purpose of communication. In all our blind babies the first babbling seemed to take the course known from normal infants.

Mary, a blind baby (7 months), at the beginning of observa-tion, enjoyed vocalizing and appeared happy playing with the sounds she could produce as she lay in her cot. This went hand in hand with her general pleasure in using her mouth for exploration.

But mouth pleasure in general seems prolonged with blind infants and children. At eating times, even with our children of nursery age, we have observed with surprise certain residues of behavior from time when they were being fed by their mothers; namely, when eating independently with a spoon, they have a tendency to wipe their mouth with the implement after every mouthful, just as the mothers had done before they fed them-selves.[1] Similarly, the mouth pleasure derived first from babbling and then from articulation seems to last longer and to play a larger role. More than is usual in childhood, besides serving communication, words are also playthings and speaking an ac-

[1] We do not forget, of course, that our children cannot watch other peo-ple having their meals, and therefore are not stimulated in the same way as the sighted to imitate more adult table manners.

tivity for its own sake. This play with words is distinctly pleasurable, it serves the child's fantasy activity even more than his contact with the external world and becomes sexualized.

When sighted infants start talking, the addition of words generally comes rapidly and continuously. With the blind the mothers tell us that just at that time, between sixteen and eighteen months, when other children are daily adding words to their vocabulary, their children rather seem to forget the few words they had learned already or at least do not increase them. There are three reasons for this.

1. So far as the verbalization of perception of the outer world normally serves fulfillment of the infant's needs and wishes, the position of the blind infant differs somewhat from the norm. The very helplessness of the child forces the mother to anticipate his wishes, thereby leaving less scope and necessity for verbal expression.

2. So far as verbalization serves communication with the mother, it is disturbed at this period by the mother's invariable depression and helplessness regarding her child with the almost inevitable withdrawal from him.

3. So far as verbalization is only one among many other ego achievements and dependent on interaction with them, it is influenced by the restriction and inhibition of motor development which has been described earlier.

PROGRESSIVE SPEECH DEVELOPMENT

On the other hand, this delay in speaking is temporary only. When the toddler stage is over, our blind children seem to have picked up speech very quickly and by the time when they have reached nursery school age it is one of their accomplishments that they speak fluently and have large vocabularies, in which they even outdo the seeing.

This is one of the spheres that mothers encourage. Speech provides a longed-for contact that the mothers have missed. They have lacked the response to their glance and to their facial expressions. Speech not only makes up for this but also reassures the mother that her child is not backward as well as blind, a fear shown by all mothers with whom we are in contact.

PARROTING

It is only normal for children to imitate their mother's speech. With sighted children this leads to no discrepancy between their concepts and the mother's because the visual impressions which are verbalized are shared by both. We find with our mothers of the blind that it is difficult or even impossible for them to realize the gulf which exists between their own ego apparatus and the child's. When naming an object the mother of a sighted child directs the child's look almost automatically. Her own glance toward something may even be enough to encourage the child's attention even if she does not say expressly "look," which she does almost all the time. It will hardly occur without instruction to the mother of a blind child to be as persistent in her urging to "feel," or "hear," or "smell" the object mentioned, or if she does so, it will not be done as naturally or automatically on her part. "Come to me" is very different for a blind child even if the voice is inviting. The expression on the mother's face, her outstretched arms create a tremendous urge toward her in the sighted child. What I mean is that by this emotional experience words such as "come" will be libidinized, and will be available earlier for independent use in the child's vocabulary.

From the foregoing it seems to us that the blind child's speech is less firmly connected with his sensory experience; also that certain words are less highly cathected than normal. On the other hand, the mother's high valuation of the child's ability to speak and the pleasure and praise she shows for this achievement open up the way to the easier path of imitation. The blind child who learns the mother's language takes an easy way out;

that is, he appears to acquire understanding while in reality he acquires only words. Since the lack in ego achievement that goes with this is not apparent to the mother, she continues to promote what seems to her a language common to both, but what is in reality her own language and not the child's. It remains to be seen and studied how far this fautly method of verbalization reveals itself later in superego formation and in certain ego characteristics such as superficiality, hypocrisy, overcompliance, which are often considered to be connected with blindness.

CONCEPTUALIZATION

Since in our nursery school work the mother's wish to make the children conform is replaced by the teacher's and observer's desire to see them develop at their own pace and on the basis of their own perceptions, we have the opportunity to watch a gradual growth of their own verbalization and conceptualization. Under such conditions they begin to verbalize their puzzlement about certain concepts insteady of merely naming them glibly. It emerges, for example, that they understand a "square" as something which has points, differentiating it in that way from something the contour of which can be followed by their hands without interference. Or, for example,

Gillian (5; 6) swings around the teacher. The teacher mentions she is going around in a circle, and Gillian asks, "What is a circle?" This is explained as feeling around an object. "But how can I go in a circle?"

It is very difficult for the children to understand the concept "round" unless the object can be contained completely in the hand. A big ball is not always recognized as round.

"In front" and "behind" are also hard to understand. We observed that when asked to grasp something behind the child, the child has to turn around to find the object.

Helen (7; 6) asks: "Where do your hands stay?" She does not seem to know where her hands are when they are not in use, a most surprising statement since we would expect such knowledge to have much less connection with vision than with the body image based an the sensations provided by its different parts.

Peter (4; 10) feels the leather belt of his teacher and asks: "Have you a collar on?" Here it is easy to find the connection since his dog has a leather collar. But the association of ideas also reveals that he thinks it quite probable that people wear collars as dogs do.

The following are some of the verbal associations to the sensations they experience.

Winnie (3; 1) plays with sand for the first time and lets it run through her fingers. She says: "Sugar."

Judy (6; 5) drops the little metal Braille letters onto her hand and says: "It feels like rain."

The children often use metaphors in an attempt to describe an object or to explain a sensation or to compare one experience with another one.

Matthew (6; 4) eats potato crisps, one of which is curved. He says: "It is like a mouth."

Alan (6; 8) shakes a tin box and is for a long time absorbed in the sound he is making. He finally said: "It sounds like people clapping."

Alan (7; 8) uses a paper puncher and remarks: "It is as if I am taking a picture."

Winnie (4; 11) swears as she often does: "Fucking'ell, fuckin'ell" and adds, "It sounds like music to me."

COLLECTING INFORMATION VIA SPEECH

People are far more attractive for blind children than inanimate objects, such as toys, etc. When they meet strangers they immediately ply them with questions: "What is your name?" "Where do you live?" "Have you children?" "Why did you come here?" These questions may seem similar to those put by institutional children, who have no real object tie and who are trying to attach themselves to every casual stranger. But with the blind the purpose of the questions is to collect information and to gain an impression of the person in place of the visual image which they cannot obtain.

The answers to their questions reveal much to them, in the tone of voice used, in the attitude of the person. They do not easily forget details which they have learned in that manner and will have them at their disposal even a year later, when a visitor returns or is discussed.

It is the same with toys or any other inanimate object. To label it by naming it serves recognition, and to recognize it again is more important to the child than the toy or the object as such. They are proud of their ability in this respect, they feel they can talk about it or ask for it again, as the seeing do. This often obscures the fact that what is cathected here by the blind child is not the person or the thing in itself but the achievement of remembering. Because of this deflection of cathexis in our blind children, memory is well developed.

ORIENTATION BY SPEECH

Questioning has still another use than those already mentioned, that is orientation. The blind children are very clever in trying to find clues for their orientation. They not only ask where they are but put other quite irrelevant questions to whoever is near. The purpose is simply to get a reply and by so doing to locate the person and in that way appreciate their own position. This question takes the place of the glance of the seeing; it serves to give the direction to where they want to go. This device is also used for objects that have fallen or are lost. "Where is it?"

Gillian (5; 10) plays with a wooden ball, listens for it, and is quite good at finding it again, but in doing so remains in constant verbal contact with the teacher, which helps her to locate her own position in the room.

As I have mentioned before, any emotional disturbance causes a child to lose his orientation; in such an instance a question resulting in an answer is the quickest way of getting reorientated.

On the occasions when the blind children visit the garden of the nursery school for normal children, the teacher of the latter is struck by the difference in the topics talked about. She comments on the constant request for orientation and the lack of the usual subjects discussed by preschool children under similar circumstances.

DRIVE TO KNOW AND UNDERSTAND

The blind child's normal drive to know and to understand, which seems to lack expression in the earliest years, finds expression following the sudden awareness that the seing know what is unknown to him. Curiosity, with the resulting urge to fathom the puzzling phenomenon of sight, sets in. Language is one of the means used for this purpose, and speech centers around the problems of blindness whenever this is not prevented for emotional reasons, as it usually is in the child's family.

Judy (5; 5), when told to pull up her sock that has slipped down, asks in a surprised tone: "How can you tell it's down?"

Matthew (5) asks the teacher whether her daughter has eyes that come out. (Matthew was born without eyes and has artificial eyes.) He is told that she has eyes that stay in. Matthew in a voice full of sympathy: "Yes, I know some people do have that sort of eyes."

Matthew (4; 8) is in the garden and calls out: "Come, and watch me water the flowers." When the teacher says she will come out, he says: "You don't have to, you can look through the glass door."

The children also want to know how to use the objects the sighted people use and mention.

Judy (6; 10) asks about pencils and how to write with them.

Matthew (6; 8), who like all boys wishes to drive cars, asks to be told about steering, gears, and about the switches, this in spite of the fact that at other times he declares that he will never be able to drive a car because he is blind.

The children get the idea that seeing is the prerogative of the adults, i.e., that children are blind but adults see.

Matthew (5; 10) asks: "Will I see when I am grown up?"

They evidently make an attempt to penetrate the puzzling abilities of the seeing world by imitating it, which leads, for instance, to the imitation of people's posture. Winnie at times walks like an old woman, an imitation of her grandmother. This might have several reasons but may also be based on a mechanism which Matthew brings to the teacher's attention quite openly in the following manner. He leans down from his chair as if looking for something and says: "I am looking at something."

At another time Matthew (5; 11) brings a yoyo to school and wants Judy "to see it, without touching it." The teacher explains that Judy cannot see it with her eyes but could feel it, to which Matthew replied: "She can stand and put her head this way," at the same time pointing with his head in the right direction, showing that he has gathered that people face in the direction in which they look.

The children also become aware of the amount of vision a person has, and differentiate between the degree of sight of two of our partially sighted children.

Judy (6; 7), who is especially interested in this, asks when Alan, a partially sighted child, drops a lid. "Can he see it?"

Alan (7; 2) keeps telling Winnie not to look at the sky when told she cannot see it. He says: "Because she is all the way blind. I am a little blind, Judy and Matthew are all the way blind."

It is obvious to us that the children continually test the correctness of what they assume from vague clues.

TALKING OF BLINDNESS A RELIEF

Once the children are able to talk about blindness in general and their own in particular it appears to give them great relief.

Judy (6; 7), when asked to come to "look" at the new cabinet, corrects the teacher: "You should not say 'see' but 'feel.' "

Judy has several times expressed the idea that blind children gain sight when they grow up. Recently she has begun to express the realization that much as she might wish to see, she would not be able to do so. In the following example she is checking up on this fact.

Judy (6; 11) asks Helen, who was visiting the nursery, whether she is blind and will be able to see when she is a big lady. Asked what she thinks herself, she quickly says: "No."

Matthew (6; 3) asked Helen the same question, whether she is blind. When she confirms it and asks about him, he admits that he is blind and changes the subject.

The ability to express their thoughts, fantasies, and disappointments about blindness has a liberating effect on the children so that they are able to verbalize other affect-laden subjects.

Judy (6; 5) has never mentioned her father directly in the three years she has been with us. But she speaks with a deep gruff voice, which is thought to be an imitation and impersonation of her father. Now, since Judy is talking of her blindness, she is able to mention her father verbally. She asks her teacher whether she can play football. When the teacher suggests that perhaps her father does, Judy says: "No, he never plays games; when I want to play with him, he says, I should not bother him." When it was put to her that he might rather talk: "No, he never talks to me . . . , he never talks to anyone, only growls at my mother." When the teacher thought he might just be shy, Judy said: "He should have got over being shy, since he is grown up now."

It is interesting that this verbalization freed Judy in her movements as well. In the music lesson that followed this conversation, she could run fast over a wide area, which she had been unable to do before.

It is noticeable that the acceptance of their blindness increases the children's curiosity about other matters and allows them to use their intelligence to draw conclusions.

Judy (6; 4) in her Braille lesson suddenly appreciates the difference between an "a" and a "g" and says: "I am feeling them [the dots]. It is going to be all right now, isn't it?" meaning, although blind, she will now be able to learn.

The children are walking along the street and come to a letter box. Matthew remembers the one in Maresfield Gardens and thinks they must be near the nursery. Judy (6; 11) corrects him and explains: "He thinks it is the same one because it is the same shape."

At another time Matthew (6) is told they are going to climb a hill and asks: "Is there a hill on the street as well as on the pavement?" Matthew is trying here to understand about inclines.

Winnie (5; 5) takes a head off a doll and tries to put it on again. "Is this how heads fit on a neck?"

While driving to a picnic the teachers explain to the children that they must not talk to the driver as she needs to concentrate on the driving. On arrival at the picnic place, they find a tree suitable for the children to climb. Matthew (6; 4) asks to be taken to it and starts to climb. He stops for a moment and says very seriously: "Please, don't help me, and don't talk to me, I have to concentrate like you do when you are driving." Matthew then climbs with great agility.

We are inevitably reminded here of the effect sexual enlightenment normally has on children in freeing their curiosity and intelligence from inhibitions. Once they are allowed to talk about their blindness, the way to the exploration of other secrets seems to be opened up for them.

It is not surprising that the subject of blindness and the difficulty of talking about it are so important. It is not only a painful subject for the mothers, but it is also treated by them as a "secret" in the sense that it is not talked about with the children, although they hear a great deal about it, as they do about sex, birth, death, illness, or other adult matters. What they do overhear can be only confusing and disturbing and in its incompleteness limiting to their intelligence. This latter effect is overcome or avoided whenever they are allowed to share and verbalize their feeling concerning it with the adult world.

There are other respects where sight and blindness become symbolic for the sex differences between children and adults, namely, the adults possessing a power and capacity which children lack. But contrary to sex, it is one of the tragic facts, with which the blind child has to come to terms, that the process to see is not acquired gradually through the process of growing up but will be lacking in his life forever.

Chapter 14

HEARING AND ITS ROLE IN THE DEVELOPMENT OF THE BLIND

At the Hampstead Child-Therapy Clinic we may soon have the opportunity of following the development of several blind infants. It therefore seems important to become aware in greater detail where their development deviates from that of the seeing infant, since only this knowledge can teach us how best to answer their needs.

When going through the literature concerned with the blind, it is interesting to note how many authors mention the lack of information regarding the blind infant's first months and years of life, a lack of information likewise existing with regard to the deaf. A.-M. Sandler (1963), in her paper on "Passivity and Ego Development in a Blind Infant," was among the first to study this subject.[1] I greatly admire her paper which I consider extremely important for the understanding of the blind child. It stimulates my wish to follow more closely the development of

---

Reprinted from *The Psychoanalytic Study of the Child*, 19:95-112. New York: International Universities Press, 1964.

[1] See also Fraiberg and Freedman (1964).

hearing and listening, to go more deeply into the role of these functions, their possibilities and effects, as well as to show the similarities and dissimilarities between hearing and the sense of vision.

A.-M. Sandler stresses in her introduction that her arguments are presented from the point of view of the child's intrapsychic development. Although she is well aware of the importance of the child's object relationship, especially to the mother, she nevertheless expresses the hypothesis that the ego deformation which occurs as a result of blindness does so in its own right.

In what follows, I shall attempt to describe the role played by the mother in furthering, or in failing to further, her infant's innate possibilities to develop. It is my contention that some of the developmental deviations of the blind children and some of the reduction in their ability to enjoy experiences are due to a lack of interaction between child and mother; i.e., they are due to the infant's failure to elicit responses from the mother in certain all-important spheres.

VISION

Looking up the role of vision in Gesell's developmental tests, one is struck by the variety of "regards" described by him for the infant. According to Gesell, the infant regards after delay, spontaneously, momentarily, starily, consistently, recurrently, prolongedly, predominantly, each type of regard having a bearing on the state of development which has been reached.

According to Gesell et al. (1934):

At 1 week the baby stares without fixation.

4-12 weeks: looks at mother's face, adults' hands and own hands; face brightens.

6 weeks: starey gaze, true inspection, follows retreating figure of mother, a moment of searching, more alert, adaptive.

16 weeks: protracted moment of staring, knows mother, sobers when he sees strangers.

24 weeks: recurrence of regard.

28 weeks: perceptual behavior; interest in own abilities, can be content alone, concentrates on an object.

40-52 weeks: inquisitive visual and motor behavior; intent on regarding what other person does; perceptive moods, gives and takes.

52-56 weeks: imitates.

Compared with these detailed differentiations in the maturing function of looking, the function of hearing does not receive a corresponding amount of attention.

MOTIONLESS ATTENTION

For some time my interest has been aroused by the immovable attention displayed by seeing infants looking or listening intently. It is a common observation, also noted many times in our Baby Clinic, that infants of five or six months are found to stare immovably at their mother's face. Several months later this motionless attention is reserved for strangers, who are looked at with a fixed stare which may be interrupted for a quick glance at the familiar face of the mother, only to be taken up again in the same manner.

It is well known, of course, that motionless attention when looking is not restricted to infants, but can be found at all ages in situations which call forth marked interest or surprise. One only needs to watch boys looking at a fast-moving electric train in a shop window, or at acrobats on a trapeze high above the ground. The best example of this behavior at present is people's motionless gazing at television. What I have in mind is the oft-repeated observation of a woman watching television while ironing; the more interesting the picture, the slower her iron goes over the material, stopping entirely at a moment of special excitement when the viewer becomes completely motionless and staring.

Corresponding observations can be made when a child is

listening. This is not surprising since discontinuing all activity reduces the sounds made by oneself and concentrates the attention on the noise listened to. I refer here to the observation of a nine-month old seeing baby who would stop crawling about the room and become motionless on hearing the clock strike. He stayed perfectly still until the clock stopped striking, when he glanced quickly at his mother sharing the experience with her. After several occurrences of this kind the child gradually lost interest and no longer paid attention to the clock. Familiarity had reduced this particular form of attentive listening.

Motionless attention, which is an interesting feature in the seeing, is, of course, of immensely greater importance in the blind. In our nursery school for the blind, we were able to observe various types of it, to which I shall refer later.

THE DEVELOPMENT OF HEARING IN THE BLIND

Although, so far, our possibilities of observing blind babies have been insufficient, some material has been collected on baby Molly from the age of six months.[2] More detailed notes have been made concerning Danny from age two years nine months over a period of fourteen months.[3] Other knowledge comes from our nursery school children (from age three years) or from reconstruction in the analysis of the blind.[4] Even with this scarcity of direct material of the earliest years of life, it has been possible to get some idea of how the sense of hearing is used by a blind child.

Molly, at 6 months, was reported to smile when her mother tickled her on her chest and made a jingling noise with a rattle. When a clock chimed, she made a slight movement toward it;

---

[2] By Cecily Legg, Doris Wills, Alice Colonna.
[3] By Doris Wills. Danny was a defective blind child.
[4] Analytic treatments of blind children of various ages were carried out by me as well as by Hanna Kennedy, Isabel Harris, Agnes Gehr, Cecily Legg, Alice Goldberger, and Dr. Max Goldblatt.

when the curtains were drawn, she stopped playing with her hands and seemed to concentrate on what was happening.

At 7 months she liked crumpling paper and listening to the sound; she scratched her pillow, listening to the sounds made by her nails.

At 11 months she did not smile when she only heard her mother's voice, but did when she was tickled at the same time.

At 1; 5, Molly now had a baby sister. When the baby cried, Molly lay quietly, listening; she banged her feet to make the baby cry, chuckled when she made the baby cry, and banged her feet again.

At 1; 6, she imitated the baby's burping and cooing noises.

At 1; 7, she reached out toward a voice and was discouraged when she was not noticed.

The points illustrated by these observations are the following:

that passive intake of noise led to active imitation of it, which was enjoyed;

that listening to the baby sister's crying could lead to a purposeful action, the purpose being the repetition of a pleasurable sound;

that cheerful noises were imitated vocally no less than noises signifying distress;

that, perhaps most important of all, no body contact can be made with a voice, and that failure in this respect leads to noticeable discouragement.

So far as I know, no one has yet explored the difference between an object which can simultaneously be seen and felt and one which can simultaneously be heard and felt. While sight is much more concerned with something material and tangible, a noise, and especially a noise the origin of which is unknown, must seem to the blind child like something disembodied and out of reach.

The following observations made on Danny are extracted from a paper by Doris Wills (1963) on "The Role of Sound in the Development of a Blind Child."

Danny (2; 9 to 3; 11) examined all objects by banging them, turning them, and banging them on each surface to get as many impressions of the objects through sounds as possible.

He patted his own body, stomach, and legs in such a manner that made it clear that he was interested in the sounds produced thereby. At times, when he was leaning against a wall or door, he would bang his head or back against it, apparently accidentally, the purpose again seeming to be the creation of noise.

The mother reported that when he dropped his bottle, he was able to get down and pick it up. This was the first object he went after and retrieved purposefully. When he was on the floor, he would throw a toy across the floor and hitch after it; having found it, he would throw it again, progressing in this way for some distance.

He drummed with his feet when he was sitting and patted cushions on the couch; these activities represented a motor discharge as well as an exercise in producing noise.

He reached for objects that he heard and wanted; when he was unable to get to the object which had produced the sound, he shook his hands and fussed.

He understood certain words ("bottle" and "car") and reacted to them so that the mother was careful not to use them unless she wanted him to have the bottle or to take him to the car. When he was having his bottle and "car" was mentioned, he dropped the bottle to go to the car.

The stages in Danny's use of sound are the following:

producing a sound and pleasure in this;
using sound production for the purpose of recognizing an object;

combining motor discharge with sound production to express
impatience;

producing purposeful sounds as a means of locating an object;

recognizing isolated words, meaningful to him.

At our nursery school for the blind it is possible to observe
how the older children (three to six years) use their hearing.
They have many different ways of listening, from the taking in
of their surroundings to the assembling of facts, to the making
of a noise for experimenting and purposeful activities. Their
reaction to what is heard is of equal interest.

By listening, the children know who is in the room and what
activities are in progress.

They orient themselves in the room, know where objects are
placed, and remember their location. This orientation and locating of objects are based on listening to conversations, or any
slight noise made by movement, by the running of the water
from the tap, the noise of the heater, etc. Whatever gives them
a clue to where the sound comes from informs them also of their
own position in relation to the sound.

They are also aware of sound beyond the room, of a dog
barking, cars passing, i.e., the background noises of everyday
life.

They seem to use their sense of hearing more efficiently than
the seeing; it may be that through practice, they are able to hear
sounds which are fainter and less distinct.

By dropping objects, banging them, throwing them against
floor or wall, knocking one piece against the other, and especially by banging an object against their own bodies, as the
younger children do, they add to their knowledge of things and
learn a great deal about shape, consistency, compactness, or hol-
lowness. An accidental happening, such as knocking bricks over,
is repeated purposefully to discover what has occurred. However, hearing is only an accompaniment of mouthing, touching,
and smelling. It is the combined sense experience which adds to

the child's knowledge. Surprisingly enough, this type of experimenting, which is repeated endlessly, does not seem to awaken further curiosity; on the contrary, it often leads to what appears like boredom or regression to autoerotic manifestations.

The fact that an object has a name attached to it is treated like a further valuable piece of information concerning it. Listening to conversations and understanding them are great sources of interest to the children and give them a feeling of power. But listening and hearing without understanding can also lead to confusion and disappointment, as in the case of some of our most backward or disturbed children who merely parrot what they hear.

The children are frequently found to imitate the sounds which they have heard. A child, apparently busy at the far end of the room, was heard to jabber away to himself apparently meaninglessly, but in reality he was reproducing a telephone conversation in the next room which was held in Danish. A boy to whom a lawnmower was explained was interested only in its noise, which he was later heard to imitate. Another child imitated the noise of workmen digging up the street by means of manipulating a plate against different surfaces.

It is also possible to follow the children's experiences in their own homes by understanding the sounds which they produce in school. One child, in which family a sister had been born, imitated the crying and cooing of the baby, her burping and sucking at feeding time, the noise made by the mother's stirring the formula for the baby's bottle. Another girl of six searched one day in the nursery for what she called her Hoover. As there was no Hoover in the nursery, every possible other object was offered to her without success until at last she came across a small dinky car, called this her Hoover, proceeded to push it on the floor and held it to her ear: the noise it made had reminded her of the Hoover her mother used at home. It is extraordinary how the children find ways of manipulating objects to make the sounds which represent their major interests. In the analysis of several of the children, the therapist was able to unravel the experiences of their past by understanding these ways.

Conversations that have made an impression are often also repeated. A boy of four years three months, after a bad experience in the hospital where his eyes had been treated without an anesthetic, repeated how they said: "Lie down," and Mummy said: "I won't have my child upset." She had in fact said this and insisted on taking him away. Another time in the nursery he kept banging doors for no apparent reason; when this was objected to, he said, "That is what my mother does when she is angry," showing how he understood moods by means of sounds.

LISTENING IN RELATION TO WITHDRAWAL

Withdrawal and apparent lack of interest sometimes prove to be different forms of listening. When a visitor enters the nursery, it often seems as if the children did not even notice. Closer observation shows at such times a moment of silent listening on their part which replaces the glance of a seeing child. A child may stand or sit at a table, apparently passive and oblivious to the activities of the other children, but later his questions reveal that he was merely listening to take in what they were doing. It is sometimes days later that a child mentions an important happening in the nursery when it was thought that he had been completely withdrawn and uninterested at the time. Very often the withdrawal serves the purpose of listening more intently. At other times the listening may be a substitute for action. One little girl, when the others were dancing, would sit with her fists in her eyes, completely withdrawn; no one could get her to take part until one day when she suddenly got up and danced by herself, making her movements appropriate to the record, showing how well she had been listening.

Even when the children prefer to be active rather than listen, they are often forced into this role. One day an older sister accompanied one of our children to the nursery. She enjoyed the nursery toys and was very active. The blind child tried to join her but was unable to participate actively and was pushed away. The result was that she just tried to stand or sit as near her sister as possible, listening to what she was doing.

A boy had brought a new whistling car to the nursery, another boy took it and made it whistle. The owner remarked softly, "It is my car." He stood in the middle of the room listening but made no effort to claim the car, nor did he make any fuss of any kind. He just stood and listened. The same situation could happen in a nursery of seeing children, but unless the child was very much younger or inhibited, he would certainly raise a great outcry.

Instead of a sound leading to activity it often does the opposite. A blind child may listen to other children playing with a toy, but remain sitting where he is, merely asking what toy they are playing with.

When one of our nursery children drops a toy or any article and it rolls away, the blind child will usually listen to it until it stops rolling; he will not try to retrieve it, but merely ask someone to pick it up for him. The effort to get it himself, to find it, is often very difficult for him, takes a long time, and just is not worth all the trouble to him.

Hearing strange or unexpected noises arouses great fear in the blind children, and in such situations they become motionless, listening. Even slight noises can cause distress. When three of the children were washing dolls which squeaked, the squeak became too much for one of them. She withdrew, sat, and listened. The barking of dogs upsets several of our children; they become anxious, stand still, and listen. Even when they are reassured that the dog is far away and separated by a fence that they have felt, the listening is still continued for a long time; or the child may be filled with terror and in a state of panic, when even listening is no help.

But stillness is also frightening. Hearing someone leave the room causes fear of separation, and the resulting stillness often arouses panic. A little girl clearly showed this when she was in the room with her therapist who happened to be motionless. She called out suddenly in panic, "Where are you? Where are you?" The most striking example of this is reported by Fraiberg and Freedman (1964) from the analysis of a nine-year-old blind boy:

> On one occasion I employed an innovation in these games [of hide-and-seek] in order to test his ability to follow cues in locating objects. I began the game with the ritual, "Good-by, Peter!" and then walked to a corner of the room clicking my heels on the wood floor to give him an opportunity to trace my movements. Then I waited in my corner, but did not give him the signal of my voice as I usually did. He started in search of me, was obviously not oriented, walked right past me, went through the door of the bathroom that communicates between his room and his parents' room, passed on into his parents' room, and then there was silence. He did not return. After a while his mother and I went in search of him. We found him lying on his mother's bed, his shoulders heaving convulsively and a look of mute terror on his face. . . . I tried to put his feelings into words and I tried to explain what had happened and that I had not been lost at all. But he refused to have anything to do with me for the rest of that hour and he would not play the hide-and-seek games with me for a very long time [p. 133].

HEARING IN RELATION TO THE MOTHER

In our work with blind children we have become convinced that it is possible to observe and understand the use made of the sense of hearing, its variations and advances, in a manner similar to the well-studied development of sight. In what follows I shall attempt to explore the role which the relationship to the mother plays in this development. Since we hope to initiate a study of blind infants in their first year, I shall, in anticipation of these more direct observations, record here material derived from our work with the various mothers of the blind, i.e., their own impressions and memories of the child's earliest stages and of their own feelings and attitudes, past and present. Almost all of these mothers had one or more seeing children besides the blind one, either before or after him. We shall have to wait and see whether the expected next step in our work will confirm or disprove the impressions gathered so far.

It is our impression that after a birth, the mother's first concern is to look at the baby, and to know that he is without physical defect. At this early moment only one mother knew about her child's blindness, i.e., the complete lack of eyes. During the early weeks the mothers learn to know their children in many ways, by looking at them, handling them, and recognizing their needs from their manner of crying.

Since infants, whether seeing or blind, react in these first weeks on the basis of reflex patterns and in accordance with satisfaction or dissatisfaction, the differences between them are not very obvious at this time. Hearing in the blind infant develops just as gradually as the sense of sight in the seeing infant. At this stage contact with the mother's body and the situation of nursing or being fed are the closest relationship. It therefore seems likely that the blind infant, as he roots and feels the mother's breast and as he sucks, also gradually notices the sounds which accompany this experience. With a bottle-fed infant the noises of the bottle feeding accompany the closeness of being held.

With the seeing children the mother's wish now is to make contact and to make them smile at her. By smiling and talking she does her utmost to elicit a response. That the blind infant naturally cannot respond as the mother desires or expects does not mean that in his own way he is not responding to the tone of her voice. What confuses the mother is the fact that the more interested the blind child is, the quieter he will become as he listens, the intentness of the listening probably being a clue to the strength of his response. This listening of the blind seems to be on a par with the staring gaze of the seeing infant—what is taken in at this time are probably the noises related to the infant's own body and to the mother's activities, her coming and going.

The mother who is concerned and disappointed because her baby does not react to her in the expected way will become more and more active with him in order to get an answering response. We know from our mothers that they have tickled their infants, even the corner of their lips to make them smile; that they have handled them roughly, done anything to get a show of feeling. According to the mothers, they often found their infants lying quietly and motionless. Possibly it was the approach of the mother to the cot which produced this *in*activity of the infant in order to listen more attentively to her footsteps and to try and differentiate the sounds. The important point here is that the mother would not be aware of the infant's listening, since she herself does not use this sense in the same manner.

While many a mother has made determined attempts to stimulate her infant, it is also natural for the mother of an inactive infant to pay less attention to him. Some mothers said of this period, "He did not seem to need me." Fraiberg and Freedman (1964) also refer to such a remark by the mother of the boy already mentioned. As a consequence the infants were receiving less stimulation even before the mothers took them to the eye hospital and had their fears confirmed that their children were blind. Often this did not happen before the fourth month, sometimes even later, although the apparent unresponsiveness of the infant and the lack of communication between mother and child may have started much earlier to slow down development. The sense of hearing probably remained unaffected by all this. On the contrary, unobserved by the mother, the infant heard more acutely, was more sensitive to noises, and had an excessive ability to differentiate between sounds.

While this was going on, the blind infant was also taking the normal steps from uncoordinated to coordinated movement and to more purposeful activity. Stretching out and thrashing about with arms and legs led to accidental encounters with objects, such as the sides or foot of his cot, which produced sounds, and the further repetition of such accidental happenings led to hitting out for the sake of the resulting noise. Tactile and acoustic impressions of the object seemingly competed for the child's attention and led to repetition. As the mothers reported, and as we could observe with other children, the infants were more active with their legs than their arms and seemed to produce more sounds with them when banging them against the bars of their cots. When the legs are more vigorous and therefore make more noise in kicking, they are naturally favored for this purpose. Interest in the sound produced is followed by interest in its variations, which in turn leads to a discrimination between objects according to the noise connected with them. This was also confirmed by the later observations of our nursery school children at play. The interest in the sounds made by their muscular activity is greater than the urge to use this same muscular power for sitting and standing or other active purposes.

Normal seeing infants during the same stage of development use their arms in preparation for pulling themselves up to sitting positions, and their leg muscles in preparation for crawling, standing, and walking. It is difficult to know how large a part vision plays in propelling them toward an aim, nor do we know how far the passivity produced in the blind by listening is a detrimental factor in slowing up this development. Whatever the answer may be, the greater interest of the blind infant in using his muscular power for making sounds seems to deflect him from using the same muscles equally for locomotion.

The mothers try to help their infants by pulling them up by their arms to create a sitting position, but this does not really remedy the situation, because this occurs in answer to the mother's wish and not in response to a stimulus arising from her child. We often find ourselves in a similar position trying to "stimulate" the interest of our blind children in the nursery school. Whenever such stimulation from our side does not answer to a spark in the child or does not coincide with it, the resulting activity remains abortive. When we give advice to the mothers, we should not forget to make use of this experience. Instead of urging them toward being active with their children, we should be able to teach them to look out for the clues which betray the child's need for activity.

For the seeing this is also the period when they watch with fascinated interest how adults and older children move about, and in play learn to imitate, as, for instance, in the game of pat-a-cake. Imitation also plays a role in the development toward sitting up and standing. I remember in this connection an observation of boy twins in the Hampstead Nurseries; one of them stood up for the first time in his cot, while the other one watched him despairingly, trying over and over again to stand like his brother, but falling back. It took him a full day more until he could follow suit.

In contrast, the blind child can imitate only sounds. Although he is aware of the mother's moving from place to place, wishes to follow her, and notices by the position of her voice whether she sits or stands, at this juncture it is impossible for him to imitate her physical postures and movements.

The most difficult period for the mothers seems to be when they learn the fact that their infant is blind. Invariably they fall into a depression and consequently withdraw from the child, instead of stimulating him when he needs it most in order to counteract the other effects of blindness. Moreover, aside from being depressed, the mother does not know how to help the child. All the mothers we have worked with have, after a period of withdrawal, done their utmost to meet the problem confronting them. Some mothers have shown thought and cleverness in the choice of measures they have taken up. They have presented their infants with all kinds of objects and toys that make a noise, given them pots and pans to play with, the noises of which were familiar from daily use; when they were in another room but within earshot, they purposefully made sounds themselves or talked to the children to keep contact, or kept the wireless on to keep the children from being bored. But these well-meaning attempts to help are not necessarily those that best answer the infant's needs.

The mothers are not the only ones who do not know how best to help these blind children; we are all groping in the dark with the same problem.

The most profitable approach to this investigation may be to try and watch what is found lacking in the development of the blind at a later age and to conclude from this retrospectively where the mother has failed to perceive his needs and therefore was unable to stimulate him appropriately.

There is nothing in the life of the blind infant which can make up for the missing interplay with the mother by means of looking and smiling at each other. For the blind, contact with the mother, apart from touch and smell, is made by hearing; but, although the mother talks and sings to her child, she does not perceive that he is building an inner world made up of sounds. Therefore his listening experience rarely affects both mother and infant in a similar manner, and does not draw them nearer to each other. As a further consequence the infant is not encouraged gradually to give up the enjoyment of the body closeness to the mother and to replace it by other means as the sighted do.

The more the infant turns to his world of sound, the less can his mother follow him. She becomes discouraged when he fails to notice that she looks at him and perhaps enjoys doing so. In her efforts to do the impossible and make the child take notice of her visually, the mother fails to follow what is possible, namely, the infant's growing interest in hearing her. She misses out on the chance to direct the child's hearing toward channels favorable for his development.

The less the infant responds to the mother, the less she enjoys him, and this sets up a vicious circle in which he is left more and more to his own devices.

These two reasons together, the mother's initial depression and her constant inability to share her visual experience with the child, are responsible for making her unable to appreciate his forward movement in development. She may not be alive to her infant's budding pleasures, his ability to notice through listening to the many sounds that make up his world, his enjoyment in the first achievements of producing sounds, banging things together, investigating objects, and exploring distances. She may not realize that his greater activity with his legs may be connected with the fact that she has missed the appropriate moment to give him incentives for using his arms. The innate urge that propels a child toward sitting, to crawling, to standing, does not seem sufficient in itself; the child also needs the mother's active participation and enjoyment in these activities (see Joyce Robertson, 1962).

What is so pleasurable for the sighted child is that his newly developing activities are accompanied by glances of approval and shared enjoyment from the mother's side, signs of approval which are missing for the blind. There is also no substitute for the seeing child's glance at the mother in moments of interest when he wants to share a pleasure. A touch or exclamation are not the same as those quick, fleeting glances accompanying actions.

Moreover, when the blind infant wants reassurance at times of doubt or anxiety, there is nothing to take the place of a reassuring glance. The blind infant probably tries to reach the mother in some subtle way at such moments, but not getting a response leads to disappointment and withdrawal on the infant's side.

Watching the mother and copying her activities are of necessity also missing, as, for instance, the pleasure when instead of being fed the seeing infant one day directs the spoon not to his own mouth but to his mother's, an action to which the mother responds with some appropriate reaction of her own, which again the seeing child watches.

With the blind infant, imitation of sound is present in the realm of speech. Since this is the main acceptable possibility of contact, the mothers pursue it energetically and the infants respond and copy them. Since this form of interplay is of such great importance for both mother and child, the learning of words is accelerated. Unfortunately, as mentioned before, this often results in parroting. The blind child's later difficulty in understanding the meaning and concepts of the language of the seeing impedes his ability to use words meaningfully. But the wish remains and the later parroting and jabbering of many blind children may be a result of this early effort of both mother and child to establish one of the few contacts possible for them.

SUMMARY

The mother who can respond only as far as her own perceptual world allows has little conception of what a blind child can do and experience. She does not encourage where it would be necessary, and expects too little in the directions where he functions well. To interrupt a blind child's apparent passivity may mean interrupting an active achievement, namely, listening. The continual shaking of noisy toys and the endless play of the wireless are not what the infant needs. Curiosity is most likely alive, but remains unnoticed. Since it is not shared with the mother, it does not lead further but results in repetitive actions, rhythmic movements (blindisms), or in boredom, at best in a lonely experience. All this leads to a slowing down of development in certain spheres; in the most favorable cases what we find is uneven and unharmonious development.

LITERATURE

There are a few articles and papers that I would like to mention, because I have found them stimulating and helpful while working on this paper.

First, in an article on "Visual Behavior of Newborn Infants," George W. Greenman (1963) notes that body movements cease when the infant is attentive (looking); that one of the earliest ways in which an infant can communicate with his mother is by looking at her; that it serves the infant "psychologically by giving more pleasure to the nurturing person and thus increases the quality and frequency of his stimulation." As an important help in diagnosis, Greenman suggests that lack of visual response in the newborn world show that something is wrong with the child, not necessarily sight.

In 1953, Peter Hobart Knapp published an article on "The Ear, Listening and Hearing." Although this paper has nothing to do with blindness, Knapp remarks on the little attention given to the ear. After a discussion of the ear as a substitute for the genital, he goes to functions of the ear: that hearing is largely unnoticed but is emotionally charged; that the ear has a remarkable capacity to pick out sound patterns against chaotic background noise; that the "act of listening . . . contributes to superego and ego functions and to instinctual gratification. It remains subordinate to the main sensory representative of reality, vision, but extends its bounds." He stresses that auditory stimuli come in constant flow; that the sense of hearing is acute and selective; and he mentions the ability not to listen so as to prevent being overwhelmed by noise.

In an article on the deaf, Robert L. Sharoff (1959) mentions the lack of information concerning either the normal or pathological development of the deaf child in the psychiatric literature. This paper contains a plea to allow mothers to communicate with their deaf children by means of signs, a communication which is prohibited by some schools for the deaf so as to force the children to speak. Sharoff contends that the child's development is retarded in consequence because of lack of communication between mother and child. He also quotes from Ruesch and Kees (1956) who write concerning a hearing child: "In the first year of life expression necessarily must occur through nonverbal means. The child literally speaks with his whole body. . . . An impoverishment of communication and character development can be observed in those children who grow up in surroundings where the verbal was emphasized too early and when messages expressed in nonverbal terms were left unanswered."

In 1961, Evelyn Omwake and Albert J. Solnit presented a detailed report of the treatment of a blind child. In a discussion of this paper, George S. Klein (1962) makes the following points: that blindness isolates the child from his environment and makes for a drastic reduction in opportunities for manipulation and stimulation; "that unless certain forms of stimulation-with-learning take place at certain as yet unknown critical periods of a child's life, it is likely that very intractable consequences for adulthood will result"; that the child has a great need of loving behavior from the mother to give him affective experience.

From what I have extracted from these papers it is clear that many people are occupied with the same problems that I have discussed here and have come to the same conclusions; they also stress the same need for more information about the first years of life of both the deaf and blind.

I would like to mention one more paper which has a bearing on the handling of blind children and seems to me important because of the ideas contained in it. This paper, "Education as Related to Perceptual Experience: Normal Developmental Learning and the Education of the Child Born Blind" (1962) by Warren M. Brodey, was written primarily for the purpose of interesting people in the Pilot School for Blind Children in Washington. The effort in this school seems to be not only to stimulate the potential sensory ability of each blind child but to try and help the teachers as well as the mothers to become aware of what blindness really means, that is, to experience blindness as far as it is possible for a seeing person. Brodey suggests, for example, that the teachers should spend several of the school hours blindfolded and try in this way to identify with the blind. Of course, it is impossible for a seeing person to go very far in actually experiencing blindness, but the attempt to do it adds a faint knowledge of some of the sense experiences and concepts of the blind, the importance of listening, the difficulties the blind child meets daily, and the skill and cleverness he needs to assemble, coordinate, and use the information collected by the other senses.

This, to my mind, is an idea well worth following. If by this means more detailed information is gathered concerning the inner life of the blind, better communication between mother and child can be established from early on and the blind child's isolation can be lessened.

Chapter 15

SOME PROBLEMS OF EGO DEVELOPMENT IN BLIND CHILDREN

When blind children are compared with their seeing contemporaries with regard to their development (A. Freud, 1963), the nature and range of their achievements tend to be underrated. Observers usually emphasize—as we have done (Chapter 13, A.-M. Sandler, 1963)—the slow rate of forward moves after the first weeks of life: that blind infants need more than the usual stimulation from the mother to respond to her; that the acoustic and tactile sensations do not seem to have the same arousing effects (Greenacre, 1959b) on the infant as the visual ones; that they do not impel him to reach out, do not excite his curiosity or, later, his urge to imitate in the same manner. Above all, the impression is created that in addition to the lack of vision itself, there is also the lack of stimulation which vision normally exercises on the other senses, i.e., a contributory or synthesizing factor

Reprinted from *The Psychoanalytic Study of the Child*, 20:194-208. New York: International Universities Press, 1965.

without which the blind child cannot make full use of hearing, touch, etc. Among the children under our observation, it was not uncommon, especially among the backward ones, to find a second sense, usually touch, employed so little that for all practical purposes it had to be considered out of action.

Due to this general slowing up of progressive processes, it is easily overlooked how much ingenuity the blind child actually expends at every stage. A mother or nurse may use endless patience or may despair while trying to teach a blind child some simple task such as fetching a toy, tying a shoelace, stringing beads; she may easily be oblivious to the fact that at the same time the blind child is busy attempting to master different experiences (Hendrick, 1943) through which he goes on his own and for which he receives neither acknowledgment nor praise.

For example, both normal and blind toddlers have the same awkwardness when learning to walk: they stumble, fall over obstacles or steps, have to hold on to keep balance, etc. With the aid of vision, however, this phase is overcome in a few weeks. Without it, the blind find it a formidable task, dominating their childhood and extending through their entire lives.

Watching our blind children, we cannot but be impressed by the variety of capabilities which they bring to bear on this task: they *remember* the position of stable fittings in their environment to avoid running into them; they *listen* acutely for sounds or echoes to tell them what has been moved from its accustomed place; they *take note* of sidewalks and fix them in their minds; later on they *count* steps; above all, they constantly control their desire for quick movement. While normal children learn about the dangers of fire, water, heights, guided by adults who have passed through the same experience in their own lives, the blind learn to protect themselves from harm in ways which are basically unfamiliar to their custodians and which are therefore not taken over by identification with them, but acquired painfully, and independently, by methods of individual trial and error.

THE PROBLEM OF MOTOR RESTRAINT IN THE
DEVELOPMENT OF THE BLIND

THE ACHIEVEMENT OF MOTOR RESTRAINT

Once we have learned to understand that control of free move-ment is an essential mode of self-protection adopted by the blind, it also becomes easier to grasp the degree of determination and will power exerted by them from a very young age for in-tentionally closing a pathway which, under ordinary circum-stances, constantly serves for discharge of the boundless energy which is present in the young and which, we may assume, nor-mal blind children have in common with the seeing.

While the seeing child hops, skips, runs or jumps, is almost always in motion and is almost invariably discontent and irrita-ble when made to sit quietly (for instance, at mealtimes) or to lie in bed (for instance, when ill), the blind child walks quietly and carefully, holding on to somebody's hand, picking his way attentively among obstacles. In the seeing child, thoughts and desires are short-circuited from moment to moment into one or the other form of action, while the blind child contains them in immobility. Throwing, hitting, kicking, which are all children's normal aggressive outlets, are automatically checked by the blind as too risky because without vision the consequences of such hostile acts cannot be assessed realistically and are over-rated. While pupils in a normal nursery school are invariably active and spontaneously occupied, the children in the Nursery for the Blind, if not compelled otherwise, will sit, motorically idle, on the floor, in a corner, often with their heads on the table.

On the other hand, it is not difficult to demonstrate that both the motor impulses and the potential pleasure in motor discharge are present, but are in fact rendered ineffective by the child's own control. As soon as conditions of absolute safety are pro-vided, the blind child too will hop and jump eagerly (for exam-ple, on the trampoline), or run and dance (when held by the teacher's hands), or even ride a bicycle (in a cleared area). The child will gladly "let go" of his own controls as soon as he is fully confident that danger arising from motility is controlled by the environment.

That self-restraint of motor activity is responsible for much of the depression, boredom, lack of spontaneity which we have learned to equate with the notion of a blind child, is borne out by the changes observed in our nursery school after such opportunities for free movement were introduced: formerly sober, pale, subdued, and restrained children acquired a sense of well-being, healthy pink cheeks, and glowing vitality. When for some reason attendance in nursery school ceases and activity is curtailed, the child adapts once more to the altered circumstances, returns to the former mastery of his desires and, with it, to his slow, sedate, deliberate, "dull" behavior.[1]

THE CONSEQUENCES OF MOTOR RESTRAINT

It is unfortunate for the blind children that a major achievement such as their sensible motor control has outwardly nothing but negative results. Immobilization is displaced from the motor area to other ego functions. The energies which are held off from their normal outlet into constructive activities flow backward and find expression in rhythmical movements, repetitiveness, and use of the musculature for other than active purposes. Since such regressions are characteristic of the mentally retarded, blind children are often classed with them even when their intelligence is basically normal.

BLINDISMS

A regressive intensification of *rhythmical* movement can also be observed in seeing children whenever they are unduly deprived of free motility by parental restriction or are partially or wholly

---

[1] In the "Sunshine Homes" and other residential schools for the blind, the need for muscular activity is fully recognized and much scope is given to it by means of climbing frames, bicycles, etc. See also Mittelmann (1957).

immobilized in illness or after surgical procedures. In the blind these rhythmical movements appear so regularly and extensively that they are regarded as characteristic behavior, which is referred to as "blindisms." This term is used for their rocking, swaying from one foot to the other, waving of the arms, twisting and turning the body, all of which take place not only when the child is unoccupied but also as an interruption of any occupation.

Doubtless, these rhythmical activities serve a dual purpose for the blind: on the one hand, as in the seeing, as sexual, autoerotic practices with the whole body and especially the musculature used as a source of pleasure; on the other hand, as their special outlet for general energy blocked otherwise. Which of the two aspects of the matter begins first and gives rise to the other, or whether they appear simultaneously, merely strengthening each other, has not yet been determined and needs further study. What is obvious, however, is the enormous effort demanded from the blind child to suppress the blindisms, which are offensive to the seeing world and do as much as anything else to set the child apart from his seeing contemporaries. It is even more difficult for the blind child to suppress blindisms than it usually is for any individual to break with autoerotic habits or their substitutes such as thumb sucking, masturbation, nail biting. No wonder, therefore, that they last far into the latency period and occasionally even through adolescence.

REPETITIVE BEHAVIOR

Repetition of specific actions serves the purpose of learning in all children and is normally given up when one particular activity has become thoroughly familiar and its performance mastered. Repetition of the familiar by the young is also known as a pleasure in itself, as shown by the demands to be told the same favorite story over and over again, in the same words. Since in the absence of vision mastery of performance is delayed and familiarity acquired more slowly, repetitive behavior inevitably lasts for longer periods.

Quite apart from his persistence which is explained by slowed-up progression to a new function next on the program for mastery, repetition of familiar (and therefore safe) actions is adopted by the blind as a welcome motor discharge and, for this reason, adhered to tenaciously.

This particular characteristic brings with it its own special difficulties for the program in the Nursery School for the Blind. In the usual nursery schools for the sighted, occupations are chosen to meet the children's insatiable curiosity and hunger for new experience, a method of selection which cannot in the same way apply to the blind since neither of the two incentives is available in them to the same degree. This leaves the teachers guessing. Left to their own devices, the children tend to "play safe" by repeating the familiar, such as opening and shutting doors, turning switches on and off, playing with the water faucets, letting water run over their hands, or filling and emptying containers, all of them actions suited to much younger children. Again, like much younger children, they cannot be coaxed away from repetition to constructive progress by a specific game or by offering them a toy; the achievement of this purpose has to rely on their personal attachment to the teaching adult. They do not progress without individual help and are at their best not in the group but alone with the teacher; in an individual person-to-person relationship they function surprisingly well.

USE OF THE BODY FOR NONACTIVE PURPOSES

While blind children, apart from uncontrollable rhythmical movements, keep their bodies immobile much of the time, bodily sensations and perceptions and other than active body uses are of the greatest importance to them. In playing with insets, for example, body contact with the cup takes precedence over the purpose of fitting it into its appointed place. A child (Winnie, 3; 6) may be seen, for instance, feeling the inset cups with her head, her forehead, her ears, her mouth, before placing them into each other; another one (Sammy, 4; 8) puts the ring on his finger each time before placing it correctly on the pegboard. Although, the children are concentrating primarily on their inner bodily sensations, including those derived from sound and touch; cues should be picked up from those areas to lead them from such preoccupations to interest in the surrounding world. But such cues are not easy to pick up, and the seeing world must learn to be more alert to them.

The blind child uses his body and musculature further to express pleasure, again in a manner which is more appropriate for the toddler stage, before communication of affect is confined to facial expression (E. Kris, 1939). When pleased, our children jump up and down on the spot, clap their hands, etc. One boy makes a funny little hop whenever he succeeds in putting a peg into the right hole, following this with handclapping and the words, "I've done it." Another child, though completely underdeveloped, used to dance up and down with peculiar body movements and wave her arms frantically for no obvious reason; when, under guidance, progressive development was initiated, these body movements were restricted to the expression of pleasure after successful achievements or while hearing music to which she was extremely sensitive.

ORIENTATION AND RECOGNITION OF OBJECTS

For a lay person, the obvious way to judge a blind child's alertness is on the basis of his orientation in space and his ability to recognize objects in his environment; nevertheless, both proficiencies are complex ones and it is easy to go astray in their assessment.

One source of error is the fact that, for the sighted adult, orientation in space as well as object recognition are taken for granted. Therefore the blind child's successes in this respect are also taken for granted, even though they represent outstanding achievements in synthesizing the remaining senses with memory, judgment, and other ego functions; his failures, on the

other hand, strike the observer forcibly when a blind child groping helplessly, searching for a door or a toy in the wrong direction with hands outstretched, is a pitiful and impressive sight.

Another difficulty in assessment is that the child's potential
competence in orientation and his actual performance are often
wide apart. Because of the very intricate interaction of functions
which underlie it, the child's effective orientation depends not
on his intelligence but on the equilibrium or disturbance of the
state of his emotions. Any unexpected happening, any increase
of stress, excitement or anxiety can overthrow the balance and
result in complete lack of orientation.

Thirdly, successful orientation is as much a function of the
desire for an object or of the wish to reach a certain place as it is
an ego function.

Sammy (4; 6), who otherwise gave no sign of being able to
orient himself, could always find his way to the trampoline,
which he loved.

Judy (6) was backward in all respects and was never able to
locate a toy on the shelf. Yet she had no difficulty in finding a
sweet in the same place.

Joan (7), usually slow to find her way, when she heard a
child say to the teacher, "Let me turn the light on," rushed from
the other side of the room and got there first to turn the switch.

If the desire is great enough, it seems that memory, concentration, and the ability to move combine quickly in order that the
wish can be fulfilled.

As mentioned in Chapter 13, we often have occasion to observe
the children's complete inability to locate a fallen toy. Again,
we would be wrong to ascribe this to a basic incapacity. On the
contrary, what impresses the observer at first sight as indifference, lack of attention, lack of understanding, etc., reveals itself
on closer inspection as a complicated mixture of very different
emotional attitudes: blind children hate to be reminded of their

defect and their limited capacity, as they are in this situation. They realize that the sighted accomplish easily what is endless trouble for them and therefore "do not bother." They may even control the movements of their bodies toward the fallen object. Occasionally a stillness can be observed in them at such times, a holding of the breath in listening, a blankness of expression, but more often it is impossible to find a clue to the child's feelings.

On these occasions, too, it is not difficult to prove that this reaction is determined by control of feelings and not lack of intelligence. It becomes obvious later that the child has been fully aware of all the happenings and has stored them in his memory: where the fallen toy has rolled to, who has tried to retrieve it, whether a broom has been used to reach under the furniture, etc. Often, as soon as the child thinks himself alone, and if his desire for the lost object is great enough, he begins to use his intelligence and, taking things in his own hands, takes appropriate action.

The following example, taken from one of our highly developed blind children, illustrates clearly how intelligence, ambition, disappointment, a sense of failure and futility, anger, pent-up rage, etc., combine in the child and determine his behavior. It also shows how easily the whole turmoil of emotions is overlooked and the child's strenuously kept-up façade of indifference and lack of involvement is taken at its face value.

Richard (4; 10), using little wood blocks, had built a village with a street down the middle, an attempt much praised by the teacher. The next day, while he was again playing with the blocks, he was pleased to find and recognize the church by the steeple. He then held up for verification an object which he called a tree. The teacher corrected him and told him its shape was like a tree but it was supposed to be a little man. A few seconds later this figure was dropped on the floor as if by accident, and soon all other objects not recognized by Richard found their way there as well. Encouragement to play as on the previous day was not accepted. Seeing him sit back idly in his chair, an adult in passing remarked how bored he looked, whereupon Richard promptly swept the remaining blocks and shapes from the table to the floor.

But even if, in this particular example, disappointment and stress have become too great to permit continuation of the action, there are many other occasions in the children's lives when frustration itself serves as a stimulation to thought, action, and further effort. In fact, closely observed, our blind children can be seen to be constantly involved in problem solving and they come up all the time with their own solutions, which are often bizarre enough—not unlike the bizarre sexual theories of infancy, which reflect a seeing child's attempt to answer questions that age-adequately are beyond his understanding.

VERBALIZATION AS A PROBLEM FOR THE BLIND

While speech comes naturally to the sighted child, in contact, communication, and identification with his first love objects, for blind children learning the language of the sighted is an intellectual feat, comparable in its formidableness to the other tasks of adaptation to a sighted world such as motor self-control, orientation in space, object recognition. The driving force behind the learning process is the wish to communicate and share experience with the object world, i.e., to arrive at mutual understanding, an ambition which is not always realized. Far from simplifying matters, learning to speak adds further problems to the blind child's life. To bridge the new gulf which opens up between him and the sighted world, the blind child once again has to take recourse to his own ingenuity and to use ego resources such as denial, pretense, withdrawal. Success or failure in this particular respect, more than in any other area of life, will be decisive for his further course in life, his schooling, his professional training, in short, his acceptance as a member of the sighted community.

Describing speech development in blind children in earlier chapters, I stated that the beginning of verbalization is delayed and that later there is a dramatic forward spurt; that by the time they enter nursery school, they speak fluently and have a good vocabulary; that they use many words which are meaningless to them, in imitation of the sighted; that they build up their own concepts gradually; that they use verbal contact in order to orient themselves in space; that they collect information by means of questioning; finally, that verbalization of thought has a liberating effect on their development (A. Katan, 1961) (as it has for the sighted). Keeping these points in mind should help as a starting point from which to probe further into the intricacies of the language of the blind.

At the time of life when normal infants make visual contact with their surroundings, learn to distinguish between people, and familiarize themselves with things by means of sight, blind infants listen to the sounds in their environment and become knowledgeable about what is going on around them, such as approaching and receding footsteps announcing the coming and going of the mother; the noises made by other family members or by strangers; things hitting against each other in the kitchen; movement in the street. There is, though, no justification for equating the two experiences. Vision brings into the infant's orbit a variety of figures and impressions. While some of them disappear and reappear periodically, others are permanent fixtures in his orbit.

Above all, during the child's waking time there is *always something or other to be seen*; so long as there is light, the field of vision is never empty. In the absence of light, fear of the darkness characteristically takes over in the seeing child, i.e., the mere absence of visual impressions creates fear. In contrast, sound is by nature intermittent, and silence, i.e., absence of acoustic impressions, is frequent in the infant's waking time. At best, there are more or less constant background noises; but if they remain meaningless, they do not fill the vacuum as visual impressions do. Moreover, visible objects are, for the most part, tangible, i.e, capable of being touched, grasped, investigated, understood, while noises are more often intangible, ephemeral, not to be contacted by any of the other senses. It is a big experience for a blind child to be able actually to reproduce a noise which he has heard (by banging things together, etc.); much more often the noise "escapes him," i.e., remains outside his jurisdiction, something which comes and goes and cannot be brought back at will. Very often, explanations from the sighted are needed to give the sightless clues to the meaning of a noise. With practice and time the blind children develop acute hearing and learn to unravel and solve the mysteries of the acoustic impressions to which they are exposed. Until that happens the blind child has every right to be fearful when he is confronted by a strange noise or silence, just as sighted children are fearful when confronted by unfamiliar visions or the dark.

There is, thus, a comparative void left in the minds of those who have to build up their world image without visual impressions, from tactile perceptions of the nearest objects and acoustic perceptions of those that are farther removed. From our observations of the blind it appears that this void is filled in part by the child's attentiveness to the sensations arising from his own body. While these do not as such differ from those in all normal children, the blind are less distracted from them by events in the external world, concentrate more on their content, and are consequently more under their dominance. Blind children are often called "withdrawn" (G. S. Klein, 1962), overinvolved with their own bodies, apparently more given to autoerotic indulgence. I believe it is more correct to say that the blind child makes use of his own body and its experiences to compensate for his lack of experiences in the external world. A child whose attention is turned in this direction cannot help but register the stirring of impulses, the changing sensations derived from affects, long before they are conceptualized psychologically.[2] Such physical representations of what will later be called love, hate, sexual desire are stored away somewhere in the memory of all children, ready for later reinforcement, but more vivid, more important, and probably more accessible in the blind than in the sighted.

Quite apart from these specific residues of prepsychological experience, what is stored in the memory, regardless of its source, is particularly important to the blind and in their case outweighs the impact of new impressions. Possibly, vision keeps the mind more firmly tied to external reality, while hearing, through its connection with verbal residues, has more links with the internal world. However that may be, we have little doubt from our close contact with blind children that they are oriented toward their own inner world and that their minds are constantly preoccupied with going over past experiences.

In lay opinion blind children are often thought of as endowed with unusually acoustic and tactile capacities, which are at their disposal to compensate for the lack of vision. In fact, this is not so. As mentioned before, in the blind child the other senses work less efficiently in the beginning since stimulation from the side of vision is missed. It is only when stimulation of other kinds is given and inhibitions are removed that hearing and touch are sharpened and placed more fully at the disposal of the ego.

On the other hand, what blind children really possess to an extraordinary degree is an excellent memory made more and more efficient by constant inward looking. During observation in the nursery school, we are constantly surprised by its scope and availability. The children not only soon know the teachers, helpers, visitors, and where the furniture and toys are placed, but remember cracks and unevennesses in the wall or floor. Every sound, once noted, whether understood or not, is remembered, to be referred to later. This attention to detail has some similarity to what happens in analysis when certain highly

[2] According to a helpful verbal exposition by Dr. H. Nagera.

cathected unconscious material is uncovered, and details appear
with photographic exactitude, their significance probably heightened by the emotional cathexis displaced onto them from the
main events. Blind children seem to possess such "photographic"
(phonographic, tactilographic) memories, the displacement in
their cases being a consequence of cathexis not being needed
for the world of sight.

Normally, speech begins after the initial vocalizations, which are
the same for all children, by the child finding words (or being
given words) for the people and things most highly cathected
with libido; i.e., finding expressions for the parents and naming
desired and familiar things in the environment. Following this
pattern, by rights, the blind child should begin to verbalize (after
the usual *ma ma* and *da da*) by giving words to his world of
sounds, tactile perceptions, and body sensations. This is what
does not happen, and the lack of it distorts the further course
of events. No words are found at this juncture for his important
experiences, since no help or pattern of identification is offered
by the adults in this respect. Since they are sighted, such words
are used less often, while verbal expression of visual experience
abounds. What the child picks up and appropriates as his own
speech is therefore a mixture of words which are meaningful to
him as verbalization of his personal experience and words which
are meaningless, since they refer to visual experience; the latter
are nevertheless important because they are offered by the parents, hold out the hope for verbal communication with them,
and because their use becomes a means of giving pleasure to
the parents. From then onward, the advances of speech in the
blind seem to proceed on two lines: one which is their own and
which they develop on their own, guided by their own intelligence and inventiveness, finding words for their own affects and
body feelings and things heard, more readily than the sighted;
and a second one which is personally strange to them but also

highly cathected as being the speech of the seeing world, i.e., the type of verbalization shared with the parents.

As the vocabulary of the blind child increases, it contains more and more words which are essentially meaningless to him. Since the intelligent blind child's wish to communicate is great, this increases his effort to understand, to clear up confusion, and not to appear stupid. Unavoidable frustration merely spurs him on to solve the riddles which are contained in the language of the seeing, a language that constantly refers to things of which he has no knowledge. In this impasse his extraordinary powers of memory are summoned to his help. It is true that many words of the seeing are meaningless insofar as they do not refer to anything in the child's experience, and that no other facts or impressions can be associated with them to explain their symbolic content. But they are still words, i.e., things heard and as such cathected, taken note of, stored; these words have been spoken by people important to the child and are cathected from that source. For this reason the blind child also appropriates words of this kind and treats them as his own, though on a different basis. He likes to use and repeat them (for which the derogatory term of parroting, speaking without under-standing, is used), even though they are likely to cause con-fusion. And he does his best to clear up confusion by attempts to digest them, to associate past experience with them, as if he asked himself: "Where have I heard this before?" "Who used this word?" "In which context?" "What did I feel at the time?" His ability to recapture internal experience thus helps him to place things, often correctly, where missing external experience leaves him guessing and confused.

In observing the speech development of our nursery school children, we find it useful to disentangle the mixture of the two divergent derivations described, i.e., to separate the expressive elements based on their own sense experience from the borrowed (parroted) ones which are filled with experience only with the help of extraneous memories. As development proceeds the difference between the two kinds tends to be obscured. What usually remains in the language of the adult blind is a certain lack of individuality, some traces of borrowed experience, and in extreme cases some phrases creating the impression of insincerity.

The following are some examples of speech observed in our nursery school.

Words Acquired Normally on the Basis of Sense Experience

A record of "Little Jack Horner Sat in a Corner" was being played when Richard (4; 1) was asked what corner meant. He explained and showed how the two adjoining walls made a corner.

Caroline (4) was helped to acquire the new word "oblong" while using a construction toy. She was heard to whisper the word many times looking very pleased with her ability to use the new word. Six months later when she felt the street sign on Maresfield Gardens by stretching up her arms to feel it, she announced correctly: "This is an oblong."

Verbalizing by Sense Association

Caroline (4; 6) was asked whether she would like to touch the guinea pig. Caroline backed away and said: "No, I don't like it, it feels like a horse."

Using Words of the Sighted World

Richard (4; 3) built a tall tower and called out to the teacher: "Come and see my tower." The teacher said she could see it from where she was. Richard corrected himself: "I mean come and feel my tower." "See" instead of "feel" is almost constantly used by all our children.

Associating from Memory to Unknown Words

Sammy (4; 8), on learning that the window he was hitting was made of glass, murmured: "Glass, glass of milk."

Caroline (4) was putting the bricks back in a corner of the shelf and said: "It is a girl in a corner in school."

Confusion between Word and Thing

Judy (4; 6) screams "off, off" whenever anything unpleasant or frightening is mentioned. If her anxiety increases, she crouches in a corner, repeating: "Turn off."

Sammy (4; 10) shows fear whenever the word "hole" is mentioned. However, he has no difficulty in touching holes. The teacher learned that the mother, in Sammy's presence, had burned a hole in a tablecloth and had been upset and excited over the incident.

Undigested Parroting

Judy (6; 10): "Once upon a time there is a bird, he has nice wedding boots, so he can put his shoes on. The fishes come along, the dogs are barking, the kittens are crying, they found their mittens." Knowing Judy, it is possible to disentangle even here the elements picked up and repeated from nursery rhymes, talk of a wedding heard at home, the expectation of some happy event as in fairy tales, and the expectation of a new outfit given to her. In her case, though, parroting speech, which encourages rambling associations, is still more prominent than the normal purposeful speech which aims straightforwardly at communication and which by now she can use in other moods.

Chapter 16

DEVELOPMENTAL CONSIDERATIONS IN THE OCCUPATIONS OF THE BLIND

One of the problems that occurs in the care of young blind children is how to find suitable occupations and appropriate toys for them. Both mothers and nursery school teachers of such children are continually at a loss as to how to interest them. The children seem to lack any desire for the objects surrounding them and consequently show no sign of a wish to play.

This differs significantly from our experience with sighted children and their inevitable curiosity: it is as difficult to keep objects from them as it is to interest the blind in the same items.

This chapter is based on a paper entitled "Occupations and Toys for Blind Children," which was read at the 25th International Psycho-Analytical Congress, Copenhagen, July 27, 1967 and published in the *International Journal of Psycho-Analysis*, 49:477-480, 1968. A somewhat different version, under the above title, was published first in *The Psychoanalytic Study of the Child*, 22:187-198. New York: International Universities Press. The chapter presented here combines both versions.

Toys for the sighted child are everywhere and in such numbers that the problem that arises is one of eliminating toys which are unsuitable or even harmful.

Much has been written about the toys and occupations of sighted infants, and a sequence has been established of the interrelation between the various stages of sensory and instinctual development and its expression in play. To quote only a few examples: putting objects into each other, next to each other, on top of each other; each of these belongs to a certain stage of development, with libidinal interest derived from notions and experimentations about the inside of the body, its dimensions, etc. To build up and then knock down a tower gives expression to both constructive and destructive urges. Pleasure in mastery is expressed by the successful handling of small copies of life-size objects.

Children are motivated to climb steps and try to attain heights on the jungle gym by the wish to be tall; both muscular and exhibitionistic pleasure is gained from gymnastics, acrobatics, and so on. Play with dolls fosters and expresses the identification with mother in girls; interest in mechanics, trains, engines, and both toy and real cars are certain signs of the boy's phallic interests. Copying games serve as a training ground for later achievements; many mechanical toys introduce the child to very real technical and scientific preoccupations of the future.

In studying these occupations and the toys and tools which serve them, we do not ask ourselves sufficiently through which sensory channel they make their appeal to the child,[1] i.e., whether they are primarily seen, heard, or felt. It is this latter problem with which we are confronted in full force when we are dealing with the blind.

When we turn from the seeing children to the blind, we suddenly find ourselves left without the yardsticks normally used to measure development. As shown in earlier publications by mem-

---

[1] With the exception of Maria Montessori.

bers of our working group,[2] progressive development of the
blind proceeds on lines quite different from the seeing. This is
so, not only with the sensory processes which are disrupted and
distorted by the absence of vision and where, at certain stages,
either touch, smell, or hearing can take precedence over the other
senses.

Equally significant for our purposes is the fact that instinct
development, i.e., sex and aggression, are affected equally by
any single one or a combination of the following factors: the
diminished contact between infant and mother at the beginning
of life, the greater importance of autoerotism, or the early repression of aggression based on the blind child's utter dependency
on his objects. Whichever of these may apply, we have seen and
described as the consequence a slowing up of development as a
whole, a prolongation of the earliest stages, and greater overlapping of the different phases, even though all these diver-
gencies are not wide enough to hinder the establishment of the
oedipal complex or the castration complex. In fact, we find the
latter reinforced by the symbolic meaning of blindness.

There is, of course, the possibility that we are wrong in judging the development of the blind child on the basis of comparisons with the sighted. What in this light appears as backward-
ness or a slowing up may turn out to be a matter of much greater
basic difference in kind. To deal with visual representations of
things, as the seeing do, is probably a much easier process than
to deal with the verbal abstractions to which the blind are confined and for which they depend wholly on the progressive
development of verbalization and its ramifications—inevitably
later occurrences.

Even before speech, seeing infants can relate directly to the
objects around them. The blind, at the same age, have to fall
back on guessing, association, concluding, and will not too fre-

2 See, e.g., Colonna (1968), Nagera and Colonna (1965), A.-M. Sandler
(1963), A.-M. Sandler and Wills (1965), Wills (1963, 1965, 1970). See also
the other chapters contained in Part II of this volume.

quently come up with the wrong answer. It seems to me that there is an expenditure of energy and intellect here which is quite formidable but often undervalued.

The question arises how these differences in development relate to the choice of toys and occupations.

THE MOTHER'S BODY AS THE FIRST TOY

With regard to play, the blind are nearest the seeing in infancy when all children have the mother's body as their plaything. The difference begins when the seeing child exchanges the mother's body for transitional objects and cuddly toys, while the blind infant is less attracted to the inanimate world and consequently remains for a long time in this first stage.

It is difficult to say where, for the blind, play ends and learning begins or vice versa, or whether it is impossible to distinguish between the two at this stage. Touching the mother's hair, nose, mouth, eyes, etc., gives the child knowledge of her face, as looking does, while at the same time the pleasure associated with touching turns this activity into play.

Mothers will need to be taught a great deal in order to alert them to the necessity of lending their bodies to the child to play with, a necessity which is much greater in the case of the blind than it is in seeing infants. Left to themselves, the mothers of blind infants will at this time tend to ignore the child's pleasure in touch; instead they express their concern over his vision by holding things near the child's eyes to test his vision or by engaging his attention for the purpose of testing his intelligence in a variety of ways. These actions are at best meaningless to the child; at worst they are distressing because, as far as vision is concerned, he cannot fulfill the mother's hopes and expectations and may easily react to her discouragement.

It may be equally important to assure the mothers that infants, and especially blind infants, not only like to play with the mother's body but also enjoy having their own bodies played with. This comes natural to the normal mother, but may be absent when a mother is depressed, and disappointed in her child, as the mothers of blind children are. Nevertheless, her play with the infant's fingers, toes, and the surface of his skin is needed to libidinize his body. When this is missing, blind children often do not develop a relationship to their own bodies until a much later age.

Contrary to the mother's concern, neither the child's play with her body nor her play with the child's overstimulates him. In fact, we believe that the opposite is the case and that the well-known blindisms, i.e., the rhythmical rocking, swaying, and eye rubbing, are the result of too little stimulation through mutual body play in infancy. According to our experience, the mother's body retains its role as a toy for the blind child far beyond infancy and certainly until nursery school age. We may, of course, be influenced in this opinion by the fact that the children we deal with have been deprived of this first "toy" by their mother's depression, withdrawal, lack of knowledge and empathy with the child.

PLAYING WITH THE FEET AND
OTHER BODY GAMES

We have observed that, in play, a blind infant prefers to use his legs and feet rather than his arms and hands. We assume that the latter are inactive since there is no visual stimulation to reaching, grasping, and holding. An additional reason for preferring the legs appears to be their greater strength and efficiency. Accordingly, to kick and push against the bars of the cot becomes a favorite game, which is endlessly repeated. The fact that this produces noise as well as muscular tension naturally serves to heighten the enjoyment.

It would be easy, at this stage, to meet the child on his own ground and to enlarge on and vary this spontaneous play. A knowledgeable mother would therefore offer the child her own hands to push against, instead of the bars; this would lead to enjoyable baby gymnastics. The main point is that the infant has made a spontaneous choice to play and should be encouraged rather than discouraged in his occupation. Instead, what usually happens to him at this stage is the experience of being offered a variety of objects which he is expected to reach for and handle—a play activity appropriate for his sighted contemporaries.[3]

In fact, the blind children's potential enjoyment of their musculature and of body play in general is much greater than one would expect from seeing them arrive at nursery school or elementary school, where they appear almost immobile, clumsy, and often apathetic. It seems that these attitudes are the consequence of the many obstacles, dangers, and accidents which occurred so often when they moved spontaneously, as well as of their mothers' efforts to keep them "safe," which, in their case, means inactive. The picture changes quickly if steps are taken to safeguard them while at the same time providing the ultimate in movement for them. Walking frames and bouncers for the toddlers would enable him much earlier to follow his mother at home as she moves about the room, thereby providing him with the enjoyment of all the exciting sensations which the sighted child enjoys in crawling and taking his first steps. In the larger space provided by the nursery school, a trampoline offers unrivaled opportunity for jumping, which is otherwise denied the blind. Children delight in the abandon of the movement while they are safe, and the rhythmical quality of the activity probably also adds to the pleasure. Children can be seen to improve further if one adds all sorts of noise-making devices on the trampoline as they jump. Jumping on the trampoline, jumping down steps or ladders while holding the teacher's hand, running while

---

[3] In a careful investigation of the search behavior of blind infants, Fraiberg et al. (1966) demonstrated that the blind infant does not intentionally reach for a lost object on sound cues alone until the age of eleven months.

holding on to her hand, or even freely running toward her hand clapping are the next stages in play. From there the children find an easy transition to climbing frames and jungle gyms, tricycles, etc., on which they become amazingly proficient.

An interesting game which is not beyond the scope of blind children is the obstacle race or its equivalent. The same pieces of furniture which frighten and hurt the child who meets them accidentally become "toys" when they are piled in an orderly fashion by the teacher, to be circumnavigated by the child. They are felt, handled, pushed into place, climbed over carefully, jumped off, and thoroughly enjoyed as props in an exciting game.

To draw the comparison with the sighted: all children, whether normal or handicapped, love body games. The difference lies in the fact that, for the blind, they play a predominant part at an age when sighted children simultaneously build, construct, explore, draw, and paint.

PLAYING WITH SOUND

In the absence of vision, sound cannot fail to play an overwhelming part in the lives of blind children. Touching and feeling the mother's body, as described, go side by side of course with listening to her. The mother's handling of things in preparation for his bottle, her picking up and putting down of objects, her footsteps, the rattle of dishes in the kitchen, the rustling of clothes, all these become familiar noises that the child soon learns to interpret correctly. This is of course crowned by her keeping contact with him through her voice, which, in the case of blind children, has to take the place of the mother's glance.

There is an obvious and convenient path here from hearing the familiar sounds to touching and handling the objects that produce them, i.e., playing with them. Unluckily, children at this early stage are unable to make their wishes in this respect known, and for this reason many mothers miss the opportunity of offering these familiar objects as playthings instead of specially constructed toys, when the pots and pans and other household articles which have announced themselves by means of sound would mean so much more to the child.

Blind children are not only attracted to playthings by sounds, they also play by producing additional sounds. This results, of course, in their handling various objects in a different manner from the seeing. Whatever they are given is pushed, scraped, dropped, hit, and banged on different surfaces, and the various noises thus produced are listened to eagerly. An impasse between mother and child frequently arises in this respect, with the mother attempting to make her child use the object purposefully, as it "should be used," while the child continues to play with it for the purpose of creating and experimenting with accoustic pleasure.

Playing with sounds soon becomes a favorite occupation and underlies many other purposes. While normal children copy what they see, the copying games of the blind consist of reproducing whatever they hear: the noises made by mother as described, as well as the noises of the street, the coming and going, and honking of cars; the noise of the gramophone, the wireless, and the television, including the squeaks, the vacuum cleaners; the sounds heard at a fair; etc.

It may be this play with sounds that not infrequently interferes with the language development of the blind children. The normal infant's babbling, which produces pleasure without serving communication, is in the blind enormously prolonged and overlaps with verbalization proper. Blind children are often found to "parrot" or use babble talk, even though they are perfectly able to talk properly. There is no doubt that they play with words. They copy everything, from different accents heard to snatches of sounds and to poetry, which is not understood. It seems to me that it would be advantageous rather than the opposite if the children were not only permitted but even encouraged and joined in extending this activity in a playful manner, by means of which many verbal copying games could be developed. This might be more helpful in the long run than placing all emphasis on offering the usual books and stories for children, which are, after all, full of visual descriptions and innumerable items without relevance for the blind. It would be a different matter if special books were devised specifically for the blind, with the content based on their own sense experience and geared to the specific stage of their intellectual and emotional development.

What extends far beyond the area of play is the blind child's interest in music. They may begin with musical toys of all kinds, such as cymbals, drums, mouth organs, xylophones, and musical games such as percussion bands, dancing to music, and may well lead on to the playing of real instruments such as the flute, the piano, the violin. It is not difficult to illustrate with examples that music meets a very real and deep need in the blind child and seems to be the nearest substitute for vision that can be found as far as emotional expression and involvement are concerned.

Many blind children invest an immeasurably greater libidinal cathexis in this activity than in any other, and at least one child proved to be very proficient in this area while she was seemingly backward in all other respects.

A COMMON TOY FOR THE BLIND: THE DOOR

The following is an example of how widely the child's own spontaneous choice of occupations diverges from the official idea of what a toy should be. If not unduly restricted, blind children of nursery school age are fascinated by playing with the doors of the room, ignoring many proper toys which are offered to them. They are inseparable from the door, which they open, shut, bang, swing on, go through, leave and find again, open and shut again, repeating single actions many times over. It takes prolonged observation of the child before one can puzzle out the appeal that this game has. What the door offers is obviously a combined exercise in muscular control, mastery, touch, and noise. In addition to the use of the senses, there is also the turning from passive into active, since the child is here leaving and returning instead of being left and returned to. There is, furthermore, the fascination of the moving object, of special interest in the phallic phase, as well as the enjoyment of controlling it.

From this door game branches off a more detached interest in the vibration felt, the meaning of space, the impact of the swing. All this makes it more understandable that blind children will leave a roomful of playthings in order to devote themselves to a door.

Unluckily, what is fascinating to the children is often discouraged by the adults, who consider this occupation not only dangerous but also annoying and exasperating in the extreme.

MASTERY OF TASKS THROUGH PLAY AND OCCUPATIONS

As observers of play we have to turn from the sighted to the blind to appreciate how many of our common toys appeal to the child only or mainly on the basis of vision. I take as an example the so-called "little world," which has become more or less a stand-by in every nursery whether at home or at school. By way of the miniature replica of the people and things of everyday life, children not only are acquainted with the world at large, they are simultaneously allowed to feel that this world is under their control and can be arranged, directed, redirected—in short, mastered by them. This is an experience on which the blind children miss out altogether. Houses, churches, fences, lampposts, human figures, domestic and wild animals, which are all part of the "little world," may look like the real thing changed only in dimensions, but they certainly neither feel, sound, nor smell like it.

For the blind child, there is not the slightest similarity between a real church and its steeple (of which he has no personal experience) and the toy which represents it. Still, blind children, when given playthings of this kind, learn by rote that this particular shape is called by the adults "church" or "fence" and therefore learn to call it by that name. Since there is, for the blind, no real personal association between such toys and the real thing, they certainly do not experience the corresponding pleasure in handling them; such toys, therefore, do not open up a path to the mastery of the real world.

What is true of the "little world" applies to a lesser degree to dolls and teddy bears. These toys have a double appeal, one of them being through touch because they are cuddly; and this pleasure is shared by the blind and the sighted alike. By both sighted and blind children these toys are not only loved but also thrown around, picked up, cuddled, banged, smacked, etc.; i.e., they are mastered and controlled and offer a channel of expression for the child's loving and aggressive feelings toward human objects. Secondly, dolls and teddy bears are also skillfully fashioned to resemble human beings and animals, a fact that heightens their usefulness for the sighted; where vision is lacking, however, this attribute remains unnoticed and detracts from their value. We only need to watch a blind child holding her doll upside down, trying to feed its legs instead of its mouth, to realize the extent to which doll play is an imperfectly maintained, learned occupation for the blind.

I should like to take as the next example the occupations offered to normal children in a Montessori nursery school, where they experience immense pleasure through the simple means of being allowed to carry out everyday tasks that are usually reserved for the adults, such as setting the table for meals, carrying dishes filled with food, filling tumblers from pitchers, washing dishes, handling hot and cold water faucets, washing clothes, etc. Not only do the children quickly show proficiency at these tasks through copying what the adults do, but their self-respect is heightened and their fantasies of being big are nourished.

According to the Montessori method, the pleasure gained thereby is sufficient to make a child persevere; praise and recognition by the teacher become superfluous.

It is an interesting problem to try and see how far these particular occupations suit the blind or in what respect they have to be varied to serve the same purpose. The overriding consideration is to leave out any part of the program which pleases the child only because it is pleasing to the eyes, and which therefore offers no enjoyment to the blind. A good example is setting the table, an activity which is most sought after by sighted children in the nursery school, where they survey the results of their efforts with great pride. In contrast, this is a chore which one should not impose on the blind child, who does not see what he is doing and cannot gauge the effect of what he has done. By this I do not mean to say that blind children cannot be taught to set the table, but only that they cannot be taught to enjoy doing it. An occupation of this kind, immensely boring to them, is maintained only artificially by the teacher substituting continual encouragement and praise for the missing pleasure.

Matters are quite different with regard to filling and emptying, carrying and fetching, especially washing dishes or clothes, i.e., occupations which either activate the child's pleasure in playing with water or in which success and failure can be felt (not seen) directly, as is the case with spilling or its opposite. Carefully selected, these occupations give the blind the same feeling of successful mastery and pride as they give to the seeing. Of special value are those activities where not only one but two senses and at least one sublimated drive derivative can come into play.

Since blind children usually are permitted to do even less at home than the sighted (to prevent damage to themselves and to the objects), the scope of "adult occupations" allowed to them at school can be correspondingly greater. Even such simple activities as turning light switches, ringing the doorbell, putting the record on the gramophone can give the child a sense of mastery. We must not forget that the blind, even more than sighted children, need constant support of their self-esteem; moreover, to do what the sighted children do is a powerful incentive for them.

Where the last two purposes are not promoted by the occupation, we find it much more difficult to engage the children's interest. I mean by this that they are much more willing to master the world around them than to cope with the difficulties they encounter in the common learning tasks. For the later instruction in Braille, a highly developed sense of touch is necessary, and many of the preschool-age games and occupations for the blind are devised with this aim in mind. Separating materials of all kinds according to texture, shape, and size, and sorting shells and marbles require much effort and give comparatively little pleasure.

Intelligent blind children in the phallic phase show the same needs for mechanical and construction toys with which we are familiar in the sighted. The wish to know how things work, what makes things move, and how they are put together is derived from sexual curiosity and interest in the difference between the sexes; these are fed by the phallic sensations which are phase-adequate. With the seeing, curiosity is constantly fed by observation, just as their pride in mastery is constantly transformed into exhibiting their functioning. Even though these incentives are missing in the blind, the blind share many interests with the sighted. When some of our blind boys were at this stage taken into the front seat of a car and allowed to move knobs, switches, levers, pedals, they showed all the excitement and pleasure of the seeing, the same identification with the omnipotent driver; they asked the same questions and acquired a smiliar level of knowledge as the sighted. They even understood traffic lights through the impact of stop and go.

On the other hand, it should not be forgotten that much of the knowledge acquired by the blind child may be less sound than it appears to be. Carried away by their excitement about car and driver, they inevitably gloss over many details and fill the gaps with undigested verbal information. In order to turn this "hearsay" knowledge into real knowledge "by acquaintance," they need, as a complement, the opportunity to play freely with large-sized wheels, cars, carts, any kind of moving vehicle which is theirs and which they can take apart and put together again, and which, in this way, can become real to them. Such toys for blind children do not yet exist, but once the need for them is recognized, there is no reason why they should not be constructed.

Building is another activity that plays a large part in both sighted and blind children, but there is a significant difference in the way in which the blind carry out this activity. The building of the seeing child is normally guided by some inner image which the child attempts to reproduce in the outside world. Such an image may be retained from actual experience or may be wholly or in part the product of the child's imagination. The more faithfully this inner image has been reproduced, the more will the builder be pleased with the result of his efforts.

Apart from very exceptional cases, the imagination of the blind does not seem to work on the same level, nor are there any visual images to be retained. Accordingly, with many such children, building may proceed aimlessly and consist essentially of knocking or throwing blocks about rather than be an organized activity. This is remedied in part by the teacher's verbal explanations. The child is taught what is high or low, underneath or on top, etc., and if he is willing to follow instructions, the result can be a pretense of spontaneous building, which in turn is praised and encouraged by the sighted adult. There is no doubt that the child "learns" a good deal about space in this manner and that this is a necessary prop for the orientation of the blind.

What I have in mind is that this can hardly be classed as play in the first instance, since it does not give expression to any of the child's instinctual needs. It is acquired rather than spontaneous, a learning activity rather than a play activity. Once learned, it can be used in the service of play.

On the other hand, building can be a spontaneous activity if we allow it to proceed in the opposite direction, i.e., from the finished product to the idea of it instead of from the imagination to the finished product. I would suggest giving the blind children the opportunity to dismantle familiar objects in their surroundings such as vehicles, trucks, pieces of furniture. This activity is easily understood by them because it gives scope to their instinctual strivings. Once the thing is dismantled, there should be a chance to put it together again; this gratifies constructive wishes of the ego and demands no effort of the imagination because this type of building is guided by the very recent experience of a whole familiar object.

CONCLUSION

The more interested we become in this subject of toys and activities for the blind, the less easily do we understand why so many children with this handicap spend hours of boredom, inactivity, and waiting; or why so many mothers despair of occupying them and of "keeping them happy." It seems that, so far, we have tapped only a minimum of the energies which lie dormant and ready to be employed pleasurably.

Chapter 17

THE RE-EDUCATION OF A
RETARDED BLIND CHILD

This paper describes in detail a backward and withdrawn child, born with multiple handicaps and subjected to pain, frustration, and lack of stimulation in her early childhood. Her therapy, carried out by Alice Goldberger within the Hampstead Child-Therapy Clinic, aimed at counteracting past damage and promoting any urge toward normal development which lay dormant in her.

PARENTS' REPORT ON PERSONAL HISTORY

The first report which the parents gave to us on Judy's history was rather scanty.

At the time of the child's birth, they were already in their middle forties, with two teenage daughters, seventeen and eleven

This paper, written in collaboration with Alice Goldberger, was presented at the third scientific meeting of the American Association for Child Psychoanalysis, Inc., New Haven, Conn., on April 20, 1968. It was first published in *The Psychoanalytic Study of the Child*, 23:369-385. New York: International Universities Press, 1968.

years old. They lived as a close-knit family in a modest house of their own, together with the maternal grandmother.

Due to the mother's high blood pressure, Judy was born in the hospital by Caesarean operation. She was "blue" at birth (not due to strangulation). Her feet were deformed, one toe folded under each foot. There was some (undefined) malformation of her mouth. At age six weeks she was found to be suffering from *congenital cataract* with her sight reduced to some light perception.

According to the parents, Judy was extremely difficult to rear from the beginning. Soon after birth, she developed a raw and blistered skin, which made her shrink from any touch, scream when handled, and dread contact with the bath water. (In later life she could not bear a clip put in her hair or a cap placed on her head.)

It puzzled the parents that her development did not resemble that of their older children. She never explored her surroundings by either smelling, licking, or touching anything. She never raised her arms to be lifted, carried, or cuddled. When she had learned to stand, her hands hung limply at her sides. She bypassed the crawling stage, but walked at the age two and a half. She was at all times oversensitive to sound and terrified of any noise to which she was not accustomed. So far as feeding was concerned, the deformity of her mouth, and later of her teeth, prevented any enjoyment of the process. The mother fed her passively until a late age and urged the intake of food to "prevent her from starving."

Toilet training was persistent, but had no result.

When speech began, Judy acquired a fairly large vocabulary fairly quickly, but it did not serve communication. Words were strung together without meaning in what the parents called her "gabble talk."

With all that, the parents stressed that the child was neither aggressive nor destructive, nor had outbursts of temper. When thwarted, she reacted with hurt withdrawal.

FIRST VISIT TO THE CLINIC

Judy was four and a half years old when she was accepted by the Clinic for observation. She was at the time a nice-looking, well-built, sturdy little girl, with large blue wide-open eyes (unseeing), appropriately and attractively dressed.

She came to the Clinic in an odd way, walking stiffly and awkwardly beside her mother, who did not hold her hand, but instead guided her by holding on to a tassel on top of her pixie cap.

When, during the interview, she sat on her mother's lap, she did so impersonally, treating the mother's body as if it were a piece of furniture. Her face remained expressionless while she chattered incessantly in a high-pitched voice; occasionally an isolated, unconnected word could be singled out from her gabble talk.

Each of her hands held an object which she did not discard during the visit; one, the plastic body of a headless and limbless doll; the other, a cup. She showed no interest in any toy offered to her. Only when a tambourine was softly drummed near her to gain her attention, she reacted by lifting an arm in front of her face as if warding off a blow.

A PERIOD OF OBSERVATION

In spite of the many oddities in Judy's appearance and behavior, it was the therapist's impression that she was neither a mentally defective nor an autistic child, and that contact could be made with her. Since touch was obviously unwelcome and words were tolerated, the latter means was chosen as appropriate for an approach.

The therapist, in a simple way, commiserated with Judy for having to meet a stranger. When the child "gabbled" in answer and the father admonished her to "talk sensibly," the therapist, again very simply and directly, explained that there was no need for this intervention, that Judy played with words as other children play with toys, and that this was her pleasure. She was gratified when there appeared an answering flicker of expression in the child's face.

Her next move was to pick out random words from the child's talk and turn them into nursery rhymes. At this Judy smiled and even attempted to construct such a rhyme herself. Contact seemed established, and further words could be used to attract her attention and amuse her. Since in her gabbling Judy gave obvious signs of copying conversations, even the intonations of TV announcers, the therapist used the device of assuming their role, thereby insinuating herself into the child's imaginary world.

On following visits, stories were made up concerning everyday events: how Judy got dressed, came to the Clinic, made her therapist wait, was welcomed by her. Judy obviously began to enjoy this entertainment, looked forward to it, and even tried to join in. The therapist realized that she had gained a first point when Judy exclaimed at the end of a session: "Next week I see you again."

It was much more difficult to elicit positive responses to touch. When a ball was rolled toward Judy, her arms would be lifted in a rejecting gesture and she would shout: "No, no, next week!"

Picking up fallen objects presented another difficult task. When the therapist prevented the mother from picking up what had dropped from the child's hand, Judy followed the directions given for her search most reluctantly ("One step toward Mummy," etc.). Gradually she accepted the therapist's interest in her clothing and began, together with her, to touch her "soft and cuddly sweater" without shrinking from the contact.

It took time until Judy cooperated in even the simplest games of the toddler stage, and there were many setbacks to be encountered on the way, Judy expressing displeasure in the place of enjoyment.

Since chocolate seemed the only sweet she liked, a piece of it was dropped into the cup held in her hand to encourage her to take it out. Unfortunately, the chocolate rattled in the cup and the noise caused her to drop both in fright. Another time, a piece of chocolate, willingly accepted and placed in her mouth, was simply let fall out.

When a toy lorry was loaded with the chocolate and wheeled toward her to be invited to "come in," she was cunning enough to defend herself by saying that she was "out, not at home." It took some time until she complied to the extent of saying: "Come in, lorry," and touched the chocolate gingerly.

Although Judy had a firm grasp on the two toys which always accompanied her, her fingers remained lifeless in contact with other objects.

Some use could be made of her perception of light. When the therapist noted some reaction on Judy's part to the turning on of lights, she tried to engage her interest in the action of the light switch and to guide her toward manipulating it herself. The father's delighted surprise about this led him to construct a special light switch for her at home, which she proceeded to turn on and off endlessly.

In any exploration of her surroundings, Judy was much hindered by her fear of sound. Any strange voice, any unexpected noise, even the wind rustling in the trees, caused a state of panic, in which she covered her ears, crouched down and begged: "Turn it off, off!"

It seemed possible to the therapist that Judy's frequent immobility marked a state of intense listening, i.e., an attempt to identify noises, thereby reducing their frightening character. With this idea in mind, she embarked on the verbalization and explanation of sounds as they presented themselves. When Judy tapped with her foot, she remarked on it and then did the same, entering into an exchange of tapping sounds. When Judy entered the room and set the chimes in motion, their soft tinkle was explained, explored, and turned into something expectable. Even though these attempts were often greeted with the usual "No, no, off, off," a growing fascination with rhythmical sounds and music gradually became apparent.

On the whole, during this observation period (which lasted approximately one year), it was possible to collect a large amount of data concerning the functioning of Judy's ego apparatus, her anxieties, and her avoidance measures.

Another gain of these first months was a clearer picture of the parental handling of the child and of the parent's own personalities. On the one hand, there was no doubt that Judy was given conscientious and loving care and that the parents spared no efforts in dealing with her handicap. On the other hand, the mother emerged as a depressed and rigid person, unable to show physical affection or to respond sensitively to the child's real needs. It was easy to picture her initial shock and revulsion when she discovered that she had given birth to an abnormal child and when she found herself unable to comfort the distressed and screaming infant. Her concern that the child would starve to death and her success in keeping Judy alive by feeding can be taken as active reactions against her guilt feelings and hostile wishes.

The father, in contrast, was affectionate and warmhearted. He tried to play with Judy, to amuse her, even to make her behave normally, but he too was handicapped in his attention to the child. Faced with his wife's severe illness at the time of her confinement with Judy, he was above all concerned with the danger to her life. Faced with her depressive reaction afterward, he attempted above all to cheer her up. This made him assume a more or less forced gaiety as a reaction to strain and worry. He approached the child on this basis, and tried to elicit the same response from her. But Judy, according to her own nature, was generally unable to respond to his efforts.

A PERIOD OF RE-EDUCATION

Judy's re-education was built on the assumption that in her early infancy she had missed out on those pleasurable experiences around which the nuclei of a normal personality are formed.

There was little pleasure to be gained from a mother who was herself despairing, guilty, and withdrawn. Her skin condition precluded any positive sensations connected with cuddling, being handled, bathed. Sucking was interfered with by her mouth condition. With vision absent, all that was left to link her with the environment was sound, but in the absence of security and comfort, sounds were as frightening as they were stimulating. Under these conditions, her own body as well as the figures of the external world remained uncathected with positive libido.

EDUCATIONAL THERAPY

The therapist accordingly set out on a program of introducing Judy to pleasurable experience. She kept the relationship to herself, playful, joyful, and companionable. She introduced sounds soft enough to be nonfrightening and pleasurable (playing a mouth organ for her, an autoharp), and toys which were pleasant to the touch. Chocolate, as described before, was used to stimulate her functioning. Contact with other adults or children in the Clinic was avoided to exclude upsets and disturbances.

Judy reacted to these arrangements with an affectionate attachment to the therapist, which took the parents completely by surprise. Their hopes were awakened and they were eager (though not always able) to follow any suggestions for different home management which were made to them. Nevertheless, it was necessary at this time to warn them that even under the most favorable circumstances a readjustment such as that necessary in Judy would take years, and that even then the outcome remained unpredictable. Ego functions would have to be coaxed into action and learning processes initiated long past the time appropriate for their emergence. Libidinal ties would have to be strengthened and widened to draw the child out of her isolation. Control of her body functions had to be established and, above all, her hands and fingers stimulated to assume their proper role.

In fact, some of these advances were made spontaneously by Judy as a by-product of her relationship to the therapist. As this developed and stabilized itself, the soiling ceased (almost immediately after attendance at the Clinic began), the wetting became intermittent, and her (archaic) fears decreased perceptibly.

What follows are illustrations extracted from Judy's attendance at the Clinic during the next two years. They are selected to highlight advances made as well as the inevitable difficulty and slowness of the task.

Fear of the Unknown

It was never possible for Judy to touch anything which she met for the first time. Her answer to such a request was invariably: "No, no, thank you." Nevertheless, if the same thing was presented to her repeatedly, on different occasions, in the form of a game, she could accept it finally and make use of it from then onward. The discouraging point was that this learning process did not extend from one object to the next. Whatever was new had to be introduced to her in the same laborious way.

It is known, in fact, that all blind children show a certain hesitation in handling new objects, probably because the reassurance provided by sight is missing. In the majority of cases this is overcome quickly. It was the therapist's surmise that Judy was handicapped more than others in this respect owing to her painful experiences with all skin contact in early infancy.

Advances in Speech

Judy's advances in verbal communication were slow but steady. Where before she had expressed her wishes with the use of one sharp word, such as "box," "door," she would now say: "Give me the box." Where before she had panicked at the sound of an aeroplane, she would now say: "The aeroplane is very noisy." Her gabble talk continued, but became less frequent, resorted to only when she was confused or frightened, or when too much was demanded of her. Although she still copied what she heard in conversation, on the wireless, or on TV, she was gradually able to use these snatches, not out of context, but with understanding.

Advances in Self-Awareness

Even at the age of four and a half, Judy had seemed not to possess an inner image of her own body. When playing body games with the therapist, she was unable to differentiate her own fingers and legs from the latter's. She behaved at times as if her clothes were part of her body. In this period she was oblivious of physical pain (in contrast to her infancy) and therefore also lacked this powerful guide to self-awareness. tI was therefore a great advance when she ceased to speak of herself in the third person and used the first person instead. When she was heard to say to her therapist: "I love you and I love myself," it was felt that she had made the forward move of differentiating herself for the first time from another person.

Denial of Emotion

In the course of Judy's attendance at the Clinic she was observed to be capable of occasionally producing a complete denial of reality. For example, when she was told that the gramophone was broken and that she would be unable to dance to her favorite tunes, she nevertheless moved the furniture around to begin dancing. When told that the therapist was going on a holiday and could not see her for a while, she reacted by saying: "See you tomorrow." When told that the therapist had been taken ill and that she would have to return home, she refused to budge, appeared stunned and speechless, and insisted on waiting until the therapist "would come."

Advances in Self-Assertion

In contrast to her former reactions of hurt withdrawal in the face of frustration, Judy gradually became able to assert herself more vigorously. When told by her father to stop twiddling with the wireless, she answered: "I did not twiddle, I put it louder so you could hear the news better." When urged to eat an apple, she said: "She does not want the apple, take it away." When offered a doll, she screamed: "I don't want the doll, I don't like dolls, and I don't want to be talked into it."

Relations with the Mother

Under the influence of the therapist, the mother began to make demands on her daughter which were long overdue, such as fetching things, washing her hands, helping to dress herself. Judy was able to comply, but apart from this there was still little warmth in their relationship.

Oedipal Attitudes toward the Father

In contrast, Judy's relationship to her father made a forward move and took on all the aspects of an oedipal attachment. When he approached, her face lit up with pleasure. She cuddled in his arms, kissed him, and called him sweetheart. She sang and danced with him. On one occasion, when told that he had to leave, she burst into tears, sobbed bitterly, and begged him not to go. On another occasion, when her mother had just got her fully dressed and she heard his voice, she proceeded in a flash to take off every single piece of clothing which her mother had laboriously put on her. She insisted: "Daddy must dress me."

It is interesting to note that this was done by the same child who, under less cathected circumstances, showed herself quite unable to undo a button or manipulate her underwear.

Wetting

For a considerable period Judy's "intermittent" wetting defied explanation. Finally, it became possible to link the occurrence of loss of bladder control with stress and confusion in her life. So long as she had no other free outlet for her feelings, notably while she was unable to weep (as she was initially), wetting served this purpose.

Early in Judy's treatment, the maternal grandmother who had

shared the family's life, died. There was the usual commotion in the house, excitement, crying, the coming and going of neighbors. Nothing of this was explained to Judy, who was thought to be unaware of the event. Here the wetting recurred, after having stopped a while ago. It persisted until the therapist took over the task of explaining and of verbalizing for Judy the emotions which she felt in the air around her and to which she responded on a body level.

She also began to wet before a visit to the dentist, which brought back a former occasion when she had been held down forcibly.

She wetted during the long summer vacation when she was separated from her therapist, and the wetting stopped when she returned to her.

Again, she wetted when a paternal uncle was found asphyxiated in the garage.

Altogether, her dry periods coincided with the times when she felt comparatively untroubled, happier, and relaxed; her wetting was associated with states of tenseness, disorientation, fear, and loneliness.

NURSERY SCHOOL

At the age of five years and ten months, after more than one and a half years of individual work, it was decided to let Judy enter our Nursery Group for Blind Children, which is under the direction of Mrs. Annemarie Curson. Although chronologically of school age, her performance was considered to be nearer to nursery school level or, if anything, below it.

For a considerable period, her attendance there was anything but a success. Although introduced to the new life gradually, by means of first once weekly, then twice weekly visits accompanied by her therapist, she was unable to show or to maintain her gains in the new surroundings, or to make use of the often undivided attention given to her by the nursery school teacher. The noise made by the other children, their talk and activities,

confused her, and she shrank from contact with them. She could often be found standing around, withdrawn and expressionless. She also resorted to gabble talk. When induced to work with Montessori insets or to sort out beads (using her color perception), she did so, listlessly, her fingers stiff, awkward, and seemingly unable to manipulate material.

It was puzzling that, in spite of this apparent rejection of her surroundings, Judy always wanted to come to the nursery school, insisted on being taken there even when she was ill, and professed that she was fond of her teacher. It led us to believe that what appeared as inactivity and indifference was, in essence, an active form of listening, and that this attempt to grasp what was going on was Judy's only way of participation.

There was only one game, on the toddler level, which Judy was ready to play with the teacher, and to repeat unendingly. It was called by her "Hello, good-bye." She would pretend to leave, saying good-bye. The teacher had to remark how sorry she was to have her go, whereupon Judy would rush back with a happy "hello" and had to be greeted lovingly. What she played out in this way was probably a fantasy of the gay, happy affectionate reciprocal mother-infant relationship which she never had occasion to experience.

With tremendous effort, patience, and encouragement on the part of the teacher, Judy finally succeeded in joining in some of the nursery school activities, such as climbing, jumping, counting, taking turns. Although little pleasure was involved in this, she could feel pleased when praised. Spontaneous enjoyment appeared only when musical activities and dancing to music were introduced.

MUSIC

As mentioned before, music played a part in Judy's re-education from the onset when her therapist played softly for her on the mouth organ to help her overcome her fear of noises. Gradually, passive listening was changed to the active production of sounds

by means of a musical box, a tambourine, a drum, and a xylophone. Primarily these served enjoyment; secondarily they also promoted the use of her fingers for handling the musical box, manipulating the drumsticks, and pressing down the keys on the keyboard of the xylophone. Music was also used to introduce simple tasks of orientation, such as tracing the location of instruments played in different parts of the room.

When introduced to a piano, Judy refused at first to touch the keys. But she soon learned to pick out tunes with one finger, and her parents were so surprised and delighted with this that they bought a piano for the home.

Her love for music took a big step forward when one of the psychiatrists of the Clinic, an active musician himself, joined forces with her therapist and came at regular intervals to play the piano for her. Judy was eager to dance to his playing. When doing this, she held herself rigid and moved her arms and legs stiffly, as if she were a puppet. Nevertheless, she kept perfect time, tapped with her feet, as in tap-dancing and responded to every change in the rhythm with abandon.

She also sang, accompanied by the piano, learned the text of a number of songs quickly and easily, and had no difficulty in beating time to the music. According to her mood of the day, she would ask with discrimination for her favorites, such as "church music" (meaning Bach) or Mozart's country dances. After a holiday (age five years ten months), she entered the room singing most appropriately "Glory, glory, hallelujah."

At the age of six years eleven months, Judy was started on formal piano lessons with Professor F. Rauter, a well-known piano teacher with experience in teaching backward children. His report on her activities with him runs as follows:

> The way I approached Judy was through asking her questions in the form of a played short melody, which could be understood as such a question. Unfailingly her answer was given in the same way. The conversation could take the form of a little opera and it gives joy to both sides. Judy seemed to

know the essentials of music without ever having been instructed.

Out of the "talking" to her through improvised melodies little special compositions arose which I put down on paper and which I numbered. Though we have recently started to learn a "real" minuet by Bach, these little pieces which I wrote for her still remain her favorites.

Judy can name and recognize each note on the piano; that is, she has perfect pitch. She is also able to find the right notes of any scale without being told, as well as to give the notes played in a chord. She plays with both hands; that is, her hands work independently in playing easy pieces. She is able to transpose single melodies into any other key. She has an excellent memory, she recognizes my symphonies and other classical music from listening to the wireless, can name them, and knows the composers. She is also aware of the various instruments which are played in an orchestra and can tell you which they are.

The inner experience of music has formed Judy's hands. It is an aesthetic pleasure to watch them when she plays, as she does naturally what sometimes needs weeks or months of teaching. Her hands are firm and when she has learned a new piece, her confidence increases and seems to spread from her fingers over her whole body and her mind. It is quite amazing how little Judy is spoiled by the music which blares from the radios and TV sets in her surrounding. She develops more and more a good taste for good things, and the time has come where I have to introduce her into a world of other composers which may be beneficial for a further development of her inner life.

What was striking to us in the Clinic was Judy's enthusiastic attitude toward her lessons and her marked expressions of enjoyment. Although, like most children, she preferred at times to play what was easy, she also tried seriously to comply with the teacher's wishes, to please him and to learn. She apologized for her mistakes and offered to "do it again." She smiled when praised, and listened entranced when a piece appealed to her. She said once: "I love Dr. Rauter and I love myself," using the same words as she had used initially to express her feelings toward her therapist.

We were left, then, with a double impression. On the one hand, there was this nursery school child, now almost eight years old, withdrawn, backward, unable to manipulate buttons or toys, or to mount the climbing frame without active help, scoring a mental age of three years ten months on the Williams intelligence scale for children with defective vision. On the other hand, the same little girl was also alert, interested, her body flexible, her hands graceful, her fingers strong and purposeful, the whole personality animated by what her teacher called "high musical intelligence."

While one part of her life seemed singularly devoid of libidinal cathexis and lay barren, the cathected part flowered and developed. The question was left open whether some of the impetus could, in the long run, be extended from there to cover other areas of her ego development.

FATEFUL EXTERNAL EVENTS

In the year that followed (age eight), Judy's life was shaken by three profoundly disturbing events: the death of her father; an operation of her own; and her mother's severe illness and hospitalization.

FATHER'S DEATH

The father's death occurred suddenly and without preparation. One day, when Judy and her mother returned from the Clinic as usual, he lay dead from a heart attack. In the ensuing confusion, Judy was sent to the neighbors where, on entering, she burst into tears and cried bitterly.

After this first outburst, Judy was found by the mother to lack any mourning response. The mother complained that the child was sitting in the living room listening to the transistor radio instead of sharing in the family's grief. On the day of the funeral she returned to her denial reaction by insisting that her Daddy should "take me to the seashore." When her therapist verbalized the happenings for her, she reacted with an obviously learned response: "My Daddy was here last year, now he is dead, he is with the angels." It was more spontaneous when she reported to her therapist two months later that "My Daddy was with me the day before," and again at another time that "He was singing" with her. Both reports presumably referred to dreams.

Apart from this, the shock showed in regressed behavior, such as clinging to the mother, wetting, return of gabble talk. It did not affect her musical ability. After a while she was able to declare sensibly: "I miss my Dad and my Mummy misses him too."

OPERATION

Judy had always been under medical care for her eye condition, her irregular teeth, and her foot deformities. At age eight and a half she was now faced with a corrective operation on her feet. This aroused concern in us that hospitalization, coupled with the many investigations and interferences, might make her lose the gains which she had achieved.

Surprisingly enough, she enjoyed the first hospital visits, including physiotherapy. She allowed herself to be handled by the medical staff and obeyed their instructions to walk, tiptoe, skip, etc. Leaving after one of her visits, she said: "Good-bye, doctors. I am coming to see you again."

Since the operation was delayed for many months, owing to the father's death, Judy's own intermittent illnesses, and other factors, there was ample time for the therapist to prepare her for the event. Fear was denied by Judy. On the contrary, she looked forward to being visited in the hospital by her therapist, to being brought her musical box, and on the very day of entering the hospital, she persisted in her denial by calling it "going on holiday."

She remained seemingly unconcerned after the operation as well, even though wires were sticking out of her toes. Accompanied by her mother and visited by her therapist, she inquired only whether the latter had really brought the musical box, as promised. She did not mind the commotion of the busy ward, nurses pursuing their activities, children running around. But she was badly put out finally by a small defective boy who declared that she was blind. She reacted to this with indignation: "He says I am blind. I am not blind."

The subject of her blindness, which had been raised unsuccessfully with her many times before, suddenly, due to the operation, seemed to have acquired significance. Possibly, also, the direct attack of the little boy had pierced her denial and laid bare a fantasy that the visit to the hospital would help her gain sight. (This would explain much of the pleasurable anticipation.) When told by the staff that nothing could be done for her eyes, she pleaded whether instead her teeth could not be made better.

There was no doubt that Judy was aware of her defects and wanted to be improved.

MOTHER'S ILLNESS AND HOSPITALIZATION

During the following holiday, soon after her own operation (age eight years two months), Judy's mother fell severely ill with high blood pressure and had to be hospitalized. Since the therapist, absent from London, could not be reached, Judy was left without support in this first separation from her mother.

Her eldest sister, by now married and with two young infants of her own, took Judy in, but she did so most unwillingly. Her home was crowded as it was, the children upset by Judy's arrival and reacting badly to their mother's preoccupation. Moreover, Judy wetted, was uncooperative, regressed and frozen; she showed no concern for the mother and refused to visit her in the hospital. In her terror that the mother might die and Judy be left on her hands, the sister talked incessantly in the child's hearing of sending her to an institution.

Altogether, this was a devastating experience for Judy.

When she could return to her own home, with the mother discharged from the hospital, she was unable to mention any of it and referred to her own recent hospitalization instead. "People turned lights on all the time and they gave me pricks." "Some wind was blowing and I went to sleep." Moreover, Judy's sister continued with her entreaties that the only sensible course of action was to send Judy to a residential home for retarded blind children. The child was well aware of this, and displayed her suspicions of her sister by shrinking from her, refusing to board a bus with her, etc.

It needed the therapist's return from holiday to put an end to this planning. She succeeded in convincing the family that even normal children find themselves unable to cope with an accumulation of events such as separation, loss of a parent, change of routine, entry into a strange household; that in Judy's situation nothing could be expected under the circumstances short of massive regression.

While the household gradually settled back into its normal routine, the therapist began to examine ways and means of safeguarding Judy's continued stay at home, her music lessons, and her therapy. Since she had outgrown nursery school, nothing except a suitable day school promised to answer the need.

ENTRY INTO SCHOOL

After much searching, the Gatehouse School, Dallington Street, London, E.C.1. was willing to accept Judy. It is a private Montessori school which makes a practice of including one handicapped child in every class of normal pupils. Judy entered on trial, at age nine, looking forward to the event with mixed feelings of fear, excitement, pride; leaning heavily on the support of her therapist, who accompanied her.

To our surprise she adapted to the school more easily than she had in our nursery school. According to the school report, she progressed well using the Montessori sensorial material; her sense of touch in particular is much stronger and more accurate. Instead of listening passively she seems to enjoy doing things. She wants to talk to the teacher and is keen on listening to what she is told. She likes being asked what she thinks, or does, and answers in a reasonable manner.

Above all, she makes progress in learning Braille, uses the Braille machine quite confidently, and has learned many letters. Reading back her Braille still presents difficulties, but her tactile sense is improving. She has also advanced in her understanding of numbers.

She relates easily and in a friendly manner to the other children who respond well to her. She is always ready to play on the piano any song the children ask for and she even played for the parents in the school concert.

BIBLIOGRAPHY

AICHHORN, A. (1925), *Wayward Youth*. New York: Viking Press, 1935.
ARMSTRONG, G. (1767), *An Essay on the Diseases Most Fatal to Infants*. London: T. Cadell.
BERGMANN, T. (1945), Observation of Children's Reactions to Motor Restraint. *Nerv. Child*, 4:318-328.
———— & FREUD, A. (1965), *Children in the Hospital*. New York: International Universities Press.
BIBRING [LEHNER], G. (1933), Referat über Traum und Okkultismus. Wiener psychoanalytische Vereinigung, May 3.
BLANK, R. (1957), Psychoanalysis and Blindness. *Psychoanal. Quart.*, 26:1-24.
———— (1958), Dreams of the Blind. *Psychoanal. Quart.*, 27:158-174.
BORNSTEIN, B. (1934), Personal communication.
———— (1948), Emotional Barriers in the Understanding and Treatment of Young Children. *Amer. J. Orthopsychiat.*, 18:691-697.
BOWLBY, J., ROBERTSON, JAMES, & ROSENBLUTH, D. (1952), A Two-Year-old Goes to Hospital. *The Psychoanalytic Study of the Child*, 7:82-94.*
BRAVERMAN, S. & CHEVIGNY, H. (1950), *The Adjustment of the Blind*. New Haven: Yale University Press.
BRETZ, A. (1940), *I Begin Again*. New York & London: McGraw-Hill.
BRODEY, W. M. (1962), Experimental Education for the Blind Holds Implications for Teaching the Gifted: I. Normal Developmental

* *The Psychoanalytic Study of the Child*, Vols. 1-25, edited by Ruth S. Eissler, Anna Freud, Heinz Hartmann, Ernst Kris, Marianne Kris, Seymour L. Lustman. New York: International Universities Press, 1945-1970.

378

Learning and the Education of the Child Born Blind. *Gifted Child Quart.*, 6:141-149.

BROUZET, M. (1754), *Essai sur l'éducation médicinale, des enfants et sur leurs maladies*. Paris: Cavalier & Fils.

BURLINGHAM, D. (1952), *Twins: A Study of Three Pairs of Identical Twins*. New York: International Universities Press.

—— & FREUD, A. (1942), *Young Children in War-time*. London: George Allen & Unwin.

—— —— (1944), *Infants Without Families*. London: George Allen & Unwin; New York: International Universities Press.

BUXBAUM, E. (1933), Über das Lügen. Presented to the Vienna Psychoanalytic Society, October 4.

—— (1936), Massenpsychologische Probleme in der Schulklasse. *Z. psychoanal. Päd.*, 10:215-240.

CADOGAN, W. (1748), *An Essay upon Nursing and the Management of Children, from Their Birth to Three Years of Age*. London: J. Roberts.

COLBORNE-BROWN, M. (1954), The Care, Training and Education of Young Blind Children in the Royal National Institute for the Blind's Sunshine Home, Residential Nurseries.

COLONNA, A. B. (1968), A Blind Child Goes to the Hospital. *The Psychoanalytic Study of the Child*, 23:391-422.

COMENIUS, J. A. [1592-1670], *Comenius' School of Infancy*, ed. W. S. Monroe. Boston: D. C. Heath, 1897.

CUTSFORTH, T. D. (1933), *The Blind in School and Society*. New York & London: D. Appleton.

DAVIS, C. M. (1928), Self-Selection of a Diet by Newly Weaned Infants: An Experimental Study. *Amer. J. Dis. Child.*, 36:651-679.

—— (1930), The Self-Selection of Diets by Infants. *Amer. J. Dis. Child.*, 40:905-906.

—— (1935a), Self-Selection of Food by Children. *Amer. J. Nurs.*, 35:403-410.

—— (1935b), Choice of Formulas Made by Three Infants Throughout the Nursing Period. *Amer. J. Dis. Child.*, 50:385-394.

DEUTSCH, F. (1940), The Sense of Reality in Persons Born Blind. *J. Psychol.*, 10:121-140.

EVELYN, J. (n.d.), *The Diary of John Evelyn*. London: W. W. Gibbings, 1890.

FRAIBERG, S. (1968), Parallel and Divergent Patterns in Blind and Sighted Infants. *The Psychoanalytic Study of the Child*, 22:264-300.

—— & FREEDMAN, D. A. (1964), Studies in the Ego Development of the Congenitally Blind Child. *The Psychoanalytic Study of the Child*, 19:113-169.

———— SIEGEL, B. L. & GIBSON, R. (1966), The Role of Sound in the Search Behavior of a Blind Infant. *The Psychoanalytic Study of the Child,* 21:327-357.

FREUD, ANNA (1936), *The Ego and the Mechanisms of Defense.* New York: International Universities Press, rev. ed., 1966.

———— (1958), Adolescence. *The Writings of Anna Freud,* 5:136-166. New York: International Universities Press, 1969.

———— (1963), The Concept of Developmental Lines. *The Psychoanalytic Study of the Child,* 18:245-265.

———— (1965), *Normality and Pathology in Childhood.* New York: International Universities Press.

FREUD, SIGMUND (1905), Three Essays on the Theory of Sexuality. *Standard Edition,* 7:125-243. London: Hogarth Press, 1953.

———— (1909), Analysis of a Phobia in a Five-Year-Old Boy. *Standard Edition,* 10:3-149. London: Hogarth Press, 1955.

———— (1920), Beyond the Pleasure Principle. *Standard Edition,* 18:3-64. London: Hogarth Press, 1955.

———— (1933), Dreams and Occultism. Lecture XXX in: New Introductory Lectures on Psycho-Analysis. *Standard Edition,* 22:31-56. London: Hogarth Press, 1964.

GESELL, A. (1940), *The First Five Years of Life.* New York: Harper; London: Methuen.

———— (1953), Development of the Infant with Retrolental Fibroplastic Blindness. *Field of Vision,* 9.

———— & AMATRUDA, C. (1960), *Developmental Diagnosis.* New York: Hoeber.

———— THOMPSON, H. & AMATRUDA, C. (1934), *Infant Behavior.* New York: McGraw-Hill.

GIBBS, N. (1949), Some Observations on Blind Children. *Young Children,* 2:1-8 (publ. Nursery School Association of Great Britain and Northern Ireland).

———— (n.d.), The Care of Blind Children. *Bull. Nat. Inst. Blind,* 18.

GREENACRE, P. (1944), Infant Reactions to Restraint. In: *Trauma, Growth, and Personality.* New York: International Universities Press, 1969, pp. 83-105.

———— (1959a), On Focal Symbiosis. In: *Emotional Growth.* New York: International Universities Press, 1971, pp. 145-161.

———— (1959b), Play in Relation to Creative Imagination. In: *Emotional Growth.* New York: International Universities Press, 1971, pp. 555-574.

GREENMAN, G. W. (1963), Visual Behavior of Newborn Infants. In: *Modern Perspectives in Child Development,* ed. A. J. Solnit & S. A. Provence. New York: International Universities Press, pp. 71-79.

GUILLET, C. (1656), *Callipaediae*, tr. L. N. Rowe. London, 1710.

HARTMANN, H. (1951), Technical Implications of Ego Psychology. In: *Essays on Ego Psychology*. New York: International Universities Press, 1964, pp. 142-154.

—— KRIS, E., & LOEWENSTEIN, R. M. (1949), Notes on the Theory of Aggression. *The Psychoanalytic Study of the Child*, 3/4:9-36.

HAYES, S. P. (1936), Twenty Years of Research: Aims and Achievements. *Proc. 33rd Ann. Convention Amer. Assn. Instructors of the Blind*, pp. 75-84.

HENDRICK, I. (1943), Work and the Pleasure Principle. *Psychoanal. Quart.*, 12:311-329.

HOLLÓS, I. (1933), Psychopathologie alltäglicher telepathischer Erscheinungen. *Imago*, 19:529-546.

JACKSON, E. B. & KLATSKIN, E. H. (1950), Rooming-in Research Project. *The Psychoanalytic Study of the Child*, 5:236-274.

JESSNER, L., BLOM, G. E., & WALDFOGEL, S. (1952), Emotional Implications of Tonsillectomy and Adenoidectomy. *The Psychoanalytic Study of the Child*, 7:126-169.

—— & KAPLAN, S. (1949), Observations on the Emotional Reactions of Children to Tonsillectomy and Adenoidectomy. In: *Problems of Infancy and Childhood*, ed. M. J. E. Senn. New York: Josiah Macy, Jr. Foundation, pp. 97-117.

JOHNSON, M. (1953), *Our Daughter Is Blind*. New York: American Foundation for the Blind.

KATAN, A. (1937), The Role of Displacement in Agoraphobia. *Int. J. Psycho-Anal.*, 32:41-50, 1951.

—— (1961), Some Thoughts about the Role of Verbalization in Early Childhood. *The Psychoanalytic Study of the Child*, 16:184-188.

KELLER, HELEN (1905), *The Story of My Life*. London: Hodder & Stroughton.

—— (1956), *Teacher*. London: Gollancz.

KELLER, W. R. (1958), Autistic Patterns and Defective Communication in Blind Children with Retrolental Fibroplasia. In: *Psychopathology of Communication*, ed. by P. Hoch & J. Zubin. New York: Grune & Stratton, pp. 64-83.

KENYON, E. (n.d.), Psychological Problems of Young Blind Children. Boston Nursery School.

KLEIN, G. S. (1962), Blindness and Isolation. *The Psychoanalytic Study of the Child*, 17:82-93.

KLEIN, M. (1932), *The Psycho-Analysis of Children*. London: Hogarth Press.

KNAPP, P. H. (1953), The Ear, Listening and Hearing. *J. Amer. Psychoanal. Assn.*, 1:672-689.

KRIS, E. (1939), Laughter as an Expressive Process. In: *Psychoanalytic Explorations in Art*. New York: International Universities Press, 1952, pp. 217-239.

LACAN, J. M. (1949), The Mirror-Stage. Abstr. in: *Int. J. Psycho-Anal.*, 30:203.

LEVY, D. M. (1944), On the Problem of Movement Restraint. *Amer. J. Orthopsychiat.*, 14:644-671.

LOCKE, J. (1963), *Some Thoughts Concerning Education*. London: Otridge & Sons.

LÖWENFELD, V. (1952), *The Nature of Creative Activity*. London: Routledge & Kegan Paul.

MACLENNAN, B. W. (1949), Non-Medical Care of Clinically Ill Children in Hospital. *Lancet*, 2:209-210.

MAHLER, M. S. (1952), On Child Psychosis and Schizophrenia: Autistic and Symbiotic Infantile Psychosis. *The Psychoanalytic Study of the Child*, 7:286-305.

MAXFIELD, K. E. (1937), *A Ten-Year Review of American Investigation Pertaining to Blind Children*. Summit, N.J. & Ann Arbor, Mich.: Edwards Brothers.

MAY, C. (1924), *Diseases of the Eye*. New York: Wood.

MEHTA, V. (1953), *Face to Face*. London: Collins.

———— (1958), Reading from Records. *Saturday Review* (Sept. 26).

MIDDLEMORE, M. P. (1941), *The Nursing Couple*. London: Hamish Hamilton Books.

MIDDLEWOOD, E. (1954), A Child—Though Blind. *New Outlook for the Blind*, March.

MITTELMANN, B. (1957), Motility in the Therapy of Children and Adults. *The Psychoanalytic Study of the Child*, 12:284-319.

MOOR, P. (1952), *A Blind Child, Too, Can Go to Nursery School*. New York: American Foundation for the Blind.

———— (1954), Meeting the Needs of the Pre-School Blind Child and His Parents. *Education*, 74:382-389.

———— (n.d.), *Toilet Habits: Suggestions for Training a Blind Child*. New York: American Foundation for the Blind.

MOSS, L. (n.d.), Work with Fathers of Blind Children in Therapy. New York Guild for the Jewish Blind.

MÜNZ, L. & LÖWENFELD, V. (1934), *Plastische Arbeiten Blinder*. Brünn: Rudolf M. Rohrer Verlag.

NAGERA, H. & COLONNA, A. B. (1965), Aspects of the Contribution of Sight to Ego and Drive Development. *The Psychoanalytic Study of the Child*, 20:267-287.

NEW YORK ASSOCIATION FOR THE BLIND
The Preschool Service of the Lighthouse (1954)
Understanding Your Blind Child (1959)

Growing through Experience (n.d.)

Services for Children at the Lighthouse (n.d.)

NORRIS, M. (1956), What Affects Blind Children's Development? *Children*, 3:(July-August)123-129.

———— ET AL. (1957), *Blindness in Children*. Chicago: University of Chicago Press.

OMWAKE, E. B. & SOLNIT, A. J. (1961), "It Isn't Fair": The Treatment of a Blind Child. *The Psychoanalytic Study of the Child*, 16:352-404.

PELLER, L. E. (1954), Libidinal Phases, Ego Development, and Play. *The Psychoanalytic Study of the Child*, 9:178-198.

PFEIFFER, E. (1958), *Study of Joe: A Blind Child in a Sighted Group*. New York: Bank Street College of Education.

POLLOCK, M. (n.d.), Visual Perception and Attention in Normal and Abnormal Children. New York: Guild for the Jewish Blind.

PRUGH, D. G. ET AL. (1953), A Study of the Emotional Reactions of Children and Families to Hospitalization and Illness. *Amer. J. Orthopsychiat.*, 23:70-106.

REIK, T. (1925), *The Compulsion to Confess*. New York: Farrar, Straus & Cudahy.

RICHTER, J. P. F. (1807), *Levana; or, The Doctrine of Education*. London: Longman, Brown, Green, & Longmans, 1848.

ROBERTSON, JAMES (1958), *Young Children in Hospital*. New York: Basic Books, 1959.

ROBERTSON, JOYCE (1962), Mothering as an Influence on Early Development: A Study of Well-Baby Clinic Records. *The Psychoanalytic Study of the Child*, 17:245-264.

ROYAL NATIONAL INSTITUTE FOR THE BLIND
Residential Nursery School for Blind Babies (n.d.)
Learning to Feed (1953)
The Education of the Young Blind Child (1957)
Lists of Toys and Equipment (n.d.)
Toys and Games for Blind Children (1964)
The Sunshine Home (prospectus) (1969)

RUESCH, J. & KEES, W. (1956), *Nonverbal Communication*. Berkeley: University of California Press.

SANDLER, A.-M. (1963), Aspects of Passivity and Ego Development in the Blind Infant. *The Psychoanalytic Study of the Child*, 18:343-360.

———— & WILLS, D. M. (1965), Preliminary Notes on Play and Mastery in the Blind Child. *J. Child Psychother.*, 1:7-19.

SCHILDER, P. (1934), Zur Psychopathologie alltäglicher telepathischer Erscheinungen: Bemerkungen zu dem Aufsatz von I. Hollós. *Imago*, 20:219-224.

SCOTT, E. (1957), The Blind Child in the Sighted Nursery School. *New Outlook for the Blind*, 51:406-410.

SENDEN, M. VON (1960), *Space and Sight*. London: Methuen.

SHAROFF, R. L. (1959), Enforced Restriction and Communication, Its Implications for the Emotional and Intellectual Development of the Deaf Child. *Amer. J. Psychiat.*, 116:443-452.

SMITH, H. (1767), *Letters to Married Women, on Nursing and the Management of Children*. Philadelphia: Mathew Carey, 6th ed., 1792.

SPEER, E. L. (1935), *A Manual for Parents of Pre-School Blind Children*. New York: The Lighthouse of the New York Association for the Blind, 7th ed., 1950.

SPENCE, J. C. (1946), *The Purpose of the Family: A Guide to the Care of Children*. London: National Children's Homes.

——— (1951), The Doctor, the Nurse, and the Sick Child. *Amer. J. Nurs.*, 51.

SPITZ, R. A. (1953), Aggression. In: *Drives, Affects, Behavior*, ed. R. M. Loewenstein. New York: International Universities Press, pp. 126-138.

——— (1955), The Primal Cavity. *The Psychoanalytic Study of the Child*, 10:215-240.

VAUGHAN, G. F. (1957), Children in Hospital. *Lancet*, 1:1117-1120.

VERNEY, F. P. & VERNEY, M. M., eds. (1647), *Memoirs of the Verney Family during the Seventeenth Century*. London: Longmans, 2nd ed., 1904.

VILLEY, P. (1930), *The World of the Blind*. London: Duckworth.

WELLS, E. (1955), Twenty-One Years of Guide-Dogging. *New Beacon*, 39:149-150.

WILLS, D. M. (1963), The Role of Sound in the Development of a Blind Child (unpublished).

——— (1965), Some Observations on Blind Nursery School Children's Understanding of Their World. *The Psychoanalytic Study of the Child*, 20:344-364.

——— (1970), Vulnerable Periods in the Early Development of Blind Children. *The Psychoanalytic Study of the Child*, 25:461-480.

WINNICOTT, D. W. (1953), Transitional Objects and Transitional Phenomena. *Int. J. Psycho-Anal.*, 34:89-97.

ZULLIGER, H. (1926), *Psychoanalytische Pädagogik: Ein Bericht über Massen- und Individualerziehung*. Zurich: Orell Füssli.

——— (1935), *Schwierige Schüler*. Bern: Huber.

INDEX